Mastering OpenTelemetry

Building Scalable Observability Systems for Cloud-Native Applications

Robert Johnson

Published by HiTeX Press

For permissions and other inquiries, write to:
P.O. Box 3132, Framingham, MA 01701, USA

Contents

Introduction

As software systems evolve and become more complex, the necessity for efficient and comprehensive observability grows in parallel. Observability, in contemporary software engineering, extends beyond conventional monitoring by furnishing insights into the internal states of systems based on external outputs. This capability is crucial in the era of distributed systems, microservices, and cloud-native architectures.

OpenTelemetry stands as a pivotal project within the observability landscape. It provides a single set of APIs, libraries, agents, and instrumentation across languages, offering a standardized method for collecting telemetry data, such as traces, metrics, and logs. As a robust open-source initiative, OpenTelemetry benefits from widespread community support and is designed to integrate seamlessly across diverse platforms and technologies.

This book, titled "Mastering OpenTelemetry: Building Scalable Observability Systems for Cloud-Native Applications," serves as a comprehensive guide to understanding, deploying, and maximizing the potential of OpenTelemetry within modern software environments. It aims to equip readers with the requisite knowledge to implement observability strategies that are not only effective but also scalable and maintainable in cloud-native contexts.

The chapters that follow cover a broad spectrum of topics essential for mastering OpenTelemetry. Beginning with foundational concepts of observability, readers will delve into the specific architectural components and the practical steps necessary for setting up OpenTelemetry in varied environments. Further exploration includes advanced techniques likely to be encountered in enterprise-level applications and insightful case studies showcasing real-world implementations.

With a dedicated focus on security and compliance, this book also addresses critical considerations necessary for safeguarding telemetry systems against vulnerabilities and meeting regulatory requirements. By the book's conclusion, readers should possess a well-rounded comprehension of both the theoretical underpinnings and practical applications of OpenTelemetry, poised to implement these insights into their respective domains.

In presenting this text, the goal is to demystify the complexities surrounding observability while providing systematic instruction that aligns with the cutting-edge demands of modern software development. Through a blend of detailed explanations and actionable guidance, readers are invited to engage deeply with OpenTelemetry, building capabilities that extend beyond mere monitoring to achieve full-spectrum observability.

Chapter 1

Introduction to Observability and OpenTelemetry

Observability represents a critical component in managing the complexity of modern software architectures by enabling visibility into system behaviors through external outputs. This chapter elucidates the core challenges faced in observing distributed systems and delineates how OpenTelemetry emerges as a comprehensive solution. It outlines the fundamental aspects of OpenTelemetry, highlighting its significance and competitive advantages over traditional observability frameworks, thereby laying the groundwork for effectively leveraging this tool in enhancing system insights and performance management.

1.1 Understanding Observability

Observability, in the context of modern software systems, is a pivotal concept that transcends traditional monitoring practices. It furnishes system operators and developers with the capacity to infer the internal states of their complex, distributed systems by scrutinizing outputs that these systems generate. The origin of the observability concept lies in control theory, specifically referring to the ability to determine the complete state of a system solely through its outputs. This is particularly relevant in software systems, as these outputs typically encompass logs, metrics, and traces.

Logs are discrete records of events that have occurred within a system. They offer a historical ledger of occurrences across the system, such as errors, warnings, and general information regarding system operations. Metrics, in contrast, provide quantitative measurements of the system's performance and health, denoting data points such as CPU usage, memory consumption, request counts, and response times. Finally, traces collect data representing a series of operations, often illustrating interactions and dependencies between system components across multiple services.

The impetus behind observability lies in its ability to enable a comprehensive understanding and insightful troubleshooting of system behavior. This is paramount given the intricacies and dynamism of modern distributed architectures, notably microservices and cloud-native applications. Observability facilitates not just the detection of system abnormalities but also aids in uncovering the root causes, thus enhancing system robustness, reliability, and performance.

The relevance of observability in modern systems is underscored by the shift from monolithic applications to microservices-driven architectures. The latter entails the devolution of an application into numerous small, independent services that communicate over a network, typically the Internet. This architecture enhances flexibility and scalability but also introduces new challenges, particularly in terms of system complexity and operational opacity. Traditional monitoring tools, once effective in monolithic setups, fall short in these distributed environments due to their limited scope and inability to provide insights beyond predefined metrics.

"timestamp":"2023-12-01T12:48:04.000Z",
"level":"ERROR",
"service":"PaymentService",
"message":"Transaction failed for user 452.",
"context":{
    "transaction_id":"bc488b6bd019",

```
"user_id":"452",
"amount":"100.00",
"currency":"USD"
}
```

Observability endeavors to bridge this gap, offering a comprehensive suite of tooling and practices that empower stakeholders to probe and comprehend system behavior under various conditions. Unlike traditional monitoring, which predominantly focuses on systemic performance indicators and predetermined alerting mechanisms, observability is centered on exploratory analysis. It provides the capacity to ask arbitrary questions about a system and receive precise, informed answers based on the collected data. This empowers the rapid identification of causal relationships, bottlenecks, and inefficiencies within a system.

Consider the example of a log entry as illustrated above. Within a service-oriented architecture, particularly a microservices pattern, such log entries are prevalent. They encapsulate critical information about interactions and state changes within and across services. Through observability practices, developers are equipped to analyze these logs in conjunction with other telemetry data such as metrics and distributed traces to diagnose issues such as transaction failures, as well as understand their underlying causes and potential ripple effects across other services.

From an implementation perspective, achieving robust observability necessitates the integration of various technologies and strategies. Central to this is the collection and analysis of telemetry data encompassing logs, metrics, and traces. Specialized tools and platforms are leveraged to standardize, collect, and visualize this data, offering a consolidated view of system operations across multiple dimensions and layers. Popular tools facilitating such capabilities include OpenTelemetry, Prometheus, Grafana, and Jaeger, among others.

```
from opentelemetry import trace
from opentelemetry.exporter.otlp.proto.grpc.trace_exporter import
    OTLPSpanExporter
from opentelemetry.sdk.trace import TracerProvider
from opentelemetry.sdk.trace.export import BatchSpanProcessor

trace.set_tracer_provider(TracerProvider())
tracer = trace.get_tracer(__name__)

span_exporter = OTLPSpanExporter(endpoint="localhost:4317")
```

11

```
span_processor = BatchSpanProcessor(span_exporter)
trace.get_tracer_provider().add_span_processor(span_processor)

def process_transaction(transaction_id):
    with tracer.start_as_current_span("process_transaction") as span:
        # Simulate processing logic
        span.set_attribute("transaction_id", transaction_id)
        return "Processed transaction {}".format(transaction_id)

print(process_transaction("bc488b6bd019"))
```

The code example above demonstrates the instrumentation of a sample Python application using OpenTelemetry, a leading open-source observability framework. Here, a transactional operation is encapsulated within a trace span, capturing pertinent attributes such as the transaction identifier. The span exporter dispatches the trace data to a designated endpoint, potentially for further processing and visualization.

Observability should not be misconstrued as merely a set of tools but rather, an integral paradigm and a state of system readiness that supports ongoing development, operations, and business objectives. It empowers users to navigate the complexity of distributed systems with confidence, fostering a deeper understanding and agile response to changing conditions. Observability is, therefore, indispensable in empowering engineers to maintain system health, optimize resource allocation, and preemptively address impending issues.

The distinctions between observability and traditional monitoring are nuanced yet substantial. Traditional monitoring is characterized by a narrow scope focused on specific metrics and often involves static thresholds that trigger alerts when exceeded. Conversely, observability equips practitioners with a dynamic, contextual awareness of their systems, enabling them to dynamically carve out ad-hoc queries and investigations post-hoc, based on real-world scenarios and evolving requirements. This adaptability is particularly vital in identifying and rectifying ambiguous performance concerns which static monitoring heuristics might overlook.

```
Alert: PaymentService CPU Usage Spike
Timestamp: 2023-12-01T12:49:00.000Z
Metric: CPU Usage
Threshold: 80%
Current Value: 92%
Instance: payment-service-1
```

A crucial aspect of observation and monitoring is the handling and analysis of metrics data. The output above illustrates a sample alert from a hypothetical monitoring system. It highlights the crossing of a pre-determined CPU usage metric threshold for a specific service instance. While such alerts are useful for quick detection of performance anomalies, the rich telemetry data available through observability enables engineers to delve deeper into the context, correlating this anomaly with logs and traces to ascertain potential root causes and downstream impacts.

Further attesting to the prominence of observability is its role in accelerating mean-time-to-recovery (MTTR). Faced with an incident or failure, practitioners can swiftly navigate through comprehensive data collected in real-time to diagnose and rectify faults with minimal downtime. This enhances system resilience and ensures continuity of services, especially critical in industries with stringent uptime requirements such as finance, e-commerce, and telecommunications.

Implementing observability in organizations mandates a cultural shift and the embracing of DevOps principles. It requires the seamless collaboration between development and operations teams and the embedding of observability practices into the software development lifecycle. This shift allows teams to continually assess the health of their systems, make informed decisions, and iteratively refine operations and processes based on empirical insights garnered from observability data.

In practice, establishing observability can initially seem daunting, given the volume and complexity of data involved. However, several frameworks and best practices can simplify this endeavor. Utilizing established models, such as the RED (Rate, Errors, Duration) or the USE (Utilization, Saturation, Errors) methods, organizations can identify crucial telemetry data points aligned with business objectives. Moreover, adopting unified logging and tracing libraries across microservices can significantly reduce the integration overhead, ensuring consistency and reliability in data collection.

Overall, understanding observability is rooted in recognizing its importance in modern software systems. It equips organizations with the necessary tools and insights to navigate the inherent complexity of distributed systems, ultimately fostering more agile, resilient, and performant applications. As modern technologies continue to evolve, observability will remain a cornerstone in ensuring the robustness and reliability of diverse software ecosystems.

1.2 Challenges with Modern Software Systems

Modern software systems, characterized largely by their distributed nature and cloud-native architecture, bring with them a plethora of challenges. These systems are composed of multiple, interconnected services, each potentially deployed across geographically dispersed data centers. While this configuration offers advantages in terms of scalability, resilience, and flexibility, it also presents a unique set of complexities and obstacles that must be efficiently addressed to ensure optimal operation and reliability.

A fundamental challenge with modern software systems lies in their inherent complexity. Traditional monolithic systems, with their centralized nature, provided a single vantage point for monitoring and management. However, distributed systems consist of a multitude of services interacting through various communication protocols such as HTTP/HTTPS, gRPC, and messaging queues. The communication patterns and data flows within these systems are more intricate and dynamic, making it difficult to achieve a cohesive understanding of the overall system behavior.

The dynamism of microservices adds another layer of complexity, with services often being updated, scaled, or replaced independently. The ephemeral nature of cloud environments, where instances are frequently created and destroyed based on load requirements, makes tracking the state and health of all components at any given time a non-trivial task. This dynamic environment necessitates robust and adaptive monitoring and diagnostic strategies to ensure system stability and performance.

```
const express = require('express');
const axios = require('axios');
const app = express();

app.get('/process-order/:orderId', async (req, res) => {
    try {
        const orderId = req.params.orderId;
```

```
    const paymentResponse = await axios.post('http://payments-service/payments',
        { orderId });
    const shipmentResponse = await axios.post('http://shipment-service/shipments
        ', { orderId });

    res.status(200).send('Order ${orderId} processed. Payment: ${paymentResponse
        .data}, Shipment: ${shipmentResponse.data}');
  } catch (error) {
    console.error('Error processing order ${req.params.orderId}:', error);
    res.status(500).send('Failed to process order ${req.params.orderId}.');
  }
});

app.listen(3000, () => {
    console.log('Order Processing Service running on port 3000');
});
```

The example above demonstrates a Node.js-based microservice responsible for order processing, integrating with both payment and shipment services. This reflects typical inter-service communication patterns in modern architectures. Each service interaction is a potential point of failure, and robust error-handling and logging are essential to identify and mitigate any issues swiftly.

Communications between services in distributed systems often face reliability and latency issues. Network partitions, latency variations, and partial failures in such environments can lead to inconsistent data states or degraded performance. Implementing fallbacks, retry mechanisms, and circuit breakers through patterns like the Circuit Breaker or Service Meshes (e.g., Istio) has become commonplace to tackle these challenges. However, these solutions introduce additional layers of complexity, necessitating a deep understanding of their configurations and implications.

Debugging in a distributed system environment is considerably more complicated than in a monolithic architecture. When an anomaly or performance issue arises, isolating the root cause requires sifting through vast amounts of log data across multiple services. The presence of microservices necessitates a distributed tracing system that can follow the lifecycle of a request as it traverses various services, providing visibility into latency bottlenecks and service dependencies.

Security is another domain of significant concern. In distributed environments, securing data in transit and at rest, protecting against unauthorized access, and ensuring compliance with security policies are paramount. Modern systems often employ techniques such as mutual TLS for secure service-to-service communication and utilize comprehensive identity and access management solutions. Nonetheless, balancing security with performance and usability in such complex infrastructures demands meticulous planning and execution.

```
apiVersion: networking.istio.io/v1alpha3
kind: VirtualService
metadata:
  name: payment-service
spec:
  hosts:
  - payment-service
  http:
  - route:
    - destination:
        host: payment-service
    retries:
      attempts: 3
      perTryTimeout: 2s
```

The YAML snippet above illustrates a simple configuration for Istio, a service mesh that provides resiliency features like retries and circuit breaking. By defining policies at the service mesh level, developers can manage communication resilience without modifying application code, thereby decoupling service logic from reliability concerns.

Data management also presents formidable challenges. In a distributed system, maintaining consistent and synchronized data presents a myriad of challenges. Systems must choose between strict consistency, availability, and partition tolerance, as dictated by the CAP theorem, each choice involving trade-offs. Consistent hashing, distributed transaction management, and eventual consistency models become necessary tools in managing distributed data but come with their own complexities and performance considerations.

Deployment and orchestration of distributed systems involve complex workflows that vary significantly from traditional deployment practices. Containerization platforms like Docker and orchestration frameworks such as Kubernetes have revolutionized deployment by providing mechanisms to define, manage, and scale applications in heterogeneous environments. However, mastering these tools requires a comprehensive understanding of concepts such as container lifecycle management, cluster scaling, service discovery, and load balancing.

The proliferation of cloud-native applications has resulted in an exponential increase in telemetry data, comprising logs, metrics, and traces. While this data is critical for understanding system behavior, its sheer volume and complexity pose challenges in storage, processing, and analysis. Advanced observability platforms, often leveraging machine learning tools, have emerged to facilitate real-time analysis and anomaly detection.

As systems scale, human oversight alone becomes inadequate to manage operations effectively. Automation, through DevOps practices and infrastructure as code (IaC) methodologies, is pivotal in orchestrating complex deployments, ensuring repeatability, and enabling continuous delivery. However, this shift necessitates the development of sophisticated pipelines and robust governance models to handle inherent security and compliance challenges.

Given these intricacies, organizations are increasingly adopting a DevOps culture combined with Site Reliability Engineering (SRE) principles. This collaborative practice emphasizes the automation of operations and continuous improvement of system reliability, performance, and operability. It fosters a culture of shared responsibility among development and operations teams, encouraging comprehensive monitoring, proactive problem-solving, and incremental system enhancements.

Modern software systems are an amalgam of diverse technologies, requiring a multifaceted approach to address their operational challenges. Through strategic implementation of advanced monitoring tools, resilience patterns, security protocols, and data management techniques, organizations can navigate the complexities of distributed environments. Coupled with a shift towards DevOps and SRE philosophies, these efforts enable the development and maintenance of robust, nimble, and scalable software systems that meet the evolving demands of the digital world.

1.3 Overview of OpenTelemetry

OpenTelemetry stands as a pivotal project in the domain of observability, offering a unified set of APIs, libraries, agents, and instrumentation tools designed to provide comprehensive visibility into distributed systems. This open-source initiative is governed by the Cloud Native

Computing Foundation (CNCF) and aims to create industry-wide standards for telemetry data collection. It supports developers and operations teams in understanding application performance and behavioral patterns through logs, metrics, and traces.

OpenTelemetry emerged from the convergence of two major projects: OpenCensus and OpenTracing. The aim was to reduce fragmentation and consolidate efforts towards a single, pragmatic observability solution. OpenTelemetry offers a vendor-agnostic platform for monitoring, simplifying the setup and configuration needed for effective observability in diverse environments. It allows developers to auto-instrument their code, ensuring that all necessary operational data is collected seamlessly.

At the heart of OpenTelemetry lie its core components, which provide the building blocks necessary for achieving effective observability. These components include the OpenTelemetry API, SDK, Collectors, and Exporters. Each component plays a critical role in ensuring that telemetry data is captured accurately and transmitted efficiently to a variety of back-end systems for storage and analysis.

The OpenTelemetry API is designed to provide a uniform instrumentation interface across different programming languages. It abstracts the instrumentation process, allowing developers to add observability capabilities into their applications without being locked into specific technologies or vendors. Through consistent APIs across languages such as Java, Python, Go, and JavaScript, developers can instrument services in diverse environments with ease.

```
from opentelemetry import trace
from opentelemetry.sdk.trace import TracerProvider
from opentelemetry.sdk.trace.export import ConsoleSpanExporter,
    SimpleSpanProcessor

trace.set_tracer_provider(TracerProvider())
tracer = trace.get_tracer(__name__)

span_processor = SimpleSpanProcessor(ConsoleSpanExporter())
trace.get_tracer_provider().add_span_processor(span_processor)

with tracer.start_as_current_span("example-operation"):
    print("Performing some operation...")
```

The example above illustrates how OpenTelemetry can be employed to create a simple span within a Python application. Here, the Con-

18

soleSpanExporter is used to print span data to the console, allowing developers to verify and understand the trace information readily.

OpenTelemetry's SDK complements the API by offering robust implementations of telemetry data collection and processing. The SDK handles the configuration of context propagation, span management, and the integration with back-end processing systems. It is modular, allowing developers to extend or customize its behavior via processors and extensions for specific use cases or environments.

To facilitate data aggregation and routing, OpenTelemetry introduces the Collector component. The Collector offers a vendor-agnostic way to process telemetry data, consolidating data from multiple sources and re-exporting it to various back-end systems. By decoupling the data collection from exporting, the Collector simplifies the configuration and management of observability pipelines.

```
receivers:
  otlp:
    protocols:
      grpc:

exporters:
  jaeger:
    endpoint: "jaeger-collector:14250"
    tls:
      insecure: true

service:
  pipelines:
    traces:
      receivers: [otlp]
      exporters: [jaeger]
```

The YAML configuration demonstrates how an OpenTelemetry Collector is set up to receive OpenTelemetry Protocol (OTLP) data and export it to a Jaeger back-end. This setup is a common scenario in production environments, where collected data needs to be analyzed and visualized using dedicated platforms.

Additionally, OpenTelemetry provides a diverse array of Exporters that enable the captured telemetry data to be sent to various back-end systems for analysis and storage. Exporters are available for popular platforms such as Prometheus, Jaeger, Zipkin, and many commercial observability solutions. By supporting standard and custom exporters, OpenTelemetry ensures flexibility and adaptability to different deployment needs and preferences.

A notable feature of OpenTelemetry is its capability to support automatic and manual instrumentation. Automatic instrumentation enables the seamless incorporation of telemetry without modifying the application source code. This is achieved through language-specific agents or instrumentation libraries that inject telemetry into application workflows. Conversely, manual instrumentation allows developers to interact directly with the OpenTelemetry API, providing fine-grained control over which aspects of their application are instrumented.

```java
import io.opentelemetry.api.trace.Span;
import io.opentelemetry.api.trace.Tracer;
import io.opentelemetry.api.GlobalOpenTelemetry;

public class DatabaseService {
    private static final Tracer tracer = GlobalOpenTelemetry.getTracer("example-
        database-service");

    public void queryDatabase() {
        Span span = tracer.spanBuilder("queryDATABASE").startSpan();
        try {
            // Simulate database query logic
            System.out.println("Executing the database query...");
        } finally {
            span.end();
        }
    }
}
```

In the Java example above, OpenTelemetry is used to manually create and manage spans within a database service. This allows developers to wrap critical application logic within spans, obtaining detailed insight into operation durations and possible bottlenecks.

Beyond instrumentation, OpenTelemetry supports various context propagation standards, ensuring that trace context is transmitted correctly across service boundaries. It integrates with multiple formats such as W3C TraceContext and B3, facilitating seamless interoperability between services that may utilize different technologies or frameworks. This ensures that distributed traces maintain continuity and integrity as they traverse disparate systems.

OpenTelemetry's flexible architecture and extensible model have catalyzed widespread adoption across the industry. With extensive community and vendor backing, it has become a fundamental component of cloud-native observability strategies. Many organizations leverage OpenTelemetry to establish a unified, standardized telemetry infrastructure that provides consistent and reliable insights into their systems' performance and reliability.

Effective use of OpenTelemetry requires a strategic approach to observability that considers both technical and organizational factors. Deployment strategies may vary depending on organizational needs and existing infrastructure, but best practices generally include automating the onboarding of services to the observability stack, maintaining configuration management as code, and using rolling deployments to simultaneously introduce OpenTelemetry to multiple services.

To maximize the potential of OpenTelemetry, collaboration between development, operations, and security teams is crucial. Regular training and alignment workshops ensure that all stakeholders understand the telemetry data being collected, its importance, and how it can be used to drive improvements. These practices remain key to achieving observability excellence, foresight into upcoming challenges, and informed decision-making.

1.4 Importance of OpenTelemetry in Observability

OpenTelemetry plays a pivotal role in enhancing observability practices, serving as a cornerstone framework that unifies and streamlines the collection and analysis of telemetry data. As systems increasingly adopt microservices, serverless architectures, and cloud-native designs, the complexity in tracing interactions across disparate components becomes profound. OpenTelemetry addresses these challenges by providing a holistic, standardized, and vendor-neutral framework that significantly augments the observability of modern software systems.

One of the quintessential benefits of OpenTelemetry is its capability to integrate seamlessly into diverse ecosystems. It provides a common protocol for exporting telemetry data—comprising metrics, logs, and traces—thereby eliminating the need for maintaining multiple incompatible tooling solutions. This integration ensures interoperability and empowers organizations to switch between observability backends without significant reconfiguration or data loss, safeguarding investments in telemetry infrastructure.

The modular design of OpenTelemetry allows for flexibility in how observability tools are deployed and managed. Developers can choose from a wealth of language-specific SDKs that cater to the nuances of their chosen platforms, whether that be Go, JavaScript, Python, or others. This flexibility ensures that OpenTelemetry can be consistently deployed across multi-language, polyglot environments—a common scenario in microservices architectures—without sacrificing the depth or breadth of observability.

Service reliability and performance are critical objectives in distributed systems where OpenTelemetry excels. By providing detailed tracing, OpenTelemetry empowers developers to visualize the complete path a request takes through a system. This visualization aids in identifying performance bottlenecks or failures that occur as requests traverse distributed services and APIs. It becomes possible to pinpoint lagging services or calls that might otherwise remain opaque within the complex web of service interactions.

```
package main

import (
    "context"
    "fmt"
    "net/http"
    "go.opentelemetry.io/otel"
    "go.opentelemetry.io/otel/exporters/stdout/stdouttrace"
    "go.opentelemetry.io/otel/sdk/resource"
    "go.opentelemetry.io/otel/sdk/trace"
    "go.opentelemetry.io/otel/trace"
    "go.opentelemetry.io/otel/attribute"
)

func initTracer() trace.TracerProvider {
    exporter, _ := stdouttrace.New(stdouttrace.WithPrettyPrint())
    resource := resource.NewWithAttributes(
        attribute.String("service.name", "example-service"),
    )

    return trace.NewTracerProvider(
        trace.WithBatcher(exporter),
        trace.WithResource(resource),
    )
}

func main() {
    tp := initTracer()
```

```go
    defer func() { _ = tp.Shutdown(context.Background()) }()

    tracer := otel.Tracer("example-tracer")

    http.HandleFunc("/", func(w http.ResponseWriter, r *http.Request) {
        ctx, span := tracer.Start(r.Context(), "handle_request")
        defer span.End()

        fmt.Fprintf(w, "Hello, World!")
        span.SetAttributes(attribute.String("request.path", r.URL.Path))
    })

    http.ListenAndServe(":8080", nil)
}
```

The Go example illustrates OpenTelemetry's role in creating spans that trace HTTP requests handled by a microservice. By capturing attributes such as request paths, developers gain detailed insights into service workloads, facilitating enhanced monitoring and optimization efforts.

Furthermore, OpenTelemetry aids in the reliable automation of alerting and incident response processes. By accurately capturing the state of systems through telemetry data, organizations leverage OpenTelemetry to feed analytics engines that provide predictive insights. This facilitates preemptive identification of potential disruptions, allowing teams to remediate issues before they impact end-users.

In addition to tracing, OpenTelemetry's robust metrics capabilities enhance the monitoring of application health and system resource utilization. By aggregating metrics across services, teams can detect anomalies such as surges in latency or CPU usage swiftly. OpenTelemetry's compatibility with popular back-ends like Prometheus simplifies these integrations, enhancing the overall observability posture.

```python
from opentelemetry import metrics
from opentelemetry.sdk.metrics import MeterProvider
from opentelemetry.sdk.metrics.export import ConsoleMetricExporter,
    PeriodicExportingMetricReader

metrics.set_meter_provider(MeterProvider())

meter = metrics.get_meter(__name__)
exporter = ConsoleMetricExporter()
reader = PeriodicExportingMetricReader(exporter)

counter = meter.create_counter(
    name="example_counter",
    description="Counts the number of example events",
    unit="1"
```

```
)

def on_event():
    counter.add(1, {"event.type": "example"})

on_event() # Increment the counter manually
```

By leveraging the metrics API in OpenTelemetry, the Python example shows how custom metrics can be defined and exported. Such metrics are critical for alerting and can be integrated into SLA/SLO (Service Level Agreement/Objective) dashboards, aligning system monitoring with business goals.

The ability of OpenTelemetry to standardize observability practices cannot be overstated. It circumvents the potential discrepancies and silos that arise from disparate observability solutions. This standardization facilitates the democratization of observability data across teams—from developers to IT operations, customer support, and business analysts—promoting a unified understanding of system health and performance.

To maintain consistency and quality, OpenTelemetry invests heavily in maintaining exhaustive documentation and thorough compliance with open observability standards. This commitment ensures users can transition from other frameworks with minimal friction, leveraging the extensive ecosystem and community resources that support OpenTelemetry's continued development and enhancement.

From a strategic perspective, enterprises are increasingly positioning observability as a business imperative. The enhanced visibility provided by OpenTelemetry contributes to superior customer experiences, as issues can be diagnosed and rectified swiftly. In industries with stringent compliance and uptime requirements, adopting a robust observability framework like OpenTelemetry is essential for safeguarding reputation and maintaining operational excellence.

Demonstrations of OpenTelemetry's value are prevalent in sectors such as finance, healthcare, and telecommunications, where latency and reliability are critical. In such domains, significant cost savings are realized through optimized resource utilization and decreased time to resolution during incidents.

The architectural complexity of modern applications continues to

24

evolve, with hybrid-cloud and multi-cloud deployments becoming more prevalent. OpenTelemetry's cloud-native orientation enables observability strategies to scale alongside these technological shifts, providing structured solutions that can adapt to more sophisticated and dispersed infrastructures.

In sum, OpenTelemetry represents a transformative advancement in the observability landscape. By addressing the myriad of challenges posed by complex distributed systems, it enables organizations to harness telemetry data more effectively and make informed decisions that enhance reliability, performance, and customer satisfaction. This underscores its vital role in not just improving observability practices, but in forging new paths toward proactive and predictive system management strategies.

1.5 Comparison with Other Observability Frameworks

OpenTelemetry is at the forefront of modern observability frameworks, yet it exists alongside a range of other tools and technologies designed to enhance system visibility. Each framework offers distinct capabilities, philosophies, and levels of integration with existing ecosystems. To fully appreciate OpenTelemetry's role and advantages within the observability landscape, it is essential to compare and contrast it with other leading frameworks, such as Prometheus, Jaeger, Zipkin, DataDog, and Elastic APM.

OpenTelemetry distinguishes itself with its comprehensive approach to observability, encompassing a broad spectrum of telemetry data, including traces, metrics, and logs. This holistic nature is particularly beneficial for organizations aiming to consolidate observability efforts under a single, unified framework. Unlike other solutions that may excel in one domain (e.g., metrics with Prometheus or tracing with Jaeger), OpenTelemetry strives to cover all bases within a single ecosystem and is supported by the Cloud Native Computing Foundation (CNCF).

Prometheus, primarily a metrics-focused system, is widely adopted for its reliability and robust querying capabilities, enabled by PromQL, a powerful domain-specific query language. Prometheus's value lies in its ability to efficiently handle multi-dimensional data and scale horizontally, particularly within dynamic, containerized environments like Kubernetes. However, it lacks native support for distributed tracing and log aggregation, which OpenTelemetry addresses by integrating these capabilities into its core structure.

```yaml
global:
  scrape_interval: 15s

scrape_configs:
  - job_name: 'otel-collector'
    static_configs:
      - targets: ['otel-collector:8888']
```

In the YAML snippet above, OpenTelemetry and Prometheus work in tandem, where Prometheus is configured to scrape metrics from an OpenTelemetry Collector. This setup showcases how organizations can leverage Prometheus to visualize and alert on metrics within an OpenTelemetry-driven observability architecture.

Tracing frameworks like Jaeger and Zipkin offer powerful tools for end-to-end distributed tracing, aiding in understanding the flow and performance of requests through microservices. Jaeger is explicitly designed with a focus on tracing and analysis, providing capabilities such as root cause analysis, service dependency graphs, and high-fidelity performance monitoring. Similarly, Zipkin offers a lightweight yet effective solution for trace data visualization and analysis, particularly valued for its integration ease with numerous back-end databases.

OpenTelemetry initially subsumed the functionalities of OpenTracing and OpenCensus to provide a singular, vendor-neutral tracing standard, unifying and extending these frameworks' capabilities. Further distinguishing itself, OpenTelemetry supports multiple propagation standards such as W3C TraceContext, enabling seamless context transfer across service boundaries in heterogeneous systems.

```javascript
const { NodeTracerProvider } = require('@opentelemetry/sdk-trace-node');
const { OTLPTraceExporter } = require('@opentelemetry/exporter-trace-otlp-grpc');
const { registerInstrumentations } = require('@opentelemetry/instrumentation');
const { HttpInstrumentation } = require('@opentelemetry/instrumentation-http');
const { Resource } = require('@opentelemetry/resources');
const { SemanticResourceAttributes } = require('@opentelemetry/semantic-
    conventions');

const provider = new NodeTracerProvider({
```

26

```
    resource: new Resource({
        [SemanticResourceAttributes.SERVICE_NAME]: 'example-service',
    }),
});

const exporter = new OTLPTraceExporter();
provider.addSpanProcessor(new SimpleSpanProcessor(exporter));

provider.register();
registerInstrumentations({
    instrumentations: [
        new HttpInstrumentation(),
    ],
});
```

The JavaScript code above leverages OpenTelemetry to trace HTTP requests, showcasing interoperability with underlying tracing systems such as Jaeger. Through instrumentations like HttpInstrumentation, developers can automatically capture relevant trace data without significant code modifications, enhancing ease of implementation and continuity.

Elastic APM provides a complete observability solution embedded within the broader Elastic Stack, renowned for log management and search capabilities through Elasticsearch. Elastic APM's strength lies in its deep integration with the existing Elastic ecosystem, offering seamless ingestion, search, visualization, and analysis of logs, metrics, and traces. However, its tight coupling with the Elastic Stack can be seen as a limitation in terms of flexibility and scalability across diverse environments outside Elasticsearch's domain.

DataDog represents a comprehensive observability platform encompassing monitoring, tracing, and logging with added operational insights through machine learning. Its cloud-native roots align well with modern enterprise architectures, and it provides an integrated view of system metrics across various dimensions and layers. However, DataDog's commercial nature often introduces cost considerations and specific deployment dependencies.

One compelling aspect of OpenTelemetry is its commitment to vendor neutrality, allowing applications instrumented with OpenTelemetry to send their telemetry data to a diverse range of observability back-ends, both open-source and commercial. This independence fosters innovation and competition, reducing vendor lock-in and enabling organizations to align their observability strategy with evolving requirements and available technologies.

This flexibility is further demonstrated through OpenTelemetry's pluggable architecture, supporting a variety of exporters for rich integrations. From Prometheus and Jaeger in a fully open-source stack to integrations with commercial SaaS platforms like New Relic and AWS CloudWatch, OpenTelemetry maximizes its reach and adaptability.

```
receivers:
  otlp:
    protocols:
      grpc:

processors:
  batch:

exporters:
  jaeger:
    endpoint: "jaeger-collector:14250"
    tls:
      insecure: true

  prometheus:
    endpoint: "0.0.0.0:8889"

  logging:

service:
  pipelines:
    traces:
      receivers: [otlp]
      processors: [batch]
      exporters: [jaeger, logging]

    metrics:
      receivers: [otlp]
      processors: [batch]
      exporters: [prometheus]
```

In the illustrative YAML configuration above, an OpenTelemetry Collector is configured to process and export telemetry data to both Jaeger for traces and Prometheus for metrics. Simultaneously, it logs telemetry data for debugging purposes. This configuration demonstrates the collector's flexibility and OpenTelemetry's broad integration spectrum.

Another strategic benefit of OpenTelemetry lies in its vibrant open-source community and CNCF backing, which ensures ongoing development, governance, and the alignment with cutting-edge practices in microservices architectures. This communal effort accelerates the creation and dissemination of best practices, educational resources, and an ecosystem of extensions and integrations that bolster observability initiatives.

On the horizon, OpenTelemetry's roadmap includes expanding support for profiling and real-user monitoring capabilities, further solidifying its role as an all-encompassing observability framework. By incorporating these features, OpenTelemetry aims to provide organizations with additional dimensions to understand software performance and user engagement holistically.

While other observability frameworks offer specialized capabilities that serve particular niches or integrations, OpenTelemetry presents an inclusive, versatile, and future-proof choice for enterprises moving towards holistic observability. Its approach transcends conventional boundaries, letting organizations build an integrated observability solution that grows in tandem with their technological ambitions and ecosystem diversity.

Chapter 2

The Architecture of OpenTelemetry

This chapter provides an in-depth examination of Open-Telemetry's architecture, detailing its core components and their interactions. It covers the foundations of tracing, metrics, and logging within the framework, offering insights into how data is captured and processed. The chapter further explores data flow mechanisms and the extensibility of OpenTelemetry, emphasizing its ability to integrate with and adapt to a wide range of existing systems and protocols. These elements collectively form the backbone of OpenTelemetry, enabling comprehensive observability across diverse environments.

2.1 Core Components of OpenTelemetry

The architectural framework of OpenTelemetry is built upon several core components that collectively offer a comprehensive infrastructure for telemetry data. These include instrumentation libraries, collectors, and exporters. Each component plays a pivotal role in efficiently capturing, processing, and transmitting telemetry data, thus enabling robust observability across various applications and services. The integration and operation of these components provide a holistic approach to monitoring and tracing distributed systems.

Instrumentation libraries are the initial building blocks within the OpenTelemetry framework. They are responsible for directly embedding within applications to automatically generate telemetry data such as traces, metrics, and logs. These libraries offer APIs and SDKs tailored to different programming languages, ensuring that developers have the necessary tools to instrument their applications seamlessly. The design of these libraries adheres to open standards, promoting uniformity and interoperability.

Consider a simple example where we instrument a Python application to generate trace data. The OpenTelemetry SDK for Python provides necessary functionalities, from creating traces to set up context propagation. Below is a code snippet illustrating the basic setup of tracing using the OpenTelemetry Python SDK.

```
from opentelemetry import trace
from opentelemetry.sdk.trace import TracerProvider
from opentelemetry.sdk.trace.export import SimpleSpanProcessor,
    ConsoleSpanExporter

trace.set_tracer_provider(TracerProvider())
tracer = trace.get_tracer(__name__)

trace.get_tracer_provider().add_span_processor(
    SimpleSpanProcessor(ConsoleSpanExporter())
)

def my_function():
    with tracer.start_as_current_span("my_span"):
        print("Hello, OpenTelemetry")

my_function()
```

In this snippet, a tracer is initialized using the Trace Provider, after which a span processor and exporter are configured to output traces to the console. The function my_function demonstrates a span being created, encapsulating its scope of execution. This basic setup exemplifies how developers can instrument applications, thus enabling the generation of valuable telemetry information.

Collectors serve as intermediaries in the OpenTelemetry pipeline. They are independent services that are responsible for receiving telemetry data, processing it, and exporting it to back-end systems or databases.

Operating as agents or gateways, collectors act as a centralized point, refining and transforming the telemetry data journey to the destination systems. They enable decoupling of data producers from consumers, offering robust management capabilities like data batching, processing, and enhancing data before export.

Here is a configuration example of an OpenTelemetry Collector using a YAML file:

```
receivers:
  otlp:
    protocols:
      grpc:
      http:

processors:
  batch:

exporters:
  logging:
    loglevel: debug

service:
  pipelines:
    traces:
      receivers: [otlp]
      processors: [batch]
      exporters: [logging]
```

This configuration sets up a Collector pipeline to receive telemetry data via the OpenTelemetry protocol (OTLP) over HTTP and gRPC, processes it with a batch processor, and finally logs the traces. Such a setup elucidates the capabilities of collectors to tailor telemetry data flow based on specific requirements before pushing data to well-adapted logging systems.

Exporters form the endpoint of the telemetry pipeline, responsible for dispatching processed data from collectors to a range of back-end systems, such as databases, analytics platforms, or third-party monitoring solutions. The exporters are effectively the bridge between the telemetry system and the analysis tools, aligning with popular formats and protocols to ensure compatibility and scalability. OpenTelemetry supports a wide array of exporters that cater to different solutions, like Prometheus, Jaeger, Zipkin, and more.

Understanding the interplay between these core components involves examining how telemetry data flows and is transformed at each stage.

In typical deployment scenarios, applications embedded with instrumentation libraries generate traces, metrics, and logs which are ingested by collectors. These collectors then apply processing strategies to enrich and aggregate the telemetry data before releasing them to exporters. The exporters dispatch this data, where it can be stored, visualized, and analyzed to yield actionable insights, thus closing the observability loop.

A crucial aspect of OpenTelemetry is its emphasis on interoperability and adherence to open standards, ensuring that each component within the architecture communicates effectively and integrates seamlessly into broader ecosystems. This capability extends to providing resilience in handling high-throughput data and accommodating a wide range of telemetry needs, from complex distributed systems to single-node applications.

As OpenTelemetry continues to evolve, its architecture becomes increasingly sophisticated with new features that enhance existing core components. Notably, adaptive sampling methods have been introduced in instrumentation libraries to manage data volumes effectively by selectively sampling critical spans or metrics based on defined criteria. Dynamic configuration options in collectors allow for flexible and responsive telemetry pipelines that adapt to changing application states or requirements. Finally, additional support for exporters ensures that OpenTelemetry remains versatile and extends its capacity to interface with emerging technologies and back-end solutions.

Thus, the core components of OpenTelemetry encapsulate a comprehensive framework designed to facilitate superior observability across complex and distributed systems. By meticulously managing each stage of telemetry data life cycle—from generation to export—OpenTelemetry enables developers and operators to gain unparalleled insights into their applications' performance and behavior.

2.2   Tracing Architecture

Tracing is a fundamental aspect of observability within OpenTelemetry, designed to capture and analyze the execution path of operations across distributed systems. The tracing architecture of OpenTelemetry is engineered to provide deep insights into how requests traverse through multiple services, uncovering latency bottlenecks and errors. This section delves into the core elements of the tracing architecture, detailing how traces are structured, captured, processed, and propagated across services.

At the core of OpenTelemetry's tracing capabilities is the concept of a *trace*, a data structure that represents a single transaction or request as it flows through a distributed system. Each trace contains a series of *spans*, individual units representing a distinct work segment within the transaction. A span records the operation's name, start and end timestamps, contextual data, and any associated attributes. The relationship between spans forms a directed acyclic graph, capturing the execution sequence and dependencies between various segments.

A trace's granularity can be illustrated by considering an example of a web application handling an HTTP request. Below is a code snippet in Python demonstrating the creation of spans within such a transaction.

```python
from opentelemetry import trace
from opentelemetry.sdk.trace import TracerProvider
from opentelemetry.sdk.trace.export import SimpleSpanProcessor
from opentelemetry.exporter.otlp.proto.grpc.trace_exporter import
    OTLPSpanExporter

trace.set_tracer_provider(TracerProvider())
tracer = trace.get_tracer(__name__)

span_exporter = OTLPSpanExporter(endpoint="localhost:4317")

trace.get_tracer_provider().add_span_processor(
    SimpleSpanProcessor(span_exporter)
)

def process_request(request):
    with tracer.start_as_current_span("handle_request") as span:
        span.set_attribute("http.method", request.method)
        span.set_attribute("http.url", request.url)
        response = call_internal_service()
        span.set_attribute("http.status_code", response.status_code)
    return response

def call_internal_service():
    with tracer.start_as_current_span("internal_api_call") as span:
        # Simulation of a delay or processing
        return MockResponse(200)

class MockResponse:
    def __init__(self, status_code):
        self.status_code = status_code
```

In this example, the handle_request span represents the processing of an incoming HTTP request, while the internal_api_call span represents an external service call. Context propagation ensures that these spans are appropriately nested, preserving the trace's structure.

OpenTelemetry ensures trace context is propagated across process barriers, which is crucial for tracking the flow of execution through multiple services. This propagation is facilitated through context carriers, typically in HTTP headers or similar protocol metadata. traceparent and tracestate headers are commonly utilized to convey this context between services.

Consider a distributed system involving multiple microservices communicating over HTTP. Below is an example of how OpenTelemetry handles trace context propagation using HTTP inject and extract methods:

```
from opentelemetry.propagate import inject, extract
from opentelemetry.trace import set_span_in_context, get_current_span
from opentelemetry.context import attach, detach, set_value
from requests import request

def client_request():
    span_context = get_current_span().get_span_context()
    headers = {}
    inject(headers=headers)

    response = request(
        method='GET',
        url='http://internal.service/resource',
        headers=headers
    )
    return response

def server_receive(incoming_headers):
    context = extract(incoming_headers)
    token = attach(context)
    try:
        span = tracer.start_as_current_span("server_process")
        # Process the request within the span's context
    finally:
        detach(token)
```

Here, the client_request function demonstrates context injection, embedding the trace context into HTTP headers when sending a request. Meanwhile, server_receive extracts the trace context from incoming headers, ensuring continuity of the trace across service boundaries.

Crucial to the productivity of distributed tracing is the implementation of sampling strategies. Sampling determines how traces and spans are collected, controlling the amount of telemetry data generated. Open-Telemetry allows for various sampling strategies, from constant sampling, where all traces are recorded, to dynamic sampling, which intelligently records specific traces based on certain criteria, such as errors or latency thresholds. These strategies allow for flexible and efficient data collection that aligns with system performance and resource constraints.

The processing of traces involves several operations, where the traces are batched, manipulated, and potentially enriched with additional metadata before being exported. Exporters within the tracing architecture dispatch traces to back-end systems, enabling storage and advanced analysis through visualization tools, dashboards, and alerting systems. Popular exporters include those for Jaeger, Zipkin, and commercial APM platforms, facilitating diverse analysis requirements and preferences.

The power of OpenTelemetry's tracing architecture is its ability to offer developers and operators an end-to-end understanding of application performance through comprehensive trace data. This understanding not only aids in diagnosing performance issues or failures but also provides an empirical foundation for optimization endeavors. Furthermore, the open standards and interoperability at the heart of Open-Telemetry ensure that trace data can be leveraged within a wide ecosystem of tools and platforms, extending its utility beyond raw telemetry ingestion.

Recent advancements in the tracing architecture have led to further innovations, such as improved span processing capabilities and enhanced support for complex trace patterns, including those generated by event-driven architectures and asynchronous workflows. The pervasive adoption and constant evolution of OpenTelemetry underscore its effectiveness and relevance in modern application observability, enabling development and operations teams to maintain excellence in application performance and reliability. The tracing architecture, by capturing the essence of each transaction within distributed systems, provides a detailed and actionable view that guides improvements in both system design and operational procedures.

2.3 Metrics Architecture

Metrics are a cornerstone of observability and performance monitoring in software systems, providing quantitative data about the operational state and processes of applications. The metrics architecture in Open-Telemetry is designed to efficiently collect, aggregate, and export metric data, offering insights into both system behavior and performance anomalies. Understanding the intricacies of OpenTelemetry's metrics architecture is crucial for leveraging this toolset to achieve a comprehensive visualization of application health.

OpenTelemetry supports three primary types of metrics: *Counters*, *Gauges*, and *Histograms*. Each metric type offers unique characteristics suited to various monitoring scenarios. Counters are non-decreasing metrics ideal for tracking events such as the number of requests received. Gauges represent a single value that can fluctuate, such as CPU usage or memory consumption. Histograms help capture distribution data over intervals, useful for tracking request latency or payload sizes.

The setup of the OpenTelemetry SDK for metrics entails defining these metrics and their collection process. Below is a Python example demonstrating how to instrument an application to collect and export metric data:

```
from opentelemetry import metrics
from opentelemetry.exporter.otlp.proto.grpc.metric_exporter import
    OTLPMetricsExporter
from opentelemetry.sdk.metrics import MeterProvider, Counter, ValueRecorder

metrics.set_meter_provider(MeterProvider())
meter = metrics.get_meter(__name__)

# Create a counter metric
request_counter = meter.create_counter(
    name="http_requests",
    description="The number of HTTP requests received",
    unit="1",
    value_type=int
)

# Create a value recorder metric
response_time = meter.create_valuerecorder(
    name="http_response_time",
    description="The duration of HTTP responses",
    unit="ms",
    value_type=float
```

```
)
# Configure metric exporter
metric_exporter = OTLPMetricsExporter(endpoint="localhost:4317")
metrics.get_meter_provider().start_pipeline(meter, metric_exporter, interval=5)

# Increment the counter for each request
def handle_request(request):
    request_counter.add(1, {"method": request.method})
    with response_time.record() as record:
        # Simulating processing time
        response = process_request(request)
        processing_time = calculate_process_time()
        record(processing_time, {"status_code": response.status_code})
    return response
```

This code initializes a counter and a value recorder, representing the number of HTTP requests and their response times, respectively. The metrics are then periodically exported via the OTLP protocol, allowing for remote monitoring and analysis.

The architecture supports efficient metric aggregation, reducing data volume while preserving statistical significance. This aggregation occurs both temporally, over periods, and spatially, across distributed systems. Spatial aggregation is particularly advantageous in systems with high cardinality, such as those with numerous microservices. Temporal aggregation, on the other hand, helps summarize metrics over defined time windows, supporting historical analyses and trend identification.

Sampling is less relevant to metrics than to tracing, primarily because certain kinds of metrics inherently involve statistical sampling, like histograms. Instead, aggregation is crucial, where metrics are summarized in ways that facilitate meaningful interpretations. For instance, while a counter records each event occurrence, the total over time is often more insightful. Similarly, aggregating values in histograms gives insights into data distribution over the measured period.

OpenTelemetry allows for configurable metric processors and exporters, tailoring metric data flow from collection to external analysis tools. Processors apply transformations and compute aggregates, while exporters emit this processed data to storage systems or real-time monitoring dashboards. Popular exporters include those for Prometheus, InfluxDB, and AWS CloudWatch, accommodating a diverse range of operational environments and

39

reporting needs.

Below is an example YAML configuration for setting up an Open-Telemetry Collector with metrics capabilities:

```
receivers:
  otlp:
    protocols:
      grpc:

processors:
  batch:
    timeout: 200ms

exporters:
  prometheus:
    endpoint: "0.0.0.0:8889"

service:
  pipelines:
    metrics:
      receivers: [otlp]
      processors: [batch]
      exporters: [prometheus]
```

This configuration defines a pipeline to receive, batch, and export metrics data to a Prometheus endpoint. Integrating OpenTelemetry with Prometheus, a widely-used open-source metrics system, enables robust metrics visualization and alerting capabilities, leveraging Prometheus's powerful query language and ecosystem.

The synchronous nature of metrics capturing in traditional settings is complemented by asynchronous settings, which are beneficial for capturing metrics from event-driven or asynchronous operations. The metrics SDKs in OpenTelemetry provide support for this by allowing the definition of callbacks that update metric values asynchronously, accommodating use cases such as monitoring event streams or message queues.

Furthermore, recent advancements in OpenTelemetry have introduced dynamic telemetry for metrics, where metric schemas can be dynamically updated at runtime, adapting to varying monitoring needs without requiring redeployment. This flexibility empowers operations teams to refine their monitoring strategy in real-time, aligning observability with current operational health and workload dynamics.

A crucial architectural strength of OpenTelemetry's metrics framework is its support for multidimensional data, enabling rich, contextual insights. Tagging metrics with dimensions such as region, instance type, or customer ID allows for comprehensive drill-down and filtering capabilities, crucial for large-scale operations that need granular insights into specific segments of their systems.

A well-architected metrics framework, as embodied by OpenTelemetry, provides substantial value by aligning metric collection closely with desired business and technical outcomes. By integrating metrics with logs and traces, OpenTelemetry achieves a single, coherent observability framework leveraging minimal mismatch across telemetry data types. This integrated approach ensures consistency and a comprehensive analytical perspective, driving well-informed decision-making across development and operations teams.

The OpenTelemetry metrics architecture continues to evolve with community-driven improvements and alignment with industry standards. The push for more sophisticated metric types and enhanced exporter support has broadened its applicability across various domains and infrastructure setups, ensuring its place as an indispensable tool for reliable and scalable observability solutions. Through efficient data capture, aggregation, and exportation, OpenTelemetry's metrics architecture empowers organizations to maintain operational excellence and continuously optimize their systems.

2.4   Logging Architecture

Logging serves as an essential facet of observability, offering detailed records of events within software systems. In OpenTelemetry, the logging architecture is designed to seamlessly integrate with existing logging frameworks while enhancing logs with contextual telemetry data. This architecture is critical for capturing granular details, tracking system behavior, and diagnosing issues, providing a foundation for comprehensive operational analytics.

OpenTelemetry's approach to logging centers around the enrichment of logs with trace and context correlation data, ultimately improving the observability capabilities within distributed systems. By correlating logs with traces and metrics, operators gain a holistic view of the system's state and behavior, facilitating more effective troubleshooting and performance tuning.

The fundamental element in the logging architecture is the *Log Record*, a structured representation of an event, typically containing elements such as timestamp, log level, message, and additional context. While traditional logging systems focus on application-level logging, Open-Telemetry enables logs to incorporate telemetry context, allowing for the linkage between logs and traces or metrics.

Consider a Python application using the OpenTelemetry logging SDK. This example demonstrates enriching log records with trace context:

```python
import logging
from opentelemetry import trace
from opentelemetry.sdk.trace import TracerProvider
from opentelemetry.sdk.trace.export import SimpleSpanProcessor,
    ConsoleSpanExporter
from opentelemetry.sdk.logging import BaggageContext, log_record
from opentelemetry.sdk.logging.export import ConsoleLogExporter

# Set up tracing
trace.set_tracer_provider(TracerProvider())
tracer = trace.get_tracer(__name__)
trace.get_tracer_provider().add_span_processor(
    SimpleSpanProcessor(ConsoleSpanExporter())
)

# Set up logging
logging.basicConfig(level=logging.DEBUG)
logger = logging.getLogger(__name__)

def example_function():
    with tracer.start_as_current_span("example_span") as span:
        logger.info("Processing data...")
        context = BaggageContext()
        log_rec = log_record.LogRecord(
            name=logger.name,
            level=logging.INFO,
            pathname=__file__,
            lineno=23,
            msg="Data processed successfully.",
            args=(),
            exc_info=None,
            trace_id=span.get_context().trace_id
        )
        ConsoleLogExporter().export(log_rec)

example_function()
```

In the example, the log record is created and enriched with trace context, such as trace ID, enabling seamless correlation with tracing events. This correlation is key to efficiently tracing transaction paths through logs in distributed systems, allowing logs to carry actionable insights in alignment with other telemetry data.

The logging architecture of OpenTelemetry offers substantial extensibility and interoperability with popular logging libraries and frameworks such as Log4j, SLF4J, and java.util.logging in Java environments, or logging in Python. This is achieved through adapters, which act as bridges between OpenTelemetry's structured logging model and the logging APIs and formats these libraries offer. Such adapters ensure that existing logging setups can easily leverage OpenTelemetry's capabilities without extensive refactoring.

OpenTelemetry logs can be exported to various back-end systems, where they are stored, processed, and analyzed. The exporter configuration plays a crucial role in defining how and where logs are dispatched. Common destinations include log management solutions such as Elasticsearch, Fluentd, or cloud-based logging services like AWS CloudWatch and Google Cloud Logging. Through these integrations, logs are centralized and can be queried for patterns, anomalies, or specific events.

Below is an example configuration of an OpenTelemetry Collector for log processing:

```
receivers:
  otlp:
    protocols:
      grpc:

processors:
  batch:
    timeout: 200ms
  resource:
    attributes:
      - key: department
        value: engineering

exporters:
  logging:
    loglevel: info
  googlecloud:
    project_id: "my-project-id"

service:
  pipelines:
    logs:
      receivers: [otlp]
```

```
processors: [batch, resource]
exporters: [logging, googlecloud]
```

This configuration illustrates a log pipeline that utilizes the Open-Telemetry Protocol (OTLP) to receive logs, applies batching and resource attribute enrichment processors, and exports logs to a local logging system and Google Cloud's log ingestion service. Such flexibility in configuration supports tailored monitoring solutions that align with organizational requirements.

An essential aspect of OpenTelemetry's logging architecture is the concept of *Semantic Conventions*. These are standardized schemas that define attribute names and types across different log contexts, ensuring consistent and understandable log representation across different applications and services. By adhering to semantic conventions, organizations can achieve consistent log analysis and querying capabilities, regardless of the application domain or infrastructure complexity.

Logging through OpenTelemetry also supports dynamic context labels, which can be appended to logs for enhanced contextual information. These labels enable filtering and aggregation of logs based on context-specific attributes like host, location, or event source, thus enriching logs with metadata that supports detailed diagnostics and forensics investigation.

Furthermore, the advancement of OpenTelemetry supports Distributed Event Logging, a concept that captures and logs events as they occur across a distributed system, simultaneously enriching these logs with relevant telemetry data. This feature aids in creating a temporal narrative of events, advantageous in incident response scenarios where understanding the sequence and context of events can be crucial.

The logging architecture is continuously evolving, with recent developments seeking seamless integration with AI-powered log analysis solutions. These integrations aim to enhance operational insights by identifying patterns and suggesting actions based on historical log data and machine learning algorithms, thus propelling log analysis beyond traditional thresholds and outlier detection.

OpenTelemetry's logging architecture, through its distributed, contextual, and semantic approach, provides a robust framework for capturing and analyzing logs in line with comprehensive observability practices. By integrating logs closely with traces and metrics, organizations can achieve a unified observability framework that drives timely and informed operational decision-making. This enables not only effective troubleshooting and root cause analysis but also predictive insights that facilitate proactive system optimization and reliability assurance. Through flexibility, configurability, and a commitment to open standards, OpenTelemetry continues to advance the log observability landscape, ensuring its relevance and utility in increasingly complex system architectures.

2.5 Data Flow in OpenTelemetry

The data flow within OpenTelemetry encapsulates the journey telemetry data undertakes from generation to its final destination in backend systems for analysis and visualization. Understanding this data flow is crucial for effectively leveraging OpenTelemetry's capabilities to enhance observability and optimize system performance. The meticulously designed data flow architecture in OpenTelemetry ensures a comprehensive, scalable, and efficient pipeline for traces, metrics, and logs across distributed systems.

The fundamental stages of data flow in OpenTelemetry include data generation, context propagation, data processing, and data export. Each stage is vital in maintaining the integrity, relevance, and utility of telemetry data, ultimately enabling robust observability and performance tuning.

Data generation is the initial stage where telemetry data is captured via instrumented applications. Instrumentation libraries integrated into application codebase utilize OpenTelemetry APIs to create and record traces, metrics, and logs. These libraries offer interfaces designed to be language-agnostic, ensuring OpenTelemetry's applicability across varied technology stacks. Below is a Python snippet demonstrating the generation of telemetry data through instrumentation:

```
from opentelemetry import trace, metrics
from opentelemetry.sdk.trace import TracerProvider
from opentelemetry.sdk.metrics import MeterProvider
from opentelemetry.sdk.trace.export import BatchSpanProcessor, ConsoleSpanExporter
```

45

```
from opentelemetry.sdk.metrics.export import ConsoleMetricsExporter

# Tracing setup
trace.set_tracer_provider(TracerProvider())
tracer = trace.get_tracer(__name__)
span_processor = BatchSpanProcessor(ConsoleSpanExporter())
trace.get_tracer_provider().add_span_processor(span_processor)

# Metrics setup
metrics.set_meter_provider(MeterProvider())
meter = metrics.get_meter(__name__)
counter = meter.create_counter("example_counter")
meter.get_meter_provider().start_pipeline(meter, ConsoleMetricsExporter(), interval
    =5)

def process_data():
    with tracer.start_as_current_span("process_data_span"):
        print("Processing data...")
        counter.add(1, {"operation": "process"})
```

In this example, an OpenTelemetry-enabled application generates spans and metrics, recording them for further processing. The span processor batches and exports trace data via a console exporter, while the meter records and outputs metric data at specified intervals.

Context propagation is a pivotal aspect, ensuring continuity and correlation of telemetry data across different services and hosts within distributed systems. OpenTelemetry manages this through context carriers embedded in communication protocols. Propagation mechanisms maintain trace and metric context through diverse interfaces such as HTTP headers or message queue properties, upholding the causality between distributed application events.

Below is an illustration of context propagation using HTTP headers:

```
from opentelemetry.propagate import inject, extract
from requests import request

def client_operation():
    headers = {}
    inject(headers=headers)
    response = request(
        method='GET',
        url='http://remote.service/api',
        headers=headers
    )
    return response

def server_process(incoming_headers):
    context = extract(incoming_headers)
    with tracer.start_as_current_span("server_operation", context=context):
        # Server-side processing logic
```

```
    pass
```

Such exemplary context propagation models ensure that telemetry data retains its contextual attributes across service boundaries, integral for coherent data analysis.

In the data processing stage, telemetry data undergoes transformation and enrichment. Collectors, deployed as agents or centralized services, perform operations such as batching, filtering, and correlating telemetry data with additional metadata. Collectors autonomously adapt to varying loads, augmenting telemetry data with node-specific identifiers, enriching it before dispatch.

A breakdown of a YAML configuration for a collector illustrates these capabilities:

```
receivers:
  otlp:
    protocols:
      grpc:
      http:

processors:
  batch:
    timeout: 200ms
  resource:
    attributes:
      - key: instance_id
        value: my-instance

exporters:
  prometheus:
    endpoint: "0.0.0.0:8889"

service:
  pipelines:
    metrics:
      receivers: [otlp]
      processors: [batch, resource]
      exporters: [prometheus]
    traces:
      receivers: [otlp]
      processors: [batch, resource]
      exporters: [logging]
```

In this configuration, a collector receives data via the OTLP receiver, processes it with batch and resource processors, and exports it to Prometheus for metrics or logs for traces. This setup facilitates flexible, efficient data flow alignment with operational priorities.

47

Finally, the export stage culminates the data flow in OpenTelemetry, defining connectivity between the collector and various back-end analytical systems. Exporters translate OpenTelemetry's telemetry data formats into formats desired by back-end observability tools. This translation and transportation establish an endpoint-independent data pathway that ensures compatibility with a multitude of telemetry-consuming systems, from open-source platforms like Jaeger and Prometheus to commercial solutions like Datadog and Splunk.

The intricacies of data flow design within OpenTelemetry continue to evolve, underscoring the goal of supporting increasingly complex telemetry demands, such as adaptive sampling and real-time event processing. Adaptive sampling dynamically adjusts telemetry data collection intensity based on involved criteria, striking a balance between insights and resource consumption. This strategic sampling minimizes telemetry overhead during regular operations, increasing fidelity when anomalies occur.

Real-time event stream processing represents a significant advancement, capitalizing on the precision and timeliness of data as it's ingested and analyzed on-the-fly, empowering operators to react swiftly to emergent events. Furthermore, deployment-agnostic data flows adjust seamlessly to varied infrastructure compositions, whether on-premises, in the cloud, or hybrid environments, enhancing Open-Telemetry's universal applicability.

Aggregated, the data flow in OpenTelemetry epitomizes a transformative paradigm for observability, unifying traces, metrics, and logs through cohesive architecture. By establishing robust connections from data generation through to exportation, OpenTelemetry delivers a reliable and responsive monitor, indispensable for operational insight, performance optimization, and incident resolution. Flexible data pathways ensure its prominence in next-gen software monitoring solutions, equipping organizations to ascertain comprehensive clarity and control over their distributed systems.

2.6 Extensibility and Interoperability

OpenTelemetry is designed with a focus on extensibility and interoperability, ensuring that it can adapt to the myriad of monitoring requirements present in diverse technology ecosystems. Its modular architecture allows seamless integration with existing observability stacks while enabling extensions that cater to specific enterprise needs. These capabilities are pivotal in maintaining OpenTelemetry's relevance and effectiveness as the de facto standard for observability.

Extensibility in OpenTelemetry involves the ability to customize and extend its inherent capabilities to accommodate additional functionalities or new telemetry formats without compromising the core system. This is achieved through its well-designed API and SDKs that offer interfaces for augmenting existing functionalities and the integration of plugins or extensions.

OpenTelemetry's extensibility is exemplified through its support for custom instrumentation. Developers can create specialized methods to capture telemetry data relevant to specific domains or applications. This process involves encoding application-specific logic that generates meaningful telemetry context. Below is an example of creating custom metrics in a Python application to track user-defined events:

```
from opentelemetry import metrics
from opentelemetry.sdk.metrics import MeterProvider

metrics.set_meter_provider(MeterProvider())
meter = metrics.get_meter(__name__)

# Custom metric for task completion
task_completion_metric = meter.create_counter(
    name="custom_task_completed",
    description="Tracks number of tasks successfully completed",
    unit="1",
    value_type=int
)

def complete_task(task_id):
    # Custom logic for task completion
    print(f"Completing task {task_id}")
    task_completion_metric.add(1, {"task_id": task_id, "status": "completed"})

complete_task("12345")
```

This snippet demonstrates how OpenTelemetry can be extended to capture new metrics that are not natively supported in the standard SDK, facilitating detailed tracking of application-specific events.

The plugin architecture in OpenTelemetry further contributes to its extensibility by enabling the addition of new exporters, processors, and other components that can be dynamically loaded and used within telemetry pipelines. This flexibility allows developers and organizations to integrate third-party solutions or proprietary systems into their observability flows without conflicting with existing deployments.

OpenTelemetry's interoperability is anchored in its commitment to open standards, ensuring compatibility with various ecosystems and standards bodies such as the Cloud Native Computing Foundation (CNCF) and OpenMetrics. Interoperability is critically important in modern IT environments, which often involve heterogeneous systems and varying operational requirements.

An example of OpenTelemetry's interoperability is its ability to export telemetry data to several widespread back-end systems, using a plethora of exporters tailored to different platforms and environments. OpenTelemetry supports exporters for popular telemetry data consumers such as Prometheus, Jaeger, Zipkin, and numerous cloud-native platforms.

A practical configuration example exporting trace data to Jaeger demonstrates this interoperability:

```
receivers:
  otlp:
    protocols:
      grpc:

exporters:
  jaeger:
    endpoint: "http://localhost:14250"

service:
  pipelines:
    traces:
      receivers: [otlp]
      exporters: [jaeger]
```

This setup leverages a Jaeger exporter to transmit trace data, illustrating OpenTelemetry's capability to seamlessly operate within existing observability infrastructures. Such integrations are pivotal for organizations looking to migrate to OpenTelemetry without disrupting their current analytics and monitoring workflows.

OpenTelemetry's adherence to open standards extends to its use of the OpenTelemetry Protocol (OTLP), a vendor-neutral protocol designed for efficient telemetry data transmission. OTLP ensures consistent data formats and exchanges across systems, enabling diverse observability solutions to communicate using common language and structures.

Beyond direct integrations, OpenTelemetry supports interoperability through data transformation tools such as processors, which can enrich, translate, and filter telemetry data effectively. These tools enable telemetry data to be adapted and aligned with specific data models required by downstream systems, ensuring that analytical and storage layers receive data in preferred schemas and formats.

The ongoing development within the OpenTelemetry community to support emerging protocols and data formats underlines its commitment to interoperability. This initiative actively incorporates community and industry feedback to refine OpenTelemetry's capabilities in addressing novel observability challenges and integrating bleeding-edge technologies.

The broader ecosystem of OpenTelemetry is fortified through its support for adaptors. These adaptors bridge OpenTelemetry with legacy or alternative telemetry frameworks, like integrating OpenTelemetry abilities into existing OpenCensus or OpenTracing setups. This feature supports incremental migration to OpenTelemetry, allowing organizations to embrace advanced observability without immediate overhaul of their entire telemetry infrastructure.

OpenTelemetry's extensibility and interoperability combine to empower organizations with the tools required for a more transparent, efficient, and adaptable observability system. These attributes secure OpenTelemetry's position as a future-proof solution, readily adaptable to unfolding enterprise requirements and technological advancements.

Extensibility and interoperability are not merely features but a strategic imperative for OpenTelemetry, ensuring it sustains its core role in evolving IT landscapes. Through a commitment to open standards and a flexible, extensible architecture, OpenTelemetry guarantees its users a robust platform for observability that blends seamlessly into existing operations while empowering them to tackle future challenges in monitoring and performance management. This readiness equips organizations with a significant advantage in a technology world driven by rapid change and relentless innovation.

Chapter 3

Setting Up and Configuring OpenTelemetry

This chapter outlines the essential steps for successfully setting up and configuring OpenTelemetry across various platforms. It guides through the installation of SDKs, the configuration of tracing and metrics, and the deployment of the OpenTelemetry Collector. Readers will learn how to export telemetry data to different backend systems and customize settings to align with distinct operational needs. Additionally, practical advice is provided for troubleshooting common setup challenges, ensuring a smooth implementation process and optimal performance from the outset.

3.1   Installing OpenTelemetry SDKs

Understanding and deploying OpenTelemetry SDKs is fundamental to utilizing OpenTelemetry's full capabilities for capturing telemetry data. OpenTelemetry SDKs are available for various programming languages including Java, Python, JavaScript, and others. Each language offers slightly different installation procedures depending on the ecosystem and package management tools prevalent in that domain.

- **Java SDK Installation:** Java is a widely-used programming language with numerous applications in enterprise environments. Ensuring proper installation of the OpenTelemetry Java SDK is crucial for capturing telemetry data. The installation typically involves adding OpenTelemetry dependencies to your build configuration.

  For Maven users, this can be accomplished by modifying the pom.xml. To include OpenTelemetry instrumentation libraries, you would edit the dependencies section as follows:

```xml
<dependencies>
    <!-- OpenTelemetry SDK and Auto-Instrumentation -->
    <dependency>
        <groupId>io.opentelemetry</groupId>
        <artifactId>opentelemetry-sdk</artifactId>
        <version>1.10.0</version>
    </dependency>
    <dependency>
        <groupId>io.opentelemetry</groupId>
        <artifactId>opentelemetry-auto-exporters-jaeger</artifactId>
        <version>1.10.0</version>
    </dependency>
    <!-- Additional instrumentation library dependencies -->
</dependencies>
```

  In a Gradle project, the build.gradle file is used. You can include the OpenTelemetry dependencies by adding:

```
dependencies {
    implementation 'io.opentelemetry:opentelemetry-sdk:1.10.0'
    implementation 'io.opentelemetry:opentelemetry-auto-exporters-jaeger
        :1.10.0'
    // Other relevant dependencies
}
```

  These instructions ensure that the necessary SDK components will be downloaded and available during your build process, enabling you to integrate OpenTelemetry into your Java applications effectively.

- **Python SDK Installation:** Python's simplicity and extensive library support make it a popular choice for developing varied applications, from web development to scientific computing. The typical installation method for OpenTelemetry SDK in Python is via pip, Python's package installer. Use the command:

```
pip install opentelemetry-api
pip install opentelemetry-sdk
```

These commands install the core OpenTelemetry API and SDK packages. For instrumenting specific libraries such as Flask or Django, additional packages are required. For instance, to instrument a Flask application:

```
pip install opentelemetry-instrumentation-flask
```

With these packages, Python applications can be instrumented to gather metrics and tracing data.

- **JavaScript SDK Installation:** JavaScript is frequently utilized for web applications and Node.js services. Installation of OpenTelemetry for JavaScript is done via npm. For Node.js, the SDK can be installed using the following command:

```
npm install @opentelemetry/api
npm install @opentelemetry/sdk-trace-node
```

For browser environments, the installation may require additional packages depending on the needs of your specific application context. Typical commands include:

```
npm install @opentelemetry/sdk-trace-web
npm install @opentelemetry/instrumentation-fetch
```

After installing these SDKs, JavaScript applications deployed on both server-side and client-side can effectively utilize OpenTelemetry's capabilities for gathering extensive telemetry data.

- **Implementation of SDKs and Instrumentation:** Once installed, each SDK typically requires a degree of configuration before telemetry data can be captured effectively. This involves setting up a tracing provider and utilizing auto-instrumentation to pivotal points in the code. Consider the following Java example:

```
// Import relevant OpenTelemetry classes
import io.opentelemetry.api.trace.Span;
import io.opentelemetry.api.trace.Tracer;
import io.opentelemetry.api.GlobalOpenTelemetry;
import io.opentelemetry.api.trace.StatusCode;
```

55

```java
public class TelemetryExample {
    public static void main(String[] args) {
        Tracer tracer = GlobalOpenTelemetry.getTracer("io.opentelemetry.
            example");

        Span span = tracer.spanBuilder("exampleSpan").startSpan();
        try {
            // Perform task and set span attributes
            span.setAttribute("task", "demonstration");
            // Simulate task execution
            System.out.println("Executing span tasks.");

        } catch (Throwable t) {
            span.setStatus(StatusCode.ERROR, "Encountered error: " + t.
                getMessage());
        } finally {
            span.end();
        }
    }
}
```

This snippet demonstrates a basic implementation of OpenTelemetry concepts within a Java environment. Similar examples are constructed for other supported languages by leveraging their respective OpenTelemetry APIs.

- **Considerations for SDK Versions and Compatibility:** Selecting the correct version of OpenTelemetry SDKs compatible with your platform and runtime environment is essential. SDKs are regularly updated, introducing new features, improvements, and occasionally deprecating older methods. Careful review of the SDK documentation concerning these changes is crucial for maintaining operational compatibility and benefiting from advanced functionality.

  Moreover, interoperability among services using different language SDKs must be considered where distributed tracing involves components written in differing languages. OpenTelemetry ensures uniformity of tracing data across disparate services, emphasizing universal standards and protocols like W3C Trace-Context and OpenMetrics.

  Engagement with the OpenTelemetry community via forums, issue trackers, and contributions can further augment understanding of the intricacies involved in SDK deployments, fostering adeptness at instrumenting and capturing telemetry data with finesse. By precisely instrumenting applications, organizations

56

can build comprehensive observability systems that illuminate the internal workings of their software systems, ensuring robust operational performance.

3.2   Configuring Tracing and Metrics

The effective configuration of tracing and metrics is crucial for leveraging OpenTelemetry's full potential in monitoring and analyzing application performance. Tracing and metrics provide vital insights into the software lifecycle, facilitating deeper understanding and debuggability of distributed systems. In this section, we delve into the intricacies of configuring tracing and metrics within OpenTelemetry, exploring different languages' SDK capabilities, instrumentations, and methodologies.

Tracing Configuration:

Tracing is a core component of observability, providing a granular view into the sequence and timing of events in software applications. Configuring tracing in OpenTelemetry involves establishing a tracer instance, setting the context, and ensuring proper propagation across service boundaries.

Setting Up a Basic Tracer:

Consider a Python application; the process starts by initializing the OpenTelemetry tracing API and SDK. Utilize the following setup for a tracer:

```
from opentelemetry import trace
from opentelemetry.sdk.trace import TracerProvider
from opentelemetry.sdk.trace.export import SimpleSpanProcessor
from opentelemetry.exporter.otlp.proto.grpc.trace_exporter import
    OTLPSpanExporter

# Setup Trace Provider
trace.set_tracer_provider(TracerProvider())

# Configure Exporter and Span Processor
otlp_exporter = OTLPSpanExporter(endpoint="localhost:4317", insecure=True)
trace.get_tracer_provider().add_span_processor(
    SimpleSpanProcessor(otlp_exporter)
)

tracer = trace.get_tracer(__name__)
```

```
# Tracing example function
def example_function():
    with tracer.start_as_current_span("example_span"):
        print("Span for example function")
```

In this snippet, an OTLPSpanExporter is used to send spans to a collector or backend at localhost. The TracerProvider and SimpleSpanProcessor facilitate the customization of the tracing logic, which can be extended for further processing.

Enhancing Tracing with Attributes and Events:

Trace attributes and events add critical context to spans. Attributes are key-value pairs associated with spans, while events represent time-stamped occurrences of meaningful incidents.

Building on the previous configuration, consider enhancing example_-function:

```
def example_function():
    with tracer.start_as_current_span("example_span") as span:
        span.set_attribute("component", "database")
        span.add_event("database_query_start", attributes={"query": "SELECT *
            FROM users"})

        # Simulate database operation
        time.sleep(0.1)

        span.add_event("database_query_end", attributes={"records_returned": 34})
        print("Span for example function with attributes and events")
```

In this enhanced tracing example, additional attributes and events provide richer contextual information, making trace data invaluable for performance diagnostics and optimization.

Metrics Configuration:

Metrics are quantitative measurements used to observe the system's state or behavior over time. OpenTelemetry provides a systematic approach to metrics, involving the configuration of metric providers, instruments, and viewers to collect and visualize data effectively.

Initializing Metric Instruments:

For Java applications, setting up metrics involves using metric instruments such as counters, gauges, and histograms. Below is a Java snippet to showcase the configuration of metrics:

```
// Import relevant OpenTelemetry Metrics classes
```

```java
import io.opentelemetry.api.metrics.Meter;
import io.opentelemetry.api.metrics.GlobalMeterProvider;
import io.opentelemetry.api.metrics.LongCounter;

public class MetricsExample {
    public static void main(String[] args) {
        Meter meter = GlobalMeterProvider.getMeter("io.opentelemetry.example");
        LongCounter requestCounter = meter
            .counterBuilder("requests")
            .setDescription("Counts the number of requests made")
            .setUnit("requests")
            .build();

        // Utilize the counter
        requestCounter.add(1);
    }
}
```

This example demonstrates initializing a LongCounter, essential for counting occurrences of a particular event, such as user requests or error counts.

Choosing the Right Instruments:

Instrument selection depends on the measurement type required:

- **Counters**: Used for values that increase monotonically, such as request counts.

- **Gauges**: Capture values that may increase or decrease, like current temperature or available memory.

- **Histograms**: Record observations of values and are ideal for measuring latency or response time distributions.

For optimal results, clarity in what is being measured should guide instrument selection, ensuring that the metrics provide meaningful insights.

Propagating Context Across Boundaries:

One of the key challenges in distributed systems is the propagation of trace context across service boundaries, which ensures continuity and consistency in tracing data. OpenTelemetry offers various propagation formats, notably the W3C Trace Context format.

In a Node.js application, context propagation can be achieved using:

59

```
const { NodeTracerProvider } = require('@opentelemetry/sdk-trace-node');
const { SimpleSpanProcessor } = require('@opentelemetry/sdk-trace-base');
const { ConsoleSpanExporter } = require('@opentelemetry/sdk-trace-base');
const { HttpTraceContext } = require('@opentelemetry/core');

const provider = new NodeTracerProvider();
provider.addSpanProcessor(new SimpleSpanProcessor(new ConsoleSpanExporter()));

// Enable context propagation
const http = require('http');
const { propagation } = require('@opentelemetry/propagation');
http.createServer((req, res) => {
    const span = provider.getTracer('example').startSpan('http_request');
    propagation.extract(req.headers);

    span.addEvent('processing request');

    res.writeHead(200, { 'Content-Type': 'text/plain' });
    res.end('Hello World\n');
    span.end();
}).listen(8080);
```

propagation.extract() is used here to extract the trace context from HTTP headers, crucial for distributed tracing implementations.

Advanced Configuration and Best Practices:

- **Tailor Sampling Strategies**: Determine which traces to record based on defined criteria. Using a probabilistic sampler can reduce the volume of recorded data, balancing granularity and overhead.

- **Tagging and Filtering Data**: Ensure spans are labeled with common attributes, such as user IDs or client types. Filters can be applied to exclude non-critical data, thus preserving storage and improving visibility.

- **Batch Processing of Spans and Metrics**: Opt for batch processing exporters to mitigate network overhead. Batches of spans lead to efficient data transmission, improving application performance.

- **Incorporate Security and Privacy Policies**: Be mindful of the data captured in traces and metrics to adhere to security and privacy standards. Scrub sensitive data before retention.

Configuring tracing and metrics, while integral, is only part of forming a proficient observability strategy. Proper implementation and ongoing optimization ensure that OpenTelemetry gives profound insights into application dynamics, empowering operators to deliver stable and performant systems.

3.3 Setting up OpenTelemetry Collector

The OpenTelemetry Collector is a crucial component for receiving, processing, and exporting telemetry data from instrumented applications to various backend systems. As a separate entity, it streamlines data collection across multiple environments, thus ensuring consistent data transformation and routing. This section details the setup, configuration, and optimization of the OpenTelemetry Collector, providing insights for effective deployment and operationalization.

Collector Overview:

The OpenTelemetry Collector comprises three core components: receivers, processors, and exporters. Each plays a distinct role in the telemetry data pipeline:

- **Receivers**: Collect data from applications in various formats (e.g., OTLP, Jaeger, Zipkin).

- **Processors**: Adapt and modify data, applying transformations, filtering, and batching.

- **Exporters**: Transmit the processed data to backend systems for storage or analysis.

The collector can be deployed as a standalone application or in an agent-collector architecture. In standalone mode, it operates independently, while in the agent-collector model, an agent runs alongside each service instance and aggregates data before forwarding it to the central collector.

Installation and Configuration:

Setting up the OpenTelemetry Collector involves downloading the binary and creating a configuration file to specify its behavior. The following outlines those steps, including more advanced configurations.

Download and Installation:

For Linux environments, OpenTelemetry provides released binaries. To download and install:

```
wget https://github.com/open-telemetry/opentelemetry-collector-releases/releases/
    download/v0.46.0/otelcol-linux-amd64
chmod +x otelcol-linux-amd64
sudo mv otelcol-linux-amd64 /usr/local/bin/otelcol
```

Using Docker is another efficient method due to its easy deployment and management features:

```
docker pull otel/opentelemetry-collector:0.46.0
```

Creating a Configuration File:

Configuration of the OpenTelemetry Collector is specified via a YAML file. This file defines components such as receivers, processors, exporters, and also pipelines that specify the flow of telemetry data. An example configuration might look like this:

```
receivers:
  otlp:
    protocols:
      grpc:
      http:
  jaeger:
    protocols:
      grpc:
      thrift_http:

processors:
  batch:
    timeout: 10s
    send_batch_size: 512

exporters:
  logging:
    loglevel: debug
  otlp:
    endpoint: "collector.example.com:4317"
    tls:
      insecure: true

service:
  pipelines:
    traces:
      receivers: [otlp, jaeger]
      processors: [batch]
      exporters: [logging, otlp]
    metrics:
      receivers: [otlp]
```

```
processors: [batch]
exporters: [logging, otlp]
```

This configuration defines two pipelines: one for traces and another for metrics. The OTLP and Jaeger receivers listen for incoming trace data, while the batch processor ensures efficient data handling. Exporters then forward data to a specified collector endpoint with logging enabled for debugging.

Advanced Configuration Features:

To leverage the full capabilities of the OpenTelemetry Collector, additional configurations can be made, including but not limited to filtering, load balancing, and custom processors.

Filtering Signals:

Filters allow selective processing of telemetry data, ensuring that only relevant data is considered. Advanced filter configurations could be used to reduce overhead by discarding completions without errors or anomalies.

```
processors:
  filter:
    include:
      match_type: strict
      services: ["frontend", "payment-service"]
```

This configuration restricts processing to specific services, optimizing resource usage and focusing observability efforts.

Load Balancing Across Exporters:

In large-scale deployments, distributing load across multiple backend systems can enhance fault tolerance and scalability. The load balancing processor supports this functionality:

```
processors:
  loadbalancing:
    protocol:
      otlp:
    resolver:
      dns:
        hostname: "backends.example.com"
        port: 4317
```

This example employs DNS-based resolution to dynamically balance the collection load across backend systems that implement the OTLP protocol.

Custom Processors and Extensions:

Advanced use cases may necessitate the creation of custom processors or extensions—code blocks that manipulate or enrich telemetry data. While OpenTelemetry provides several standard processors, custom implementations can extend functionality to suit unique operational needs.

Deployment and Monitoring:

Deploying the collector necessitates strategic considerations concerning placement, redundancy, and monitoring:

- **Placement**: Determine whether to place collectors in proximity to monitored applications (e.g., as a sidecar/agent) or as centralized nodes. The choice impacts latency, network traffic, and fault domains.

- **Redundancy**: Use clustering or intelligent routing to provide high availability. This prevents single points of failure in telemetry data pipelines.

- **Monitoring**: The collector itself should be monitored for health metrics, throughput, and errors. Consider using OpenTelemetry itself, or tools like Prometheus and Grafana for visualizing the collector's performance metrics.

Security Considerations:

Data security within OpenTelemetry Collector setups requires robust measures:

- **Data Encryption**: Ensure data is encrypted in transit using TLS configurations, notably for OTLP over gRPC endpoints.

- **Authentication and Authorization**: Implement authentication mechanisms for receivers and exporters to secure endpoint communications.

- **Compliance**: Maintain compliance with policies and standards (e.g., GDPR) by filtering sensitive data and using retention and deletion policies.

Case Study: Multi-Environment Ingestion:

Consider a case where a company operates in both cloud and on-premises environments. Deploying OpenTelemetry Collector in such environments entails considering data ingress from varied sources without compromising data consistency or integrity. Use case-specific custom processors to resolve environmental differences, convert timestamp formats, or normalize metric names before export.

Both centralized and decentralized setups might be employed, each having merit based on specific internal policy drivers and architectural constraints, enabling this holistic ingestion model.

By thoroughly understanding and correctly setting up the OpenTelemetry Collector, teams can capture, transform, and export rich telemetry data flexibly and efficiently, forming the backbone of a state-of-the-art observability solution tailored for complex, distributed systems. Through rigorous adherence to design best practices, security measures, and continuous monitoring, the deployment of the OpenTelemetry Collector can significantly contribute to achieving operational excellence and deep system insights.

3.4   Exporting Data to Backend Systems

The capability to export telemetry data to various backend systems is crucial in designing effective observability architectures with OpenTelemetry. This process enables the consolidation, visualization, and analysis of telemetry data, turning raw trace and metric data into actionable insights. Different backend systems provide varying capabilities for storage, query, and analysis, necessitating careful consideration of the appropriate systems for specific operational needs.

Understanding exporter architecture:

Exporters in OpenTelemetry serve as conduits between the collected telemetry data and backend systems. Implemented as modules within the OpenTelemetry Collector or SDKs, exporters can channel data to numerous backend systems, including open-source solutions like Prometheus and Elasticsearch, and commercial platforms like Google Cloud Monitoring and Amazon CloudWatch.

The role of an exporter involves:

- Translation: Adapting telemetry data into the formats or protocols understood by the backend.

- Transmission: Handling connectivity and ensuring secure, reliable data transmission.

- Optimization: Managing resources to minimize impact on application performance and ensuring scalable data flow.

Configuring exporters in OpenTelemetry SDKs:

Exporters are typically configured via code or configuration files loaded by SDKs or agents. For instance, consider exporting trace data for a Python application using an OTLP exporter:

```
from opentelemetry import trace
from opentelemetry.sdk.trace import TracerProvider
from opentelemetry.sdk.trace.export import BatchSpanProcessor
from opentelemetry.exporter.otlp.proto.grpc.trace_exporter import
    OTLPSpanExporter

trace.set_tracer_provider(TracerProvider())

otlp_exporter = OTLPSpanExporter(endpoint="localhost:4317", insecure=True)
trace.get_tracer_provider().add_span_processor(
    BatchSpanProcessor(otlp_exporter)
)

# Initialize the tracer for use in the application
tracer = trace.get_tracer(__name__)
```

This setup provisions an OTLPSpanExporter to forward traces to a specified endpoint, often configured to point at the OpenTelemetry Collector or a compatible backend service. Parameters such as endpoint, headers, and transmission protocols require specification based on desired system integration.

Exporter types and backend selection:

Choosing the correct exporter type depends on the backend system in use and the operational requirements. Below are popular exporter-backend combinations along with practical considerations:

- Prometheus Exporter: Primarily used for metrics, Prometheus exporters facilitate metrics collection by offering endpoints for Prometheus server scrapes.

```
exporters:
  prometheus:
    endpoint: "0.0.0.0:9464"
```

Prometheus suits environments demanding high availability and flexible query capabilities through Prometheus Query Language (PromQL).

- Jaeger Exporter: Optimized for trace data, Jaeger offers distributed tracing capabilities with efficient storage indexes for fast queries.

```
exporters:
  jaeger:
    endpoint: "http://jaeger-collector:14268/api/traces"
```

Jaeger excels in microservice architectures, providing a robust UI for tracing visualizations and dependency analysis.

- Elasticsearch Exporter: Versatile for both traces and metrics, Elasticsearch provides sophisticated search and analytic capabilities through its aggregation framework.

```
exporters:
  elasticsearch:
    endpoint: "http://elastic-search-cluster:9200"
```

Elasticsearch is ideal for environments focused on real-time analytics, complex query requirements, or archival retrieval needs.

Custom exporter development:

For unique requirements, developing custom exporters allows integration with proprietary or less mainstream systems. OpenTelemetry provides interfaces to develop and plug custom exporters, adaptable for core trace, metric, or log functionalities.

The custom exporter interface mandates methods for exporting collected data batches. A simplified abstraction for traces in Java can be exemplified as follows:

```java
import io.opentelemetry.sdk.trace.export.SpanExporter;
import io.opentelemetry.sdk.trace.data.SpanData;
import java.util.Collection;
```

```
public class CustomTraceExporter implements SpanExporter {

    @Override
    public ResultCode export(Collection<SpanData> spans) {
        // Implement export logic, e.g., convert spans to custom format
        // Send data to backend system
        return ResultCode.SUCCESS;
    }

    @Override
    public ResultCode flush() {
        // Implement necessary cleanup
        return ResultCode.SUCCESS;
    }

    @Override
    public void shutdown() {
        // Resource cleanup requirements on shutdown
    }
}
```

This Java example provides a framework for pushing spans to a bespoke endpoint. Implementing robust error handling and performance tuning measures are crucial for custom development.

Operational considerations:

Practical deployment of exporters within observability architectures depends on operational factors that ensure efficient and secure data export processes:

- Security and Compliance: Implement stringent security measures like TLS encryption, API keys, or other authentication protocols to protect data in transit. Compliance with data regulations, for example, GDPR or HIPAA, mandates careful selection and physical localization of data storage.

- Network and Performance Overhead: Exporters can incur network usage and system resource load. Optimize batching configurations, transmission intervals, and compression settings to mitigate overhead.

- High Availability and Fault Tolerance: Configure exporters within redundant environments to prevent data loss. Retry and buffering mechanisms ensure continuous data transmission in face of transient network failures.

- Interoperability and Versioning: Align data formats and versions across systems to maintain interoperability between Open-Telemetry components and backend platforms.

Case study: Hybrid deployment with mixed backends:

Consider an organization utilizing both cloud and on-premises backends—GCP for cloud-native applications and a local Elastic Stack deployment for legacy systems. This hybrid strategy requires configuring appropriate exporters for both endpoints.

Telemetry data versatility allows:

- Seamless method integration for dynamic system segments.

- Enhanced granularity by mixing metrics storage in GCP and Elastic Stack for traces, each backend exploiting its strength.

- Conversion of data from formats incomprehensible by the other system, intermediary pipelines within the collector can format conversions or enable format-agnostic transfers.

Comprehensive and efficient telemetry in hybrid architectures predicates the successful orchestration of these diverse pipelines, fundamentally reliant on well-engineered OpenTelemetry exporters and adaptable process configurations.

Effective exportation of data through OpenTelemetry's exporter mechanisms ensures robust data delivery and underpins data-driven performance evaluation, anomaly detection, and strategic planning within modern, distributed system architectures. By aligning exporter configurations with backend capabilities, architectural goals, and security standards, organizations can extract maximum value from their telemetry data, driving operational excellence and innovation.

3.5 Customizing OpenTelemetry Settings

Customizing OpenTelemetry settings is pivotal in tailoring its functionality to meet specific application requirements and operational environments. Customizations allow observability systems to capture precise telemetry data aligned with organizational objectives, catering to unique performance, security, and compliance demands. This section details various avenues for customization across different OpenTelemetry components, illustrating approaches for optimizing data collection, processing, and exportation.

Instrumentation and SDK Configuration:

Starting with the fundamental layer of customization, the OpenTelemetry SDKs offer various configurational parameters. Determining appropriate instrumentation levels, SDK options, and extended settings is vital in collecting the right data effectively and minimally impacting application performance.

Adjusting Trace and Metric Intervals:

Configuring intervals for trace and metric reporting can significantly affect data granularity and resource consumption. For example, configuring the Python SDK for specific time intervals:

```
from opentelemetry.sdk.trace.export import BatchSpanProcessor

trace.set_tracer_provider(TracerProvider())

# Configure a batch span processor with custom reporting intervals
span_processor = BatchSpanProcessor(
    exporter=OTLPSpanExporter(),
    schedule_delay_millis=5000, # custom flush interval in milliseconds
    max_export_batch_size=1024 # custom maximum batch size
)
trace.get_tracer_provider().add_span_processor(span_processor)
```

Adjusting schedule_delay_millis refines how frequently the data is sent, balancing the trade-off between timeliness of data and overhead.

Setting Resource Attributes for Contextual Data:

Resource attributes provide metadata about the origin of telemetry data, facilitating targeted analysis across diverse application segments. Configuring these attributes allows insights linked to particular services, hosts, or deployment environments. An example in Java could be:

```
import io.opentelemetry.sdk.resources.Resource;
import io.opentelemetry.api.common.Attributes;

// Configure resource attributes
```

```
Resource resource = Resource.getDefault()
    .merge(Resource.create(Attributes.builder()
        .put("deployment.environment", "staging")
        .put("service.version", "1.2.3")
        .build()));

OpenTelemetrySdk.builder()
    .setTracerProvider(SdkTracerProvider.builder()
        .setResource(resource)
        .build())
    .build();
```

These attributes can notably influence data aggregation and visualization in complex environments where multiple service versions and environments coexist.

Processor and Pipeline Customization:

Processors in OpenTelemetry Collector offer a powerful means to transform telemetry data to meet organizational needs before data export occurs.

Batching and Queueing Adjustments:

Efficient data flow often necessitates customizing the batch processor. For instance, increasing the batch size might enhance data transmission efficiency for high-throughput environments:

```
processors:
  batch:
    timeout: 5s # time to wait before sending data
    send_batch_size: 512 # number of spans/metrics per batch
    send_batch_max_size: 2048 # upper limit on batch size
```

These settings can balance throughput and latency, especially crucial for metrics needing more rapid delivery than traces.

Utilizing Attribute Processors:

Customizing attributes can refine or standardize values before export. Leveraging processors to handle dynamic enrichment and masking is often necessary for adding custom fields or preserving privacy:

```
processors:
  attributes:
    actions:
    - key: "http.url"
      action: "insert"
      value: "{.value} - path only"
```

Attribute processors can also be configured to anonymize sensitive information to ensure compliance with privacy policies like GDPR or HIPAA.

Advanced Exporter Configuration:

Refined control over exporter behavior supports integration efficiencies and environmental constraints. Exporters can be fine-tuned to suit network limitations, security mandates, and compatibility requirements.

Export Format Conversion and Adaptation:

In cases where backends require specific data formats, leveraging exporters that adapt OpenTelemetry data can ensure interoperability without altering fundamental system behavior. Java applications, for example, require modular transformations:

```
public class CustomJsonExporter implements SpanExporter {

    @Override
    public ExportResult export(Collection<SpanData> spans) {
        for (SpanData span : spans) {
            // Transform SpanData into a custom JSON format
            String jsonData = convertToCustomJson(span);
            // Send jsonData to the backend
            sendDataToBackend(jsonData);
        }
        return ExportResult.SUCCESS;
    }
}
```

This strategy includes custom logic to adapt telemetry data to backend requirements, potentially reducing integration costs and complexities.

Security and Compliance Customization:

Security-centric environments impose stringent demands on observability components. Customizing settings to align with security policies encompasses encryption, masking, and access controls.

Data Encryption:

Encrypting telemetry data in transit is pivotal for complying with policies safeguarding sensitive information. Utilize transport layer security configurations such as TLS to maintain data integrity and confidentiality:

```
exporters:
```

```
otlp:
  endpoint: "collector-secure.example.com:4317"
  tls:
    insecure: false
    ca_file: "/etc/certs/ca.pem"
    cert_file: "/etc/certs/cert.pem"
```

Ensuring proper TLS setup guards against man-in-the-middle attacks and unintended data exposure.

Access Control Customization:

Customization can extend to access permissions, leveraging identity and access management frameworks to create strict controls:

```
receivers:
  otlp:
    protocols:
      grpc:
        authentication:
          username: my_user
          password: my_secure_password
```

Implementing authentication methods using API keys or OAuth2 grants can further ensure that data is accessed only by authorized entities, enhancing security postures across telemetry channels.

Optimization and Performance Tuning:

Fine-tuning OpenTelemetry setups for performance involves configuring it to minimize impact on application lifecycles while ensuring data completeness and correctness.

- **Instrument Selection and Sampling:** Careful instrument selection and sampling techniques can capture essential insights without overwhelming data processing pipelines or storage systems.

- **Resource Allocation:** Allocate appropriate computational resources, including CPU and memory, tailored to expected telemetry volumes, ensuring collector components operate efficiently and uninterruptedly.

- **Infrastructure Scaling:** Dynamically scaling infrastructure using auto-scaling groups can mitigate server overloads, improve throughput, and maintain data fidelity.

Customizations within OpenTelemetry environments transform basic setups into sophisticated observability frameworks, adeptly tuned for the operational realities and demands of modern applications. Through deliberate configuration and refinement of OpenTelemetry settings, organizations can capture insights that are rich, relevant, and actionable—fueling strategic improvements and operational excellence.

3.6   Troubleshooting Common Setup Issues

Deploying OpenTelemetry across complex systems, though highly beneficial, can present several challenges. Troubleshooting common setup issues is vital for ensuring that telemetry data is accurately captured and effectively utilized. This section discusses prevalent setup challenges, methods for diagnosing and resolving these issues, and best practices for preventive configurations.

Diagnosing Missing or Incomplete Data:

When telemetry data appears missing or incomplete, the problem often lies within configuration mismatches or network connectivity issues.

SDK Misconfiguration:

SDK misconfigurations are frequent culprits affecting data collection. Verify that:

- The correct instrumentation libraries are included in your project.

- Appropriate initialization of the Tracing and Metric providers.

- Correct endpoint configurations in exporters.

Consider a Java trace initialization check:

```
TracerProvider tracerProvider = SdkTracerProvider.builder()
    .setResource(Resource.getDefault().merge(serviceResource))
    .addSpanProcessor(SimpleSpanProcessor.builder(new OTLPSpanExporter(endpoint
        )).build())
    .build();
```

74

```
OpenTelemetrySdk.builder().setTracerProvider(tracerProvider).build();
```

Double-check that the endpoint points to a valid and reachable Open-Telemetry Collector or backend.

Collector and Exporter Verification:

Ensure the collector is correctly configured and running without errors. Review configuration files for discrepancies in receiver, processor, or exporter settings:

```
receivers:
  otlp:
    protocols:
      grpc:
exporters:
  logging:
    loglevel: debug
  prometheus:
    endpoint: "0.0.0.0:9464"
```

Utilize logging exporters to view telemetry data in real-time and confirm its flow through the collector.

Network Connectivity:

Network issues can hinder data transmission between applications, the OpenTelemetry Collector, and backend systems. To diagnose:

- Ping services to test connectivity and ensure the host machine can reach the endpoints.

- Validate any applied firewall restrictions aren't blocking telemetry ports.

```
ping collector.example.com
curl localhost:4317
```

Network debugging tools, such as tcpdump and wireshark, can offer deeper insights into packet flow issues.

Resolving Data Quality Issues:

Inaccuracies in telemetry data can result from ill-configured timing, sampling, or data processing:

Adjusting Sampling Strategies:

Improper sampling configurations can skew data impressions. Sampling is pivotal for managing the volume of traces and ensuring meaningful data subsets are collected. Validate sampling rates carefully:

```
SdkTracerProvider.builder()
    .setSampler(Sampler.traceIdRatioBased(0.5)) // 50\% of traces are sampled
```

Ensure a sampling rate aligns with your data retention capability and performance analysis requirements.

Examining Timing and Synchronization:

Data aggregation and processing might be affected by misaligned timing or clock synchronization issues. Deploy timesync services like NTP to keep system clocks precise:

```
sudo apt install ntp
sudo ntpdate pool.ntp.org
```

Ensuring clocks across distributed components are synced can prevent inconsistencies in trace-and-metrics data timestamps.

Troubleshooting Security and Configuration-Related Errors:

Security and configuration issues can stop data flow due to stricter access controls or incorrect credentials:

Authentication and Authorization:

Check if authentication configurations affecting data transmission endpoints are correct. Keep secrets, API keys, certificates, or credentials correctly set and periodically validated.

```
receivers:
  otlp:
    protocols:
      http:
        auth:
          tls:
            ca_file: "/etc/certs/ca.pem"
```

Utilize and examine logs to identify authentication failures, mismatched signatures, or credentials expiry.

Compliance and Data Privacy:

Ensure data pseudonymization or anonymization practices meet regulatory requirements—improper processing might lead to setup issues.

Regularly audit your data handling mechanisms for adherence to privacy standards such as GDPR. Pay particular attention to fields involving personal or sensitive data and apply encryption as needed.

System Resource Contention and Optimization:

High resource consumption can manifest symptoms like delayed trace or metric logs, requiring direct evaluation:

Profiling Collector and SDK Resource Usage:

Understand and document resource usage profiles for both SDKs and the OpenTelemetry Collector by utilizing profiling tools:

- Employ top, htop on Unix-based systems for high-level resource tracking.

- Use language-specific profilers like Java's VisualVM or Python's cProfile for deeper visibility into processing loads.

Optimize attributes like buffer sizes and timeout parameters to better suit available system memory and CPU quotas.

Scaling Infrastructure Dynamically:

As applications scale, ensuring telemetry pipelines are appropriately robust involves dynamic infrastructure scaling strategies using orchestration platforms (e.g., Kubernetes):

```
kubectl scale deployment otel-collector --replicas=3
```

Horizontally scaling the OpenTelemetry Collector ensures high availability and balances load, alleviating system pressure.

Best Practices for Troubleshooting Prevention:

- **Maintain Documentation**: Keep detailed records of configurations, SDK versions, and environment-specific particulars.

- **Automate Monitoring and Alerts**: Use monitoring frameworks to automate the detection of anomalies within telemetry data flow and trigger alerts.

- **Implement CI/CD Testing for Telemetry**: Include tests within CI/CD pipelines to simulate telemetry transmissions; ensuring configurations meet expected outcomes.

- **Regular Training**: Ensure teams remain updated on OpenTelemetry developments and industry standards, reducing inadvertent setup mishaps.

By adopting a comprehensive troubleshooting framework sensitive to the nuances of OpenTelemetry, users can proficiently handle setup challenges. Through rigorous attention to configuration, authentication precision, and resource optimization, common challenges can be met head-on, bootstrapping the operational resilience and effectiveness of OpenTelemetry deployments across sectors and environments.

Chapter 4

Instrumentation: Tracing, Metrics, and Logging

This chapter delves into the methods of implementing instrumentation in applications using OpenTelemetry, focusing on tracing, metrics, and logging. It provides detailed strategies for creating and managing trace spans, collecting and analyzing metrics, and integrating logging to offer contextual insights. By exploring both automated and manual instrumentation techniques, the chapter equips readers with knowledge of best practices and effective strategies for enhancing observability with minimal system overhead. Additionally, guidance is provided on retrofitting instrumentation into existing systems, ensuring comprehensive visibility and performance monitoring.

4.1   Understanding Instrumentation

In the context of software observability, instrumentation refers to the implementation of additional code within an application to collect data about its execution. This data typically includes metrics, logs, and traces, which are used to monitor, diagnose, and optimize the application's performance. Within OpenTelemetry, a widely adopted observability framework, instrumentation plays a critical role in providing comprehensive visibility into application behavior by capturing essential metadata during execution.

Instrumentation is the process of integrating observability capabilities into software applications. This includes embedding code that can produce telemetry data such as metrics, logs, and traces. The primary objective is to capture the dynamic operational characteristics of an application, which can then be analyzed to understand how different components interact, pinpoint performance bottlenecks, and identify anomalies or failures in real time.

Utilizing OpenTelemetry, developers can instrument their applications to automatically capture detailed telemetry data, fostering a deeper understanding of application state and behavior. This integration enables precise context propagation and correlation of telemetry data across distributed systems and services, thus providing consistent and comprehensive insights.

Instrumentation within OpenTelemetry is highly configurable, allowing it to be applied to various application layers, from infrastructure to user interfaces. Furthermore, it supports multiple programming languages, offering community-contributed instrumentation libraries for popular frameworks and tools. These libraries simplify the process of attaching custom telemetry to an application, significantly reducing the overhead associated with manual instrumentation.

```
from opentelemetry import trace
from opentelemetry.sdk.trace import TracerProvider
from opentelemetry.sdk.trace.export import BatchSpanProcessor, ConsoleSpanExporter


# Set up TracerProvider
trace.set_tracer_provider(TracerProvider())

# Create an exporter for stdout (console)
console_exporter = ConsoleSpanExporter()
```

```
# Create a span processor and attach the exporter to it
span_processor = BatchSpanProcessor(console_exporter)

# Add span processor to the tracer provider
trace.get_tracer_provider().add_span_processor(span_processor)

# Define a tracer
tracer = trace.get_tracer(__name__)

# Example function with instrumentation
def process_data():
    with tracer.start_as_current_span("process_data_span"):
        print("Processing data...")

process_data()
```

In this Python example, we establish a basic instrumentation setup using OpenTelemetry by initializing the tracing provider and configuring a span processor that exports spans to the console. The process_data function reflects the embedding of a custom span, offering newfound visibility into that segment of code execution.

- Importance of Instrumentation in Observability

  Instrumentation is intrinsically linked to observability—a system's ability to infer its internal states based on the outputs. Observability expands beyond monitoring by leveraging instrumented data to establish a broader understanding of an application's operation under diverse conditions.

- Enhances Visibility: Instrumentation captures real-time telemetry data, furnishing developers and operators with actionable insights into application's runtime behavior. This visibility is imperative for ensuring applications perform efficiently, even under unpredictable load.

- Facilitates Troubleshooting: By tracing application processes and recording logs, instrumentation aids in swiftly identifying issues and bottlenecks. Developers can analyze collected data to address failures or optimize underperforming components.

- Supports Performance Tuning: Metrics derived from instrumented code help in recognizing performance trends over time. Optimization strategies can be formed based on collected data about resource usage, execution times, and throughput.

81

- Promotes Proactivity through Anomaly Detection: Alerts can be configured to trigger on detected anomalies, thus enabling proactive remediation strategies before users are impacted.

- Instrumentation Techniques

  The process of instrumentation can vary significantly depending on the requirements and the architecture of the application. Broadly, these techniques can be classified as either automated or manual.

- Automated Instrumentation

  Automated instrumentation involves using pre-built libraries or tools that automatically insert tracing and logging code into applications. These are often provided as language-specific SDKs or libraries by OpenTelemetry.

  Advantages of automated instrumentation include:

  - Time Efficiency: Significantly reduces the workload for developers as it requires minimal code changes. - Consistency: Provides a uniform approach to data collection across different services and applications. - Low Error Potential: Minimizes human error in data collection code, enhancing the accuracy of collected telemetry.

  However, automated methods may not cover all custom requirements specific to a unique business logic or system architecture.

- Manual Instrumentation

  Manual instrumentation requires developers to insert code for data collection at strategically chosen points within an application. This approach allows developers to:

  - Customization: Provides precise control over what data to collect and how to handle it, thus enabling fine-tuning to specific use cases. - Granularity: Offers detailed insights at very precise points in the application flow, essential for capturing domain-specific metrics.

  While manual instrumentation offers enhanced flexibility, it does introduce additional complexities and potential overhead in terms of development and maintenance efforts.

```
const opentelemetry = require('@opentelemetry/api');

// Retrieves a tracer from the global tracer provider
const tracer = opentelemetry.trace.getTracer('custom-instrumentation');

function simulateExternalRequest(url) {
  const span = tracer.startSpan('simulateExternalRequest', {
    attributes: { url: url }
  });

  setTimeout(() => {
    console.log('Simulating request to ${url}');
    span.end();
  }, 1000);
}

simulateExternalRequest("http://example.com");
```

In this Node.js snippet, we manually specify a custom span to trace a simulated external request. The function simulateExternalRequest leverages the OpenTelemetry tracer to encapsulate execution within a span, thus enriching trace visualization with user-defined attributes.

- Data Models for Instrumentation

  Effective instrumentation requires a comprehensible data model to structure the telemetry information generated by applications. Common data models include:

  - Traces: A trace represents a journey through a system consisting of a series of operations. Each operation is known as a span, and spans capture start and end timestamps, attributes, status, and other context. - Metrics: Metrics are quantitative representations of resource usages or application performance. Examples include request counts, memory usage, and latency. They are typically represented as counters, gauges, or histograms. - Logs: Logs provide detailed, timestamped records of discrete events occurring within a system. They often contain informational messages or warnings outside the span context.

  Each model complements one another to provide a multi-faceted view of the applications' behavior.

- Implementing OpenTelemetry Instrumentation

  Starting with OpenTelemetry involves incorporating one or more

83

language-specific SDKs into your application. This process typically includes:

- Initialization: Configure a global instance of telemetry providers such as TracerProvider for tracing, and MeterProvider for metrics.
- Integration: Dependency on OpenTelemetry libraries enables the necessary hooks to your application's execution context. - Export Configuration: Define the destinations where telemetry data should be exported, such as APM tools, dashboards, or even simple log files. - Instrumentation: Apply either automated or manual instrumentation strategies as per the application and domain necessity.

```java
import io.opentelemetry.api.trace.Span;
import io.opentelemetry.api.trace.Tracer;
import io.opentelemetry.api.GlobalOpenTelemetry;
import io.opentelemetry.context.Scope;

public class OpenTelemetryExample {

    private static final Tracer tracer = GlobalOpenTelemetry.getTracer("demoTracer");

    public static void main(String[] args) {
        Span span = tracer.spanBuilder("sampleSpan").startSpan();
        try (Scope scope = span.makeCurrent()) {
            System.out.println("Hello, OpenTelemetry!");
        } finally {
            span.end();
        }
    }
}
```

Here, the Java example demonstrates how to begin using OpenTelemetry by obtaining a Tracer from the GlobalOpenTelemetry and creating a basic span. This architecture positions developers to instrument code execution segments, capturing telemetry data essential for observability tasks.

It is crucial that OpenTelemetry components seamlessly align with an organization's broader observability strategy, permitting real-time performance diagnostics and data-driven decision making. Through effective instrumentation, developers can significantly enhance the operational insights into complex distributed systems, leading to improved reliability, efficiency, and customer satisfaction.

84

4.2 Tracing in OpenTelemetry

Tracing is a fundamental element of observability, providing insights into the flow of requests across complex, distributed systems. Within OpenTelemetry, tracing is accomplished by capturing and linking together units of work within an application, referred to as spans. This section explores the implementation of tracing in applications, detailing the creation, management of spans, and context propagation which are integral to stitching together a coherent trace across various services.

- **Key Concepts of Tracing**

A trace represents a transaction or a sequence of activities triggered by a request in a distributed system. This may include API calls, interactions with external services, or database operations. Each operation in the trace is recorded as a span.

- Span: The primary building block of a trace, representing a single operation. Each span encompasses a start and end time, along with contextual metadata.

- Parent Span: The preceding span that identifies the origin of another new span within the trace.

- Child Span: A span that is invoked by the parent span, continuing the flow of operations in the trace.

- Trace Context: A set of identifiers and metadata necessary for seamless context propagation across process boundaries.

Understanding these key components is paramount for setting up effective distributed tracing, as they aid developers in identifying and rectifying performance issues and ensure trace context is correctly maintained through microservices architectures.

- **Implementing Tracing in Applications**

Developers can integrate tracing within applications by leveraging OpenTelemetry's SDKs available across multiple programming languages. These libraries are structured to automatically capture common tracing data with minimal configuration while also providing options for customization.

• Setting Up Tracing

Implementation typically begins by setting up a Tracer Provider, the core element responsible for generating and managing traces. Here is an example of setting up tracing in a Java application:

```
import io.opentelemetry.sdk.OpenTelemetrySdk;
import io.opentelemetry.sdk.trace.SdkTracerProvider;
import io.opentelemetry.sdk.trace.export.SimpleSpanProcessor;
import io.opentelemetry.exporter.otlp.trace.OtlpGrpcSpanExporter;

// Create an exporter instance
OtlpGrpcSpanExporter spanExporter = OtlpGrpcSpanExporter.builder().build();

// Configure the tracer provider
SdkTracerProvider tracerProvider = SdkTracerProvider.builder()
    .addSpanProcessor(SimpleSpanProcessor.create(spanExporter))
    .build();

// Initialize OpenTelemetry SDK with the tracer provider
OpenTelemetrySdk openTelemetry = OpenTelemetrySdk.builder().setTracerProvider(
    tracerProvider).build();
```

This code snippet illustrates the configuration of a tracer provider using the OpenTelemetry Java SDK. The OtlpGrpcSpanExporter is utilized for exporting trace data over gRPC. The SdkTracerProvider is configured to create spans which can be enriched with metadata, such as attributes and status.

• Creating and Managing Spans

Following the establishment of a tracer, developers can begin defining spans around segments of code which hold significance in the trace.

```
import io.opentelemetry.api.trace.Span;
import io.opentelemetry.api.trace.Tracer;
import io.opentelemetry.context.Scope;

Tracer tracer = openTelemetry.getTracer("io.demo.tracer");

void performOperation() {
```

86

```
Span span = tracer.spanBuilder("operationSpan").startSpan();
try (Scope scope = span.makeCurrent()) {
    // Perform the operation
    System.out.println("Operation in progress");
    span.setAttribute("operation.status", "in-progress");
} finally {
    span.end();
}
}
```

In this example, a span called operationSpan is initiated, representing a single logical unit of work during the application's execution. The scope ensures the span's context remains active within the method call. Attributes like operation.status provide rich contextual information imperative for trace analysis.

- **Context Propagation**

For multi-service interactions, propagating context becomes essential. Context propagation ensures that trace identifiers are maintained as requests traverse service boundaries, allowing disparate spans to be linked into a single cohesive trace.

OpenTelemetry SDKs provide comprehensive context propagation capabilities in adherence with standards like W3C Trace Context.

- **Propagation Example**

Here is a simplified example in Python illustrating context propagation using OpenTelemetry.

```
from opentelemetry import context
from opentelemetry.trace import TracerProvider, get_tracer
from opentelemetry.propagate import inject
import requests

trace.set_tracer_provider(TracerProvider())
tracer = get_tracer(___name___)

def send_request():
    with tracer.start_as_current_span("client-request") as span:
        current_context = context.get_current()
        headers = {}
        inject(headers=headers, context=current_context)
        response = requests.get("http://service.endpoint/api", headers=headers)
        span.set_attribute("http.status_code", response.status_code)

send_request()
```

87

In this snippet, the context is propagated within a request made to an external service. The inject function is used to insert trace context into the HTTP headers, ensuring downstream services can continue the trace by extracting the context.

- **Instrumenting Key Transactions**

While automatic instrumentation can capture significant telemetry, manual instrumentation may be necessary to capture domain-specific operations critical for business. Choosing the right depth of instrumentation aids in balancing overhead and data utility.

- Server-Side Instrumentation: Instrument server request handlers to begin spans upon the receipt of each request, capturing metadata like HTTP method, URL, and response status.

- Database Operations: Span database queries to include details regarding query execution times, query types, and impacted records.

- External API Calls: Instrument outbound API calls for dependency monitoring, capturing destination URL, request/response statuses, and latency.

```
const http = require('http');
const { trace } = require('@opentelemetry/api');

const tracer = trace.getTracer('server-instrumentation');

function requestHandler(req, res) {
    const span = tracer.startSpan('handleRequest', {
        attributes: { method: req.method, url: req.url }
    });

    res.end('Hello, Tracing!');
    span.setAttribute('http.status_code', 200);
    span.end();
}

const server = http.createServer(requestHandler);
server.listen(3000, () => console.log('Server is running on port 3000'));
```

Here, a basic HTTP server in Node.js is instrumented to create spans for every incoming request. Attributes such as the HTTP method and URL are attached to the span to enrich trace data, making it more valuable for diagnostic purposes.

88

- **Analysis and Visualization**

Once trace data is captured and exported, visual analysis within observability platforms like Jaeger or Zipkin becomes invaluable. These tools depict traces as directed acyclic graphs that represent the temporal ordering of spans, enabling:

- Bottleneck Identification: Identifying spans with excessive durations which may indicate performance bottlenecks.

- Root Cause Analysis: Isolation of erroneous spans originating from failures or exception sites.

- Dependency Mapping: Observing service interaction paths to understand service dependencies and latencies.

Effective analysis can subsequently drive decisions to enhance application architecture, scale services appropriately, or streamline inefficient processes, underpinned by tangible tracing data.

- **Best Practices for Tracing**

To maximize the value of tracing, organizations should heed these practices:

- Selective Instrumentation: Focus on high-impact operations. Avoid exhaustive tracing that may introduce significant overhead or data deluge.

- Structured Metadata: Consistently incorporate structured attributes into spans for streamlined querying and filtering.

- Configuration Management: Use environment-specific configurations for controlling tracing levels, tailoring sampling strategies based on the traffic patterns and critical path insight demands.

- Scalable Storage: Ensure backend storage of trace data can scale with the system load to retain seamless performance insights over time.

The implementation of these best practices ensures organizational tracing efforts yield productive, intuitive insights, ultimately leading to enhanced service reliability and operational excellence. By harnessing OpenTelemetry's tracing capabilities, developers can gain a comprehensive understanding of application behavior in real time, forming the bedrock of an effective observability strategy.

4.3 Working with Metrics

Metrics serve as a fundamental component of observability, providing quantitative data that reflects the performance and health of an application over time. They allow developers and operations teams to gain insights into system behavior, track performance anomalies, and optimize resource utilization. Within OpenTelemetry, metrics are collected, aggregated, and exported seamlessly, forming an integral part of an observability framework alongside tracing and logging.

- **Counters**: Increment-only instruments used to track the number of times an event occurs. Commonly used for counting requests, errors, or processed records.

- **Observers**: Instruments that capture samples of values over time, often utilized to monitor statistical distributions of data such as response times or heap memory usage.

- **Histograms**: Designed to capture the distribution of a set of measurements. They provide detailed statistical insights like min, max, mean, and quantiles.

- **Gauges**: Instruments that record the current value of a particular variable, accommodating both increments and decrements. Typically employed for measuring system or application load, such as CPU usage or memory consumption.

Metrics in OpenTelemetry are designed to offer high-level statistical data which is pivotal for both real-time monitoring and historical analysis. Unlike logs or traces, metrics data is often aggregated before it is exported, allowing for reduced network and storage overhead.

Implementing Metrics: An Overview

Establishing a metrics pipeline involves setting up a Meter Provider, defining instruments, collecting data, and finally exporting it to a backend capable of visualizing and analyzing the metrics.

Configuring the Meter Provider

The Meter Provider serves as the primary entry point for creating and managing metric instruments. Through this component, applications are configured to record and report metric data.

For instance, in a Python application, the setup of a Meter Provider with OpenTelemetry can be achieved as follows:

```python
from opentelemetry import metrics
from opentelemetry.sdk.metrics import MeterProvider
from opentelemetry.sdk.metrics.export import ConsoleMetricExporter,
    PeriodicExportingMetricReader

# Initialize a MeterProvider
meter_provider = MeterProvider()
metrics.set_meter_provider(meter_provider)

# Configure metric exporter to console
exporter = ConsoleMetricExporter()
meter_provider.start_pipeline(meter_provider, exporter, 5)
```

In this example, the 'MeterProvider' is configured with a 'ConsoleMetricExporter' which outputs metrics data to the console every 5 seconds. This setup is essential for configuring pipelines to export data for further analysis.

Creating and Using Metric Instruments

Once the Meter Provider is configured, the next step involves defining the various metric instruments that will capture key performance data.

For example, here is a demonstration of defining and using counters and observers in a Java application:

```java
import io.opentelemetry.api.metrics.GlobalMetricsProvider;
import io.opentelemetry.api.metrics.LongCounter;
import io.opentelemetry.api.metrics.DoubleValueObserver;
import java.util.Collections;

public class MetricsExample {

    private static final LongCounter requestCounter = GlobalMetricsProvider.getMeter
        ("demo")
            .longCounterBuilder("processed_requests")
```

91

```
        .setDescription("The number of requests processed")
        .build();

private static final DoubleValueObserver memoryUsageObserver =
    GlobalMetricsProvider.getMeter("demo")
        .doubleValueObserverBuilder("memory_usage")
        .setDescription("Tracks the application's memory usage")
        .setCallback(result -> {
            double usedMemory = (double) (Runtime.getRuntime().totalMemory() -
                Runtime.getRuntime().freeMemory()) / (1024 * 1024);
            result.observe(usedMemory, Collections.emptyMap());
        })
        .build();

public void processRequest() {
    requestCounter.add(1);
}
}
```

In the Java example, a 'LongCounter' is defined to track processed requests, incremented with each request processed. A 'DoubleValueObserver' is set up to monitor memory usage periodically, which can be extremely useful for identifying memory pressure scenarios.

Aggregating and Exporting Metrics

Aggregation is a powerful feature of metrics that minimizes data volume by summarizing metrics data over time, allowing for efficient storage and analysis. In typical use, metrics instruments aggregate data into temporal windows before results are subjected to export.

Exporting aggregated metrics data to visualization and alerting systems can be completed with ease through various OpenTelemetry exporters. Here is an example illustrating metrics export configuration using the Prometheus exporter in JavaScript:

```
const { MeterProvider, ConsoleMetricExporter } = require('@opentelemetry/sdk-
    metrics-base');
const { PrometheusExporter } = require('@opentelemetry/exporter-prometheus');

const exporter = new PrometheusExporter({
    startServer: true,
});

const meterProvider = new MeterProvider({
    exporter: exporter,
    interval: 1000,
});

const meter = meterProvider.getMeter('example-meter');

const requestCount = meter.createCounter('request_count', {
```

```
    description: 'Counts the number of incoming requests',
});

requestCount.add(1, { path: '/api/user', method: 'GET' });
```

The Prometheus exporter facilitates the scrapping and inspection of metrics data by Prometheus, a powerful metrics visualization tool. Given the setup, metric data for request_count is made available to Prometheus, ensuring real-time system observability.

Use Cases and Analysis

Metrics play an essential role across various business functions:

- **Performance Monitoring**: Metrics provide insights into application behavior and performance, allowing teams to identify trends and proactively address potential issues before they impact users.

- **Capacity Planning**: By analyzing metrics over time, organizations can make informed decisions about infrastructure scaling and resource allocation to efficiently handle projected loads.

- **Alerting and Incident Response**: Metrics can trigger alerts in response to predefined thresholds, enabling immediate action in response to anomalies or degradations in service.

Domain-Specific Instrumentation

Different domains and environments necessitate unique instrumentation strategies to fully capture the breadth of operational insights desired. Here are some domain-specific considerations:

- **Web Applications**: Focus on request rate, latency, error rates, and user interactions.

- **Microservices**: Monitor inter-service communication, network latency, throughput, and failure rates.

- **Databases**: Capture query execution times, connection pool occupancy, and successful transaction rates.

- **Cloud Services**: Track resource utilizations like CPU, memory, I/O operations, and cloud provider specific metrics.

93

```python
from opentelemetry import metrics
from opentelemetry.sdk.metrics import MeterProvider
from opentelemetry.sdk.metrics.export import ConsoleMetricExporter

# Initialize MeterProvider
meter_provider = MeterProvider()
metrics.set_meter_provider(meter_provider)

# Create a ConsoleMetricExporter
exporter = ConsoleMetricExporter()
meter_provider.add_metric_reader(exporter)

# Create custom counters and observers
meter = meter_provider.get_meter("advanced-example")

responseTimeObserver = meter.create_value_observer(
    "response_time",
    "Observes response time latency",
    callbacks=[
        lambda result: result.observe(get_latency(), labels={"endpoint": "/users"})
    ]
)

responseCounter = meter.create_counter(
    "response_count",
    "Count number of responses sent"
)

# Function to simulate a request handling
def handle_request():
    responseCounter.add(1, {'route': '/users'})
    response_latency = simulate_request_latency()
    responseTimeObserver.observe(response_latency)

# Simulate request handling
handle_request()
```

This advanced illustration using Python features a value observer that calculates response time latencies associated with a specific endpoint. Simultaneously, a counter records the volume of responses, enhancing granularity in reporting and analysis.

Best Practices for Effective Metrics

To derive maximum benefit from metrics, the following practices should be considered:

- **Efficient Aggregation**: Always leverage aggregation to minimize data volume and maintain focus on high-level insights, reducing noise from raw data.

- **Dynamic Thresholds**: Implement dynamic, context-aware

94

threshold rules that reflect business priorities and load patterns for adaptive alerting.

- **Integrated Dashboards**: Utilize comprehensive dashboards that present multi-dimensional data views, enabling stakeholders to monitor various aspects of the system effortlessly.

- **Regular Calibration**: Periodically review and calibrate metric definitions and alert rules in response to evolving system architecture and user expectations.

Through these practices, organizations can harness the potential of OpenTelemetry's metrics capabilities, promoting informed decision-making and operational robustness in complex environments. Metrics provide the foundational data needed to enhance strategic oversight and facilitate high-performance, reliable system operations.

4.4   Integrating Logging

Logging is a pivotal component of software observability, delivering essential insights and contextual information about application behavior and events. Effective logging can significantly facilitate debugging, error tracking, and understanding application flow. This section elucidates the integration of logging within OpenTelemetry, orchestrating a symphony of logs, traces, and metrics to produce a comprehensive and cohesive observability strategy.

- **Fundamentals of Logging**:

   Logging involves writing informational outputs to record events, errors, and other significant occurrences within a program. These logs serve as an audit trail that offers insights into application execution, user interactions, system resources, and error conditions.

   - **Log Levels**: Logs are typically categorized based on severity levels such as DEBUG, INFO, WARN, ERROR, and FATAL. This categorization helps prioritize issues and optimize log filtering for particular operational needs.

- **Structured Logs**: In contrast to plain-text logs, structured logs encapsulate log messages in a machine-readable format, such as JSON. Structured logging facilitates powerful querying, automatic extraction, and analytics.

- **Log Context**: Contextual information, such as request identifiers, session details, and user metadata, enhances log utility, enabling easier correlation of events across distributed systems.

- **OpenTelemetry and Logging**:

  OpenTelemetry's ecosystem encompasses logging as an integral aspect of observability, neither supplanting nor encapsulating logging libraries but ensuring logs are a centralized piece of the observability puzzle by correlating with traces and metrics.

- **Log Correlation with Traces**:

  One of the principal challenges in distributed systems is correlating log entries from different sources with corresponding traces. OpenTelemetry addresses this by providing mechanisms to attach trace identifiers to log messages, making it straightforward to cross-reference logs and traces for the same request or process.

- **OpenTelemetry Logging Interface**:

  While OpenTelemetry does not provide a direct API for log events, it integrates with existing logging frameworks to enrich log messages with trace context. The 'LogEmitter' interface enlists the capabilities to offer trace metadata with log records.

- **Implementing Logging with OpenTelemetry**:

  The integration of logging within an application utilizing Open-Telemetry involves multiple steps, mainly centered around configuring logging frameworks to embed trace information. This is demonstrated in several languages below.

- **Python Logging Integration**:

  Python's rich ecosystem includes the 'logging' library, widely used for generating log messages. Here's how OpenTelemetry

96

can seamlessly augment Python logging by automatically injecting trace context:

```python
import logging
from opentelemetry import trace
from opentelemetry.instrumentation.logging import LoggingInstrumentor

# Initialize logging
logging.basicConfig(level=logging.INFO)
logger = logging.getLogger(___name___)

# Attach OpenTelemetry trace context to logs
LoggingInstrumentor().instrument(set_logging_format=True)

# Example function
def perform_task():
    with trace.get_tracer(___name___).start_as_current_span("example-
        operation") as span:
        logger.info("Performing a task")
        if span.is_recording():
            span.set_attribute("task.status", "completed")

perform_task()
```

In this code, 'LoggingInstrumentor' is employed to bind trace context to each log message. The 'instrument' method is utilized to automatically format logs to include additional trace-related information, such as trace and span identifiers, enhancing trace-log correlation.

- **Java Logging Integration**:

  Java's ecosystem features robust logging solutions such as SLF4J and Log4J. OpenTelemetry can be integrated with these libraries to incorporate trace identifiers into log outputs. Below is a demonstration using SLF4J:

```java
import org.slf4j.Logger;
import org.slf4j.LoggerFactory;
import io.opentelemetry.api.trace.Tracer;
import io.opentelemetry.context.Context;
import io.opentelemetry.context.Scope;
import io.opentelemetry.extension.trace.propagation.B3Propagator;

// Initialize the logger
Logger logger = LoggerFactory.getLogger("DemoLogger");

Tracer tracer = openTelemetry.getTracer("sampleTracer");

// Example method with tracing and logging
void exampleMethod() {
    Context context = tracer.spanBuilder("exampleOperation").startSpan().
        makeCurrent();
```

```
try (Scope scope = Context.current().makeCurrent()) {
    logger.info("Executing business logic with trace context");
} finally {
    context.close();
}
}
```

By utilizing SLF4J along with OpenTelemetry Tracer and Context objects, trace identifiers can be seamlessly appended to logs, aiding in pinpointing the causal chain of events and operations.

- **Best Practices for Effective Logging**:

  To maximize the utility of logs in conjunction with OpenTelemetry, adhere to these best practices:

  - **Log Enrichment**: Enhance logs with contextual data like trace identifiers, user IDs, and geo-location information to support intricate debugging and auditing.

  - **Consistent Log Structure**: Ensure logs are consistently structured, enabling efficient parsing, querying, and automatic analyses. Implement structured logging for clarity and integration with analytics platforms.

  - **Selective Logging**: Focus on logging strategic events and states to balance log verbosity and requisite information. Avoid logging sensitive information unless necessary and use encryption where possible.

  - **Instrumentation Alignment**: Synchronize logging efforts with tracing instruments to cover complex operation flows comprehensively, supporting swift incident resolution.

- **Enabling Advanced Log Analysis**:

  With logs tagged with trace metadata, they become an asset for advanced analysis, allowing organizations to:

  - **Perform Root Cause Analysis**: Trace individual log entries back to specific requests and operations to identify fault origins and propagation paths.

98

- **Monitor Security and Compliance**: Audit logs for policy violations or security threats while maintaining trace visibility.

- **Optimize Performance**: Assess logged response times, and request processing stages to determine and optimize slow points.

- **Cross-Language Insights and Example Scenarios**:

  OpenTelemetry enhances logging capabilities across diverse languages, providing a unified framework for context propagation. Consider the following comprehensive Node.js example that augments Express.js logging with OpenTelemetry:

```
const express = require('express');
const { context, trace } = require('@opentelemetry/api');
const { getTracer } = require('@opentelemetry/api');
const app = express();

// Initialize tracer
const tracer = getTracer('express-example');

app.use((req, res, next) => {
    const span = tracer.startSpan('incoming_request', {
        attributes: { method: req.method, url: req.url }
    });

    context.with(trace.setSpan(context.active(), span), () => {
        console.log(`traceId: ${span.context().traceId}, Handling ${req.
            method} request for ${req.url}`);
        next();
    });

    res.on('finish', () => {
        span.end();
    });
});

app.get('/', (req, res) => {
    res.send('Hello OpenTelemetry!');
});

app.listen(3000, () => console.log('Server listening on port 3000'));
```

  In this example, the Express middleware starts a span for each incoming request, logs trace identifiers alongside basic request information, and ends the span upon request completion. Such integration fosters traceability within complex API interactions, elucidating service responsiveness.

99

- **Toward Effective Observability**:

  The integration of OpenTelemetry with logging frameworks transforms standard logging into a powerful observability tool. Enabling developers to perceive logs as components of a larger story comprising traces and metrics reveals insights into application behavior and performance at multiple levels.

  Continuously evolving, OpenTelemetry's logging capabilities increasingly center on enabling more profound insights, improved automation, and greater alignment with other observability signals. Through understanding and leveraging the synergy between logging and OpenTelemetry, teams gain the ability to swiftly diagnose problems, improve system performance, and enhance overall operational excellence.

4.5 Automated vs Manual Instrumentation

Instrumentation is the cornerstone of effective observability, vital for gathering insights into how software operates in various environments. It involves embedding code or leveraging libraries to collect telemetry data such as metrics, logs, and traces, which reveal application performance, user interactions, and operational health. Instrumentation methods can be broadly categorized into automated and manual approaches, each with distinct methodologies, trade-offs, advantages, and challenges. Understanding these paradigms allows developers to make informed decisions about integrating observability capabilities into their software systems.

Automated Instrumentation

Automated instrumentation leverages pre-built libraries or tools that automatically embed instrumentation code without requiring developers to modify their original codebase significantly. This approach emphasizes ease of use and rapid deployment, making it a popular choice for enhancing observability across complex systems.

Characteristics of Automated Instrumentation

- Library-Based Approach: Automated solutions often involve using language-specific libraries or platforms that can instrument codebases with negligible manual input.

- Minimal Code Invasion: Instrumentation code is added with little to no modifications of the original codebase, preserving the software's architectural integrity.

- Time Efficiency: Instrumentation is executed swiftly, typically requiring developers to only integrate specific packages or enable features.

Automated instrumentation is often implemented through OpenTelemetry auto-instrumentation layers that harness language runtime capabilities to examine applications dynamically and place instrumentation points strategically.

Advantages of Automated Instrumentation

1. Speed and Simplicity: Fast to implement and particularly well-suited for teams seeking rapid deployment or prototyping of observability solutions.

2. Reduced Error Potential: With automatic configuration, the probability of human error is minimized, providing consistent and reliable instrumentation.

3. Comprehensive Coverage: Offers blanket coverage for widely-used frameworks and libraries, thus capturing a broad range of telemetry data with minimal effort.

Challenges of Automated Instrumentation

- Limited Customization: May not cater to specific business logic or bespoke algorithms where deeper insights are required beyond standard metrics or traces.

- Dependency on Library Versions: Consistency and effectiveness are often linked to specific versions of libraries or frameworks, potentially resulting in hurdles during upgrades.

- Overhead Management: The inclusion of extensive auto-generated data may lead to additional overhead if not configured properly, affecting system performance.

Example of Automated Instrumentation

Consider the Java agent instrumentation utilizing OpenTelemetry, which automatically covers a broad range of libraries and application servers:

```
java -javaagent:path/to/opentelemetry-javaagent.jar -jar myapp.jar
```

This command demonstrates using the OpenTelemetry Java agent to instrument an application without modifying the underlying code. It automatically adds instrumentation to compatible libraries and frameworks, providing access to collected telemetry with minimal configuration.

Manual Instrumentation

Manual instrumentation, in contrast, entails developers inserting custom instrumentation code at precise application points. This technique offers fine-grained control over what telemetry data is collected, enabling bespoke observability strategies.

Characteristics of Manual Instrumentation

- Detailed and Customizable: Users exercise explicit control over instrumented code, capturing domain-specific metrics or traces tailored to application objectives.

- Explicit Code Insertion: Developers manually write and integrate instrumentation libraries into their code, applying instrumentation at strategically determined application points.

- Sophisticated Analysis Potential: Allows capturing and analyzing complex operations related to business logic, unique use cases, or specific user requirements.

Advantages of Manual Instrumentation

1. Customization and Flexibility: Provides unrivaled customization, empowering developers to fine-tune data collection to specific application needs.

2. Granular Insights: Enables analysis at a granular level, essential for capturing significant events, intricate interactions, or business critical operations.

3. Integration with Business Logic: Facilitates the gathering of data specific to domain or logic-specific requirements, offering enhanced visibility into particular application segments.

Challenges of Manual Instrumentation

- Time-Intensive: Requires considerable developer resources to embed, manage, and maintain instrumentation throughout continuous integration cycles.

- Higher Risk of Errors: As manual coding is involved, it presents a higher potential for human-induced errors or inconsistencies.

- Inherent Complexity: Typically involves a steeper learning curve and more substantial setup than automated solutions, especially for distributed system architectures.

Example of Manual Instrumentation

Here is a Node.js example where custom spans are added manually around specific application logic to enable detailed understanding and optimization potential:

```
const { trace } = require('@opentelemetry/api');
// Create a tracer instance
```

```
const tracer = trace.getTracer('manual-example');

function handleRequest(req) {
    const span = tracer.startSpan('handleRequest', {
        attributes: { method: req.method, path: req.path }
    });

    // Perform business logic
    setTimeout(() => {
        console.log('Handling request');
        span.setAttribute('operation.status', 'success');
        span.end();
    }, 200);
}

handleRequest({ method: 'POST', path: '/api/resource' });
```

The above code sample showcases manual instrumentation by explicitly creating a span around business logic execution within a request handler. This approach allows developers to ensure meaningful telemetry is collected for operation-specific insights.

Trade-offs and Considerations

Selecting between automated and manual instrumentation necessitates balancing diverse factors to align with organizational goals, application architecture, and developer resources.

1. Speed vs. Precision: Automated instrumentation excels when time-to-value is primary, offering widespread coverage without the need for exhaustive coding. Manual instrumentation suits environments where precision and insight into bespoke algorithms are crucial.

2. Scalability vs. Customization: In systems exhibiting high variability or frequent scaling, automated instrumentation supports swift deployability. Conversely, manual instrumentation empowers deeper customization ideal for static domain environments or critical systems.

3. Resource Allocation: Automated options alleviate substantial developer resource burdens, while manual solutions necessitate allocation of time, expertise, and maintenance due to their intricate nature.

4. Integration with CI/CD: Both require seamless integration with continuous deployment. Automated instrumentation readily fits into DevOps pipelines, while manual instrumentation demands concerted orchestration to ensure resilience.

Strategic Recommendations

Developers and architects can adopt a hybrid approach, utilizing a combination of automated and manual instrumentation for optimal outcomes. By strategically selecting the advantages of each:

- Leverage Automated Tools for Coverage: Apply automated instrumentation for framework-level observability to cover a wide range of system interactions.

- Strategically Embed Manual Code: Identify key performance areas, critical pathways, or unique algorithms and manually instrument these components for refined insights.

- Evaluate System Evolution: As software systems evolve, reassess instrumentation methods to ensure alignment with current performance monitoring and business goals.

Such strategies equip organizations to identify and act upon resilience challenges, capacity constraints, and performance bottlenecks with improved efficacy.

4.6 Adding Instrumentation to Existing Applications

Integrating instrumentation into existing applications is a critical step in enhancing observability, providing developers with rich insights into application performance and behavior. Instrumentation involves embedding telemetry to collect metrics, logs, and traces, vital for diagnosing issues, optimizing resources, and ensuring seamless user experiences. This process, while powerful, must be approached strategically, especially when dealing with incumbent applications that might not have been initially designed with observability in mind.

- **Complexity**: Legacy applications often embody intricate architectures that may not be fully understood, complicating the insertion of telemetry without affecting existing functionality.

- **Performance Overhead**: Care must be taken to ensure that added instrumentation does not incur significant performance overhead or alter the application's timing-sensitive operations.

- **Minimal Disruption**: Instrumentation efforts must be minimally invasive to reduce potential disruption or interference with ongoing operations.

- **Dependency Management**: Updating dependencies to support modern instrumentation frameworks may involve substantial refactoring, requiring careful planning and testing.

Successfully integrating instrumentation within existing applications involves creating a thoughtful strategy that assesses existing architecture, identifies key areas for visibility, and balances performance considerations.

- **Assessing Current State**: Conduct a comprehensive analysis of the application architecture to understand key components, data flows, and potential bottlenecks. This assessment informs decisions on focal points for instrumentation.

- **Selecting the Right Tools**: Choose appropriate instrumentation tools and frameworks that align with the application's technology stack, ensuring compatibility and long-term support.

- **Defining Clear Objectives**: Determine the primary objectives of the instrumentation, such as improving request latency, enhancing error tracking, or achieving granular resource monitoring.

- **Incremental Integration**: Adopt an incremental approach, starting with small pilot projects, validating telemetry results, and gradually scaling up implementation to cover more components.

When retrofitting existing applications, specific techniques can be leveraged to implement instrumentation while mitigating potential challenges.

Utilize OpenTelemetry's Auto-Instrumentation

Automated instrumentation using OpenTelemetry provides a rapid, non-invasive method to introduce observability into existing codebases. Language agents or SDKs can attach to runtime environments, automatically capturing telemetry.

```
java -javaagent:/path/to/opentelemetry-javaagent.jar -jar your-application.jar
```

This command showcases utilizing the OpenTelemetry Java Agent to instrument an application. The agent dynamically adds instrumentation to the runtime, capturing spans from supported libraries and frameworks without code changes.

Implement Lightweight Manual Instrumentation

Where automated tools fall short, implementing lightweight manual instrumentation at crucial application points can provide additional granularity and context.

```python
from opentelemetry import trace, context

tracer = trace.get_tracer(__name__)

def crucial_function():
    with tracer.start_as_current_span("crucial_operation") as span:
        span.set_attribute("custom.attribute", "value")
        # existing logic
```

In this Python snippet, manual instrumentation involves wrapping a critical function with a custom span named crucial_operation, enriching the trace data with specific attributes corresponding to business logic.

Employ Progressive Integration

For larger applications, progressive integration, focusing on high-impact areas first, allows for controlled growth of observability practices:

- **Start with Infrastructure Components**: Instrument core components such as network interfaces, databases, or messaging queues to gain insights into system-wide bottlenecks.

- **Move to Business Logic**: Expand to instrument business processes and domain-specific logic, capturing critical interactions and decision points.

- **Extend to User Interactions**: Finally, instrument user-facing components, tracking user transactions, interface performance, and experience metrics.

Instrumenting existing applications demands consideration of the specific technologies and ecosystems involved. Here's how various platforms can be successfully instrumented:

Web Applications

- **HTTP Traffic Monitoring**: Instrument request handlers and middleware to monitor request patterns and latency.

- **Database Call Tracing**: Enhance visibility into database interactions by tracing query execution and optimizing slow queries.

```
const express = require('express');
const { trace } = require('@opentelemetry/api');
const app = express();

const tracer = trace.getTracer('express-tracer');

app.use((req, res, next) => {
    const span = tracer.startSpan('incoming_request');
    res.on('finish', () => span.end());
    next();
});

app.get('/', (req, res) => {
    res.send('Hello OpenTelemetry');
});

app.listen(3000, () => console.log('Server running on port 3000'));
```

In this Express.js example, middleware initializes a span per request, capturing throughput and latency metrics that feed into performance analysis.

Microservices Architectures

- **Service Interaction Tracing**: Capturing distributed traces across microservices to understand latency and inter-service communication patterns.

- **Load Balancing and Caching**: Monitoring traffic flows through load balancers, caches, and service meshes to ensure efficient resource utilization.

Cloud-Native Deployments

- **Dynamic Resource Instrumentation**: Automatically instrumenting cloud-native applications using container orchestration and serverless frameworks through OpenTelemetry is key for maintaining observability with dynamic resource allocation.

- **Distributed Context Propagation**: Ensuring trace context is accurately propagated across service boundaries provides a cohesive picture of the multi-service environment.

Upon integration, it is essential to continually monitor and validate the instrumentation setup to assure consistency and accuracy in telemetry data:

- **Data Quality Audits**: Set up monitoring dashboards to audit captured telemetry data, verifying expected metrics are accurately represented.

- **Performance Benchmarks**: Regularly benchmark system performance to ensure that added telemetry does not introduce significant latency or resource consumption.

- **Feedback Loops**: Establish feedback mechanisms involving development and operational teams to iterate on instrumentation strategies, discovering insights and optimizing approaches continually.

To maximize business value from retrofitting instrumentation:

- **Align with Business Goals**: Instrumentation efforts should be driven by overarching business objectives, such as increasing application responsiveness or tracking customer engagement metrics.

- **Establish KPIs**: Develop quantifiable key performance indicators (KPIs) tied to the instrumentation, offering meaningful analytics that guide decision-making.

- **Foster Collaborative Environments**: Encourage collaboration between developers, operations staff, and business stakeholders to adapt instrumentation as technology and marketplace dynamics evolve.

Successfully integrating instrumentation into existing applications enhances their observability capabilities, unlocking insights into performance, efficiency, and user interaction like never before. By making strategic choices between automated and manual methods, integrating carefully selected tools, and maintaining a clear focus on performance impacts, organizations can enrich their legacy systems with state-of-the-art observability frameworks, ensuring continued reliability, efficiency, and alignment with business goals. Through careful planning, testing, and the incorporation of feedback, the road to full observability becomes navigable and rewarding.

4.7 Best Practices for Effective Instrumentation

Instrumentation is a critical component of observability, providing the necessary telemetry data to gain insights into application performance, diagnose issues, and optimize system operations. Effective instrumentation avoids excess overhead, ensures data accuracy, and delivers granular visibility into operational states. Recognizing effective practices for implementing instrumentation can significantly enhance the utility and efficiency of monitoring, tracing, and logging efforts, leading to greater reliability and performance optimization. This section outlines best practices for implementing effective instrumentation.

- **Prioritize Key Areas for Instrumentation**: To maximize the value of instrumentation, focus on key areas that exert the most impact on business operations and system performance. This strategic focus includes:

- **Critical Paths**: Identify application pathways critical to business processes and operational success. Instrument these paths to capture latency, resource consumption, and potential bottlenecks.

- **User Interactions**: Capture metrics related to end-user interactions, such as page load times, transaction durations, and user flow efficiency, to enhance user experience and satisfaction.

- **Resource-Intensive Operations**: Identify and instrument operations that are resource-intensive, like database queries, asynchronous workflows, or large-scale data processing, to evaluate performance and optimize where possible.

- **Maintain Minimal Overhead**: Instrumentation inherently introduces some level of overhead. Effective practices involve minimizing this impact to maintain system performance:

  - **Granular Sampling**: Implement granular sampling strategies, capturing only a representative subset of telemetry data pertinent to current analysis objectives.

  - **Dynamic Configuration**: Use runtime configurations to adjust the level of instrumentation dynamically, scaling telemetry collection in response to system metrics or operational priorities.

  - **Efficient Data Handling**: Prioritize pre-aggregation of telemetry data on the client-side to reduce transmission and processing overhead downstream, employing batch processing for increased efficiency.

```python
from opentelemetry.sdk.trace import TracerProvider
from opentelemetry.sdk.trace.sampling import TraceIdRatioBased

# Configure a tracer provider with sampling
tracer_provider = TracerProvider(sampler=TraceIdRatioBased(0.1))
trace.set_tracer_provider(tracer_provider)

tracer = trace.get_tracer(__name__)

def perform_operation():
    with tracer.start_as_current_span("operation-span") as span:
        # Actual business logic here
```

```
    pass
perform_operation()
```

In this Python example, a TraceID ratio-based sampler is configured to sample 10% of all traces, enabling effective management of telemetry data volume while maintaining insight coverage.

- **Ensure Consistent Context Propagation**: Accurate context propagation is vital for meaningful trace and log correlation. Consistency in context propagation ensures that telemetry reflects true relationships across service interactions:

    - **Use Standard Protocols**: Implement and adhere to protocols such as W3C Trace Context Specification for context propagation, ensuring compatibility and standardization across services and programming languages.

    - **Cross-Service Correlation**: Ensure trace context is propagated through inter-service communication via REST, gRPC, messaging queues, and other integration points.

    - **Contextual Logging**: Embed trace and span identifiers in log records, enhancing the traceability and contextual navigability of logs in conjunction with other telemetry types.

- **Example of Consistent Context Propagation**: Below is a simple Java example demonstrating context propagation through HTTP requests using OpenTelemetry's ContextPropagators.

```java
import io.opentelemetry.api.GlobalOpenTelemetry;
import io.opentelemetry.api.trace.Span;
import io.opentelemetry.api.trace.Tracer;
import io.opentelemetry.context.propagation.TextMapPropagator;
import java.net.HttpURLConnection;
import java.net.URL;

Tracer tracer = GlobalOpenTelemetry.getTracer("example");

void sendHttpRequest() throws IOException {
    HttpURLConnection connection = (HttpURLConnection) new URL("http://
        example.com/api").openConnection();
    Span span = tracer.spanBuilder("outgoingRequest").startSpan();
    try {
        TextMapPropagator propagator = GlobalOpenTelemetry.getPropagators().
            getTextMapPropagator();
```

```
        propagator.inject(Context.current(), connection, HttpURLConnection::
            setRequestProperty);
        connection.connect();
    } finally {
        span.end();
    }
}
```

- **Implement Structured Logging**: Transition from simple text-based logs to structured logging. Structured logs facilitate deeper insights, easier parsing, and effective integration with advanced analytics platforms:

  - **Standard Format**: Use well-defined formats like JSON to structure log entries, making logs easily queryable and machine-readable.

  - **Enriched Metadata**: Incorporate additional context into logs, such as trace IDs, user/session identifiers, and environmental data to enhance analytical depth.

  - **Consistent Logging Schema**: Maintain consistency in log schemata across services to simplify data aggregation and streamline analysis workflows.

- **Align with Business Objectives**: Instrumentation should align with business priorities to ensure that technical efforts support broader organizational goals. To that end:

  - **Define Goals-Based Metrics**: Collaborate with business stakeholders to identify performance indicators that resonate with business outcomes, and ensure those are adequately instrumented.

  - **Feedback Loops**: Develop feedback loops to align ongoing instrumentation efforts with evolving business needs and market conditions.

  - **Performance Benchmarks**: Conduct regular assessments of observed telemetry data against performance goals to determine the value delivered through ongoing instrumentation efforts.

- **Ensure Comprehensive Coverage**: Instrumentation should provide comprehensive coverage across system layers and modules:

- **End-to-End Tracing**: Implement end-to-end tracing that spans from user interaction through backend services and integrations. This approach provides a complete trajectory of transactions, highlighting response times and inter-service dependencies.

- **Middleware and Service Interfaces**: Instrument middleware components, APIs, and service interfaces to capture the flow of data and interactions between isolated subsystems.

- **Database and I/O Operations**: Include instrumentation for database operations, file accesses, and other I/O interactions to ensure resource utilization and latency measurements are accurately recorded.

- **Adoption of Automation and CI/CD Integration**: Leverage automation and integrate instrumentation within CI/CD pipelines to ensure timely deployment and uniformity in observability across development environments:

  - **Automated Instrumentation**: Exploit automated instrumentation tools that complement manual efforts to ensure broad, standardized coverage.

  - **Inclusion in DevOps**: Integrate instrumentation within CI/CD pipelines to facilitate a continuous observability approach capable of adapting to code changes and evolving systems.

  - **Discoverability**: Ensure instrumentation infrastructure is readily discoverable by development teams, allowing for immediate utilization and fostering a culture of observability-first design.

- **Example: CI/CD Integration**: Using GitHub Actions, here is a YAML example guideline to enforce instrumentation testing and deployment as part of a CI/CD pipeline:

```
name: Instrumentation CI Pipeline

on:
  push:
    branches:
```

```
    - main

jobs:
  build-and-deploy:
    runs-on: ubuntu-latest

    steps:
    - uses: actions/checkout@v2

    - name: Install Dependencies
      run: npm install

    - name: Run Tests
      run: npm test

    - name: Instrumentation Check
      run: npm run check-instrumentation

    - name: Deploy
      if: success() && github.ref == 'refs/heads/main'
      run: npm run deploy
```

In this GitHub Actions example, instrumentation validation is integrated into the CI pipeline, ensuring instrumentation-related checks are enforced before deployment, sustaining quality and conformity across environments.

- **Set Up Alerts and Notifications**: Implement alerting strategies based on observed telemetry data to enable proactive response to emerging issues, with considerations such as:

  - **Dynamic Alert Thresholds**: Configure thresholds that adapt based on historical patterns, peak loads, or business calendars, enhancing accuracy and reducing noise.

  - **Contextual Alerts**: Ensure alerts include sufficient contextual data to facilitate immediate action, including root causes and potential remediation steps.

  - **Escalation Mechanisms**: Design escalation policies for critical alerts to minimize response latency and orchestrate swift interventions.

By adopting these best practices, developers and operations teams can unlock the full potential of their instrumentation efforts. This results in increased application reliability, performance intelligence, and a deeper understanding of systems dynamics, driving forward an organization's capacity to innovate and compete effectively. Through strategic planning, operational alignment, and technology integration, effective instrumentation supports a robust foundation for achieving observability excellence.

Chapter 5

Working with OpenTelemetry in Cloud-Native Environments

This chapter addresses the unique considerations of deploying OpenTelemetry within cloud-native environments, focusing on the intricacies of containerized and orchestrated applications. It offers practical insights into integrating OpenTelemetry with platforms such as Kubernetes and OpenShift, managing scalability, and ensuring effective observability across microservices and serverless architectures. Readers will gain an understanding of optimizing performance while maintaining low telemetry overhead and will learn how to handle challenges associated with dynamic environments. These insights are critical for maintaining comprehensive observability in environments characterized by rapid deployment and scaling.

5.1 Characteristics of Cloud-Native Environments

Cloud-native environments are fundamentally designed to exploit the capabilities of cloud computing architectures, emphasizing scalability, resilience, and continuous delivery. These environments embrace modern practices and methodologies to ensure efficient resource utilization, rapid deployment cycles, and robust application performance, especially within distributed systems. Understanding their characteristics is crucial for effectively implementing and utilizing tools like OpenTelemetry for observability.

- **Microservices Architecture**
  Microservices architecture is a defining feature of cloud-native environments. It involves developing applications as a suite of small, independently deployable services. These services communicate over lightweight protocols, often HTTP/REST or gRPC, and are organized around specific business capabilities. This modularity allows for enhanced scalability and easier maintenance.

  The independence of services facilitates continuous deployment and rapid iteration, which is essential in today's fast-paced development cycle. Each microservice can be developed, tested, and deployed independently, allowing for greater flexibility in managing updates and scaling.

- **Containerization**
  Containers, often orchestrated using platforms like Docker, are a fundamental unit of deployment in cloud-native settings. They encapsulate an application's code, configurations, and dependencies into a single artifact that can be uniformly deployed across environments. This ensures that applications run reliably regardless of where they are moved, making development and deployment more predictable and manageable.

  The following Dockerfile illustrates a simple setup for a containerized application:

```
FROM python:3.9-slim
```

```
WORKDIR /app

COPY requirements.txt requirements.txt
RUN pip install -r requirements.txt

COPY . .

CMD ["python", "app.py"]
```

This Dockerfile establishes a Python environment, installs the necessary dependencies from requirements.txt, and specifies the start command for the application. Such a setup allows developers to ensure consistency across different stages of development and production environments.

- **Scalability and Elasticity**
  Cloud-native systems are inherently designed to be scalable and elastic. Scalability refers to the system's ability to handle increased load by adding resources, whereas elasticity pertains to the system's capability to adapt to changing workloads by provisioning and de-provisioning resources as needed. These characteristics are essential for maintaining optimal performance and cost efficiency in dynamic environments.

For instance, Kubernetes offers built-in mechanisms for automatic scaling of applications using Horizontal Pod Autoscaler. This component scales the number of pods in a deployment based on observed CPU utilization or other specified metrics.

```
apiVersion: autoscaling/v2beta2
kind: HorizontalPodAutoscaler
metadata:
  name: my-app-hpa
spec:
  scaleTargetRef:
    apiVersion: apps/v1
    kind: Deployment
    name: my-app
  minReplicas: 2
  maxReplicas: 10
  metrics:
  - type: Resource
    resource:
      name: cpu
      target:
        type: Utilization
        averageUtilization: 50
```

119

This YAML configuration example sets up a Horizontal Pod Autoscaler for a Kubernetes deployment named my-app, allowing the number of replicas to scale between 2 and 10 based on CPU utilization metrics.

- **DevOps and Continuous Integration/Continuous Deployment (CI/CD)**
  DevOps culture is built into the ethos of cloud-native environments. It focuses on the integration of development and operations processes with an emphasis on automation, monitoring, and collaboration throughout the product lifecycle. CI/CD pipelines allow for regular, automatic updates to software applications, which significantly reduces the time-to-market and ensures that feedback loops are closed faster.

Automation of build, test, and deployment processes is achieved through a combination of tools like Jenkins, GitLab CI, or GitHub Actions. An example GitHub Actions workflow file for deploying a Dockerized application could be structured as follows:

```yaml
name: CI/CD Pipeline

on:
  push:
    branches:
      - main

jobs:
  build-and-deploy:
    runs-on: ubuntu-latest
    steps:
    - name: Checkout code
      uses: actions/checkout@v2

    - name: Set up Docker
      uses: docker/setup-buildx-action@v1

    - name: Build Docker image
      run: docker build -t my-app:latest .

    - name: Log in to Docker Hub
      uses: docker/login-action@v1
      with:
        username: ${{ secrets.DOCKER_USERNAME }}
        password: ${{ secrets.DOCKER_PASSWORD }}

    - name: Push Docker image
      run: docker push my-app:latest

    - name: Deploy to Kubernetes
      run: |
```

```
kubectl apply -f k8s/deployment.yaml
```

In this workflow, a Docker image is built and pushed to Docker Hub when changes are pushed to the main branch, and subsequently deployed to a Kubernetes cluster, demonstrating a streamlined CI/CD process.

- **Observability and Monitoring**
  Observability is a critical aspect of cloud-native environments. With the advent of distributed systems, traditional monitoring techniques become insufficient. Observability involves extensive instrumentation to achieve insights into the system's health, performance, and behavior through metrics, logs, and traces.

  Tools like OpenTelemetry facilitate observability by providing a unified framework for tracing and metrics collection. OpenTelemetry agents are deployed within the application stack to instrument services automatically. This data is then exported to observability tools like Prometheus or Jaeger for analysis and visualization.

- **Resilience and Fault Tolerance**
  Resilience is the ability of a system to recover from failures and continue to operate without behaving incorrectly. Fault tolerance involves the design techniques used to achieve resilience. Cloud-native systems are designed to cope with failures, be it infrastructure outages or software defects.

  Patterns such as circuit breakers, retries, and fallbacks are employed to enhance fault tolerance. Likewise, orchestrators like Kubernetes inherently provide mechanisms for health checks and restarting failed services, ensuring continuous availability.

- **Infrastructure as Code (IaC)**
  Infrastructure as Code is a methodology where infrastructure provisioning and management are performed through code, using descriptive languages or domain-specific languages like Terraform or AWS CloudFormation. This approach ensures consistency and reproducibility, and supports version control, auditing, and collaboration.

  The following Terraform script demonstrates provisioning an EC2 instance:

121

```
provider "aws" {
  region = "us-west-2"
}

resource "aws_instance" "example" {
  ami = "ami-0c55b159cbfafe1f0"
  instance_type = "t2.micro"

  tags = {
    Name = "terraform-example"
  }
}
```

Terraform scripts like the one above enable automated deployment and scaling of resources, crucial for dynamic cloud-native environments.

- **Service Mesh**
  Service mesh is an increasingly popular approach within cloud-native applications for the handling of inter-service communication. It abstracts the management of service-to-service interactions by providing capabilities such as load balancing, traffic shaping, and secure communication across microservices, all managed through a control plane.

  Istio is a widely adopted service mesh platform that provides robust solutions for traffic management, security, and observability.

- **Ephemeral Infrastructure**
  Characterized by short-lived workloads, ephemeral infrastructure is a hallmark of cloud-native environments, further accelerated by container orchestration. Applications are designed to expect transient lifecycles, preparing them to recover from infrastructure volatility seamlessly.

With such attributes fundamental to cloud-native environments, effective deployment and management practices are essential. Through a deep understanding of these characteristics, leveraging tools like OpenTelemetry for comprehensive observability and monitoring is feasible, thereby improving the reliability and performance of cloud-native applications.

5.2 Deploying OpenTelemetry in Containers

The deployment of OpenTelemetry within containerized environments requires thoughtful integration to harness its full capabilities. Containers provide a lightweight, consistent runtime environment, which aligns well with the modular, scalable nature of cloud-native applications. Utilizing OpenTelemetry within this context enables the capture and processing of telemetry data, providing valuable insights into application behavior and performance. This section explores the various aspects and methodologies for effectively deploying OpenTelemetry in containerized applications.

Containerized Application Stack Overview

Before delving into the deployment of OpenTelemetry, it is essential to understand the typical setup of a containerized application. At its core, a container encapsulates the application code, along with its libraries, dependencies, and environment settings. Container orchestration platforms like Docker provide tools to manage the lifecycle of these containers seamlessly.

A basic Dockerized application typically involves creating a Dockerfile, which defines the environment configuration and includes instructions to build the application's image. The following Dockerfile example demonstrates the encapsulation of a simple Go-based application:

```
# Use the official Golang image as the base image
FROM golang:1.17-alpine

# Set the Current Working Directory inside the container
WORKDIR /app

# Copy go mod and sum files for dependencies
COPY go.mod go.sum ./

# Download all dependencies
RUN go mod download

# Copy the source code into the container
COPY . .

# Build the Go app
RUN go build -o main .

# Command to run the app
CMD ["./main"]
```

This Dockerfile establishes a basic Go development environment, installs necessary dependencies, copies the source code, and compiles the application, preparing it to run within a containerized setup.

Integrating OpenTelemetry SDKs

OpenTelemetry provides language-specific SDKs, which need integration within the application's codebase for telemetry data collection. This involves instrumenting application code to capture metrics and traces. Here, we illustrate how OpenTelemetry can be integrated using a Go example:

```
// Import the necessary OpenTelemetry packages
import (
    "go.opentelemetry.io/otel"
    "go.opentelemetry.io/otel/exporters/stdout/stdouttrace"
    "go.opentelemetry.io/otel/sdk/resource"
    "go.opentelemetry.io/otel/sdk/trace"
    "go.opentelemetry.io/otel/trace"
    "context"
)

// Setup function to initialize OpenTelemetry
func setupTracer() (func(), error) {
    exp, err := stdouttrace.New(stdouttrace.WithPrettyPrint())
    if err != nil {
        return nil, err
    }
    tp := trace.NewTracerProvider(
        trace.WithSampler(trace.AlwaysSample()),
        trace.WithSpanProcessor(trace.NewSimpleSpanProcessor(exp)),
        trace.WithResource(resource.NewWithAttributes(
            semconv.ServiceNameKey.String("example-service"),
        )),
    )
    otel.SetTracerProvider(tp)

    return func() {
        // Shutdown will flush any remaining spans.
        tp.Shutdown(context.Background())
    }, nil
}
```

In this setup, OpenTelemetry's Go SDK is used to establish a tracer provider, with the tracer data being exported to stdout in a formatted output. The 'setupTracer' function initializes this configuration, and a deferred function is set to ensure proper cleanup and data flushing.

Configuring OpenTelemetry Collectors

While SDKs manage local data collection, OpenTelemetry Collectors serve as a crucial intermediary for batching, processing, and exporting telemetry data to various backends. Deploying a collector within a containerized environment involves creating a configuration file and defining container specifications, typically using Docker.

A sample Docker Compose file to deploy an OpenTelemetry Collector alongside a containerized application is presented below:

```
version: '3.8'

services:
  app:
    build: .
    image: my-app:latest
    container_name: my_app_container
    ports:
      - "8080:8080"
    depends_on:
      - otel-collector

  otel-collector:
    image: otel/opentelemetry-collector:latest
    container_name: otel_collector
    ports:
      - "4317:4317"
    volumes:
      - ./otel-collector-config.yml:/etc/otelcol/otel-collector-config.yml
    command:
      ["--config", "/etc/otelcol/otel-collector-config.yml"]
```

This Docker Compose configuration spins up two services: the application and an OpenTelemetry Collector. The collector is configured to listen on the OpenTelemetry Protocol (OTLP) port 4317, ensuring it can receive telemetry data from the instrumented application.

The 'otel-collector-config.yml' file will often resemble the following:

```
receivers:
  otlp:
    protocols:
      grpc:

processors:
  batch:
    timeout: 5s

exporters:
  logging:

service:
  pipelines:
    traces:
```

125

```
receivers: [otlp]
processors: [batch]
exporters: [logging]
```

In this configuration, the collector is set to receive traces via the OTLP receiver, process the batches, and export them using a logging exporter. This setup logs telemetry data to the console and can be extended to include other exporters, such as those supporting Prometheus or Jaeger.

Ensuring Network Connectivity

When deploying OpenTelemetry in a containerized application, it is crucial to ensure proper network configuration for containers to communicate effectively. Docker Compose provides an inherent networking structure where containers can reach each other by service name. This property simplifies the setup by letting the application send telemetry data to the collector without the need for explicit IP addresses.

Additionally, it is recommended to define specific network policies when working in more extensive orchestrated environments like Kubernetes. Tools such as Kubernetes Network Policies can control the network flow between pods, facilitating secure communication pathways for telemetry data.

Handling Resource Allocation and Limitations

Running OpenTelemetry adds overhead to your application, and while light, it must be monitored to avoid performance degradation. Proper resource allocation, including CPU and memory limits, ensures that the monitoring processes do not overconsume resources, potentially starving the application itself.

The following Docker Compose snippet illustrates the application of resource constraints:

```
services:
  otel-collector:
    ...

    deploy:
      resources:
        limits:
          cpus: "0.5"
          memory: "256M"
        reservations:
          cpus: "0.25"
```

```
memory: "128M"
```

By configuring these constraints, you can ensure that the collector and the application itself operate within the available resources, preserving both application performance and telemetry fidelity.

Advantages of Using OpenTelemetry in Containers

Deploying OpenTelemetry in containers offers numerous benefits beyond enabling detailed observability:

1. *Consistency* - Once configured within an image, the telemetry setup remains consistent across development, testing, and production environments. 2. *Scalability* - The ability to scale telemetry collection seamlessly alongside service scaling ensures continuous data accuracy as demand fluctuates. 3. *Portability* - Containerized telemetry setups can easily be transferred and executed on different environments without modification, fostering a seamless flow from local development to cloud deployment.

Deploying OpenTelemetry within a containerized environment requires a blend of thoughtful instrumentation, comprehensive collector configuration, and attention to resource management. By leveraging the traits of containers, OpenTelemetry enhances the understanding and observability of application performance, which is crucial for maintaining efficient, robust, and high-performing cloud-native systems.

5.3 Integrating with Kubernetes

Kubernetes has emerged as the de facto standard for container orchestration, providing a robust platform for deploying, managing, and scaling containerized applications. Integrating OpenTelemetry into Kubernetes environments enhances observability by collecting, processing, and exporting telemetry data such as metrics, logs, and traces. This section delves into the methodologies and considerations for successfully integrating OpenTelemetry with Kubernetes, offering insights into deployment strategies, configuration, and observability enhancement techniques.

Understanding Kubernetes Architecture

Kubernetes follows a master-worker architecture where the control plane manages the cluster's overall state and operations, while worker nodes run the applications. Key components include:

- **API Server**: Exposes Kubernetes APIs and acts as the central management entity.

- **Controller Manager**: Oversees the orchestration of clusters, maintaining desired states.

- **Scheduler**: Allocates resources to newly-created pods based on specified requirements.

- **Kubelet**: Manages the node, ensuring that containers are running in pods.

- **Kube-proxy**: Handles networking, ensuring communication across services.

OpenTelemetry must interact with this architecture, integrating within pods to collect telemetry data flowing through Kubernetes-managed applications.

Deployment Strategies

There are two primary strategies for OpenTelemetry deployment in Kubernetes: *as an agent* or *as a collector*. Each serves different purposes and can be adapted based on specific use cases.

Agent Deployment: With this strategy, OpenTelemetry is integrated directly into each application pod, often as a sidecar container. This allows for the direct collection of telemetry data from within the application environment, ensuring granularity and immediate data availability.

Consider the following Kubernetes YAML configuration, deploying OpenTelemetry as a sidecar within an application:

```
apiVersion: apps/v1
kind: Deployment
metadata:
  name: my-app
spec:
  replicas: 3
```

```
selector:
  matchLabels:
    app: my-app
template:
  metadata:
    labels:
      app: my-app
  spec:
    containers:
    - name: app-container
      image: my-app-image:latest
      ports:
      - containerPort: 8080
    - name: otel-agent
      image: otel/opentelemetry-collector:latest
      args: ["--config=/etc/otelcol/config.yaml"]
      volumeMounts:
      - name: config-volume
        mountPath: /etc/otelcol
    volumes:
    - name: config-volume
      configMap:
        name: otel-config
```

In this example, an OpenTelemetry agent runs alongside the application container, with a ConfigMap providing configuration details.

Collector Deployment: Alternatively, collectors can be deployed as dedicated pods, aggregating telemetry data from multiple sources. This model is scalable and centralized, simplifying configuration and management for large clusters.

The following YAML snippet demonstrates how to deploy a standalone OpenTelemetry Collector:

```
apiVersion: apps/v1
kind: Deployment
metadata:
  name: otel-collector
spec:
  replicas: 2
  selector:
    matchLabels:
      app: otel-collector
  template:
    metadata:
      labels:
        app: otel-collector
    spec:
      containers:
      - name: otel-collector
        image: otel/opentelemetry-collector:latest
        ports:
        - containerPort: 4317
```

```
volumeMounts:
  - name: config-volume
    mountPath: /etc/otelcol
volumes:
  - name: config-volume
    configMap:
      name: collector-config
```

Here, the collector listens on port 4317 to receive telemetry data, with configurations supplied through a ConfigMap.

Configuration Management with ConfigMaps

ConfigMaps in Kubernetes provide a key-value store for configuration data, independent from container images. This is especially beneficial for OpenTelemetry, as configurations may need frequent updates. ConfigMaps allow dynamic configuration without re-building container images.

Here's an example ConfigMap for configuring an OpenTelemetry Collector:

```
apiVersion: v1
kind: ConfigMap
metadata:
  name: collector-config
data:
  config.yaml: |
    receivers:
      otlp:
        protocols:
          grpc:

    processors:
      batch:

    exporters:
      logging:

    service:
      pipelines:
        traces:
          receivers: [otlp]
          processors: [batch]
          exporters: [logging]
```

This ConfigMap specifies that traces should be received via gRPC, processed in batches, and logged. Any updates to this configuration can be seamlessly applied by merely updating the ConfigMap resource in the cluster.

Networking and Service Discovery

In Kubernetes, services are used to expose applications running on a set of pods. OpenTelemetry components, like the collector, may require service objects to ensure they can be accessed over the network, both internally within the cluster and externally through ingress controllers if needed.

A simple service definition to expose an OpenTelemetry Collector could look like this:

```
apiVersion: v1
kind: Service
metadata:
  name: otel-collector
spec:
  ports:
  - port: 4317
    protocol: TCP
    targetPort: 4317
  selector:
    app: otel-collector
```

This service provides a stable endpoint for applications to send telemetry data, leveraging Kubernetes' native DNS-based service discovery.

Authentication and Security

Security is paramount when handling telemetry data. Kubernetes provides several mechanisms to secure OpenTelemetry integration:

- **Role-Based Access Control (RBAC)** - Limits permissions for pods and users interacting with resources like ConfigMaps and Kubernetes APIs.

```
apiVersion: rbac.authorization.k8s.io/v1
kind: Role
metadata:
  namespace: default
  name: otel-config-reader
rules:
- apiGroups: [""]
  resources: ["configmaps"]
  verbs: ["get", "list", "watch"]
```

- **Network Policies** - Define rules that control traffic flow at the IP address level between resources within a Kubernetes namespace.

```
apiVersion: networking.k8s.io/v1
kind: NetworkPolicy
metadata:
  name: otel-restrict-access
spec:
  podSelector:
    matchLabels:
      app: otel-collector
  ingress:
  - from:
    - ipBlock:
        cidr: 10.0.0.0/24
```

These configurations ensure that telemetry data remains secure and accessible only by intended services.

Monitoring and Troubleshooting

Once integrated, monitoring OpenTelemetry's performance is essential to ensuring its own health and the fidelity of telemetry data. Kubernetes offers several built-in tools, such as the metrics server and dashboard, along with third-party solutions like Prometheus and Grafana, to facilitate this.

OpenTelemetry itself can expose metrics about its operations, enabling you to monitor metrics such as spans collected, spans dropped, and exporter timeouts. These insights can help fine-tune the collector's configurations and resources.

Here's how OpenTelemetry metrics may look in a configuration:

```
receivers:
  otlp:
    protocols:
      grpc:

processors:
  batch:

exporters:
  prometheus:
    endpoint: "0.0.0.0:8889"

service:
  pipelines:
    metrics:
      receivers: [otlp]
      processors: [batch]
      exporters: [prometheus]
```

By exporting metrics to Prometheus, they can be visualized and analyzed in Grafana for comprehensive monitoring.

Successfully integrating OpenTelemetry with Kubernetes involves careful consideration of its architecture, deployment strategies, configuration management, networking, security, and ongoing monitoring. By adhering to these practices, OpenTelemetry can significantly enhance the observability of applications running in Kubernetes, providing actionable insights that drive performance optimization and ensure reliability in dynamic cloud-native systems.

5.4 Handling Dynamic Scaling and Auto-Healing

Dynamic scaling and auto-healing are pivotal features in modern cloud-native environments that enhance system resilience, adaptability, and cost efficiency. As applications face variable loads and potential failures, the ability to automatically adjust resources and recover from disruptions becomes essential. This section explores the mechanisms and strategies for implementing dynamic scaling and auto-healing, focusing on their interplay with OpenTelemetry to maintain observability in changing conditions.

Understanding dynamic scaling often referred to as autoscaling, involves automatically adjusting the computational resources allocated to an application based on current demand. This can happen both vertically, by altering resource limits within a single unit, and horizontally, by changing the number of units (such as pods in Kubernetes).

Horizontally scaling an application involves adding or removing instances of application components. In Kubernetes, this is typically managed through a controller known as the Horizontal Pod Autoscaler (HPA). The HPA dynamically adjusts the number of pod replicas in a deployment based on observed metrics like CPU utilization, memory usage, or custom application-level metrics provided by OpenTelemetry.

A basic Horizontal Pod Autoscaler configuration using HPA can be defined as follows:

```
apiVersion: autoscaling/v1
```

```
kind: HorizontalPodAutoscaler
metadata:
  name: my-app-autoscaler
spec:
  scaleTargetRef:
    apiVersion: apps/v1
    kind: Deployment
    name: my-app
  minReplicas: 1
  maxReplicas: 10
  targetCPUUtilizationPercentage: 50
```

In the configuration above, the HPA monitors the CPU usage of pods within the my-app deployment, aiming to maintain CPU utilization around 50%. If the average utilization exceeds or falls below this threshold, the number of replicas is adjusted to meet demand.

Integrating telemetry for enhanced metrics while basic metrics like CPU and memory are supported natively by Kubernetes, application-specific metrics can provide a more accurate basis for scaling decisions. OpenTelemetry can instrument applications to emit such custom metrics, which can then be utilized by the Kubernetes metrics server to influence scaling behaviors.

For example, consider a web application where the number of active HTTP sessions better indicates load. OpenTelemetry SDKs can be used to emit real-time metrics reflecting this.

```
// Import OpenTelemetry metric packages
import (
    "go.opentelemetry.io/otel"
    "go.opentelemetry.io/otel/metric/global"
    "go.opentelemetry.io/otel/metric/instrument"
    "context"
)

// Setup function to create a custom metric
func setupCustomMetric() {
    meter := global.Meter("myapp-metric")
    activeSessions, err := meter.Int64ObservableGauge(
        "http.active_sessions",
        instrument.WithDescription("Number of active HTTP sessions"),
    )
    if err != nil {
        // Handle error
    }

    ctx := context.Background()
    meter.RegisterCallback(
        []instrument.Asynchronous{activeSessions},
        func(ctx context.Context, a instrument.Observer) {
            a.ObserveInt64(activeSessions, getCurrentSessionCount())
```

```
    },
  )
}
```

This example sets up a gauge metric for tracking active HTTP sessions. When registered, the metric system automatically collects this data and makes it available for scaling policy logic.

Auto-healing mechanisms refer to the system's capability to detect and rectify faults automatically. Kubernetes provides several auto-healing capabilities through probes and the restart behavior of pods. There are three primary types of probes used to assess container health:

- Liveness Probes: Determine if the application is running. If a liveness probe fails, the container is restarted.

- Readiness Probes: Indicate whether a pod is ready to accept traffic.

- Startup Probes: Used when an application may take a long time to start; only run at startup.

Configuring a liveness probe for an application container might look like this:

```
apiVersion: apps/v1
kind: Deployment
metadata:
  name: my-app
spec:
  replicas: 3
  selector:
    matchLabels:
      app: my-app
  template:
    metadata:
      labels:
        app: my-app
    spec:
      containers:
      - name: app-container
        image: my-app-image:latest
        ports:
        - containerPort: 8080
        livenessProbe:
          httpGet:
            path: /healthz
            port: 8080
          initialDelaySeconds: 15
          periodSeconds: 20
```

Here, the liveness probe checks the /healthz endpoint on port 8080 every 20 seconds, restarting the container if the endpoint is unhealthy after an initial delay period.

The role of OpenTelemetry in auto-healing, while Kubernetes manages basic health checks, OpenTelemetry adds deeper insights into application behavior and performance patterns. By analyzing telemetry data, one can identify anomalies or degradation trends before they manifest as critical failures. This proactive approach to observability enables more effective preventive measures and adjustments.

By leveraging OpenTelemetry traces, for example, you can pinpoint specific services or components responsible for slowdowns, allowing focused troubleshooting and mitigation, often performed automatically by workflows defined in integration platforms like Argo Workflows or Tekton Pipelines.

Integrating OpenTelemetry in scalable architectures for effective scaling, integrating OpenTelemetry with Kubernetes goes beyond basic data collection. A robust setup will involve:

- Establishing centralized telemetry collection through OpenTelemetry Collectors to aggregate and process distributed metric and trace data.

- Utilizing cloud-specific managed services for telemetry (such as AWS CloudWatch, Azure Monitor, or Google Cloud Operations) to optimize data storage and analysis.

- Implementing service mesh solutions, like Istio, to enhance telemetry-related observability across microservices, including data on inter-service communication and failure points.

Example: dynamic scaling with custom autoscaler. To implement custom scaling policies using OpenTelemetry metrics, one may employ a custom controller or integrate solutions like the Kubernetes Custom Metrics API. Suppose an application experiences cyclical load with known usage patterns influencing specific scale-up criteria. OpenTelemetry-provided metrics can drive the logic of a custom scaler, which might adaptively adjust resources by leveraging machine learning models trained on historical telemetry data.

```yaml
apiVersion: metrics.k8s.io/v1beta1
kind: PodMetrics
metadata:
  name: http.active_sessions
spec:
  scaleTargetRef:
    kind: Deployment
    name: my-app
  maxReplicas: 15
  minReplicas: 2
  behavior:
    scaleUp:
      stabilizationWindowSeconds: 60
      selectPolicy: Max
      policies:
        - type: Pods
          value: 4
          periodSeconds: 60
    scaleDown:
      stabilizationWindowSeconds: 60
      selectPolicy: Min
      policies:
        - type: Pods
          value: 2
          periodSeconds: 60
```

This scalable configuration responds to the http.active_sessions metric, leveraging Kubernetes' extensibility to precisely scale deployments based on dynamic criteria beyond simple CPU or memory utilization.

Challenge mitigation and future outlook implementing dynamic scaling and auto-healing mechanisms can present challenges such as configuration complexity, ensuring security and privacy of telemetry data, and avoiding metric overload and alert fatigue. OpenTelemetry's modular design and community-driven enhancements ensure it evolves alongside changing operational needs.

In the future, tighter integration with advanced analytics, AI-driven decision-making for auto-scaling, and fine-grained policy controls are anticipated. These enhancements will improve the accuracy and transparency of scaling operations, providing organizations with a powerful toolset to maintain optimal system performance, resilience, and cost efficiency in highly dynamic environments.

By effectively deploying OpenTelemetry within Kubernetes, organizations do not only achieve baseline observability but position themselves to harness advanced dynamic scaling and auto-healing methods, allowing them to meet demand with precision and reliability. Through comprehensive instrumentation and automated response strategies, enterprises can ensure their systems remain robust, responsive, and aligned with business objectives in an ever-evolving technological landscape.

5.5 Managing Microservices with Open-Telemetry

Microservices architecture has become a dominant paradigm for building scalable and maintainable software systems. This approach decomposes applications into small, loosely coupled services, each responsible for a specific domain. These services often have independent deployment pipelines and can be developed with various technologies and languages. As beneficial as microservices architecture is, it also introduces complexity, especially in observability. OpenTelemetry, a unified observability framework, plays a vital role in managing these complexities by providing comprehensive insights into the interactions, performance, and dependencies of services within a system.

The Nature of Microservices

Microservices are designed to overcome the limitations of monolithic architectures by promoting agility, scalability, and independent deployment. However, with these advantages come challenges such as managing service discovery, load balancing, redundancy, and especially monitoring.

A typical microservice-based system might involve several components interacting over network protocols like HTTP/REST, gRPC, or messaging queues like Kafka or RabbitMQ. Each service runs its database, uses different libraries, and communicates with others through Application Programming Interfaces (APIs). This highly decentralized approach demands sophisticated monitoring techniques to ensure everything functions cohesively and efficiently.

Observability Challenges in Microservices

The move to microservices shifts the monitoring focus from individual components to services and their interactions. Important challenges include:

138

- Disparate Technologies: Services can be written in different languages and run on various environments or platforms. This diversity complicates the monitoring process across the architecture.

- Scaling Issues: Each service scales independently, which may affect how telemetry data is collected, stored, and analyzed.

- Inter-Service Communication: Understanding how services communicate is essential for diagnosing issues, which requires capturing distributed traces and metrics.

- Service Dependencies: As the number of services grows, understanding dependencies and their impact on application health becomes challenging.

OpenTelemetry addresses these challenges by offering a cohesive framework to capture and analyze telemetry data across diverse services and environments.

OpenTelemetry Basics for Microservices

To effectively manage microservices, developers must integrate OpenTelemetry within each service. This process typically involves setting up the SDK for the chosen language, instrumenting code to generate telemetry data (traces, metrics, and logs), and configuring the OpenTelemetry Collector to process and export this information to a backend observability tool.

Consider a simple microservice written in Python using Flask. To instrument this service with OpenTelemetry, we integrate code as follows:

```
from flask import Flask, request
from opentelemetry import trace
from opentelemetry.instrumentation.flask import FlaskInstrumentor
from opentelemetry.sdk.trace import TracerProvider
from opentelemetry.sdk.trace.export import SimpleSpanProcessor
from opentelemetry.exporter.otlp.proto.grpc.trace_exporter import
        OTLPSpanExporter

# Set up tracing
trace.set_tracer_provider(TracerProvider())
tracer = trace.get_tracer(__name__)

# Create a span exporter
otlp_exporter = OTLPSpanExporter(endpoint="localhost:4317")
```

139

```
# Add span processor to the tracer
span_processor = SimpleSpanProcessor(otlp_exporter)
trace.get_tracer_provider().add_span_processor(span_processor)

app = Flask(___name___)

# Instrument the Flask application
FlaskInstrumentor().instrument_app(app)

@app.route('/api/greet')
def greet():
    name = request.args.get('name', 'World')
    message = f"Hello, {name}!"
    return {"message": message}

if ___name___ == "___main___":
    app.run(host="0.0.0.0", port=5000)
```

In this Python Flask service, the OpenTelemetry Flask Instrumentor is used to automatically create spans for incoming HTTP requests. These spans are exported to a local OpenTelemetry Collector, which processes and sends them to a back-end system.

End-to-End Tracing

One key benefit of OpenTelemetry is its ability to contextually trace requests through a system of interconnected microservices. This end-to-end visibility is critical to identify and troubleshoot performance bottlenecks or failures.

Consider a flow where a user's request to a service propagates through several other services, each executing part of the workflow. OpenTelemetry tags each service interaction with a unique trace ID and span IDs representing the operation performed. This contextual data allows reconstructing the entire user journey across services:

- **Start Span**: Marks the initiation of a service operation. Each span records the start time, end time, attributes, events, and status.

- **Propagate Context**: OpenTelemetry's context propagators ensure trace correlation information travels across service boundaries. This can be handled automatically by OpenTelemetry SDKs if configured to instrument network libraries like HTTP clients.

140

- **End Span**: At the completion of each operation, the span ends, capturing the total duration and success/failure status.

Example of context propagation in Python using HTTP requests:

```
import requests
from opentelemetry.propagate import inject

def call_another_service(url):
    headers = {}
    inject(headers) # inject trace context into headers
    response = requests.get(url, headers=headers)
    return response.json()

with tracer.start_as_current_span("process user request") as span:
    response = call_another_service("http://service-b/api/process")
```

Here, the 'inject' method propagates the current trace context to ensure the trace continues through external service calls.

Metrics Collection for Microservices Performance

Besides tracing, metrics provide quantitative measurement of service performance and resource usage. OpenTelemetry allows developers to define custom metrics relevant to application performance, like request counts, latencies, error rates, and resource utilization.

Using OpenTelemetry Metrics API, developers can instrument services to emit relevant metrics data actively:

```
from opentelemetry import metrics
from opentelemetry.sdk.metrics import MeterProvider
from opentelemetry.sdk.metrics.export import ConsoleMetricExporter,
    PeriodicExportingMetricReader

metrics.set_meter_provider(MeterProvider())

meter = metrics.get_meter(__name__)
requests_counter = meter.create_counter(
    "http.server.requests",
    description="Number of HTTP requests",
)

def greet_handler():
    requests_counter.add(1) # Increment counter for each request
    # ... Handler logic
```

This script sets up a counter metric for HTTP requests within the service, allowing tracking over time. These records are periodically exported and analyzed to manage scaling, capacity planning, and identifying unusual patterns indicative of service anomalies or outages.

Correlation and Dependency Analysis

In microservices architecture, understanding dependencies is crucial for diagnosing failures or performance degradation. OpenTelemetry traces can be visualized to reveal these service dependencies and their health. This visualization can highlight problem areas where services might be performing suboptimally or where external factors cascade into other services.

For instance, by analyzing OpenTelemetry data, one might find that a slow database query in one service is impacting response times of multiple downstream services.

To support such analysis, it's common to export telemetry data to a backend like Jaeger or Grafana, which provides visualization capabilities. These platforms allow breadcrumbs tracing of requests across services, enabling deeper insights into performance.

Advanced Visualization for Microservices Observability

Ultimately, raw OpenTelemetry data becomes most useful when visualized in ways that make it actionable for development and operations teams. Tools like Grafana, Jaeger, and Zipkin integrate with Open-Telemetry to provide intuitive interfaces for telemetry exploration.

- **Grafana**: Provides dashboards for visualizing metric data with customizable panels to capture trends and anomalies.

- **Jaeger**: Specializes in distributed tracing, allowing developers to track the paths and dependencies of requests within the system.

- **Zipkin**: Another tracing tool that captures timing data for requests and visualizes trace trees and timelines.

When deployed at scale, these visualization tools empower teams to maintain actionable observability over their microservices, reducing the mean time to resolution (MTTR) for issues, and confidently managing service health and performance.

Managing microservices with OpenTelemetry represents both a necessary observability shift and an opportunity to enhance service performance. OpenTelemetry provides comprehensive tooling to navigate the complexities of distributed architectures, collecting critical insights through metrics, traces, and logs. By effectively deploying OpenTelemetry instruments across microservices, teams can ensure robust monitoring and resilience, paving the way for adaptable and high-performing cloud-native applications.

5.6 Using OpenTelemetry in Serverless Architectures

Serverless computing has revolutionized the landscape of cloud applications by abstracting infrastructure management and allowing developers to focus purely on code. Prominent platforms like AWS Lambda, Azure Functions, and Google Cloud Functions enable functions to be executed in response to events, automatically scaling with demand and charging only for actual execution time. Alongside these advantages, however, come unique challenges in observability due to the ephemeral and stateless nature of serverless functions. OpenTelemetry offers a robust framework to address these challenges, providing visibility into function invocations, performance, and dependencies.

Characteristics of Serverless Architectures

Serverless architectures are epitomized by their focus on execution rather than infrastructure management. Key characteristics include:

- **Event-Driven Execution**: Functions are triggered by events such as HTTP requests, file uploads, or message queue events.

- **Automatic Scaling**: Functions automatically scale based on incoming demand, without explicit provisioning of resources.

- **Short-Lived and Stateless**: Functions execute quickly, often within milliseconds or seconds, and do not retain state between invocations.

These traits significantly reduce the operational burden of managing underlying infrastructure. However, they also introduce complexity in monitoring execution context and performance, as traditional infrastructure metrics are less applicable.

Observability Challenges in Serverless

Observing serverless functions requires nuanced approaches to capture relevant telemetry data, given the constraints and unique patterns in serverless environments:

- **Ephemeral Nature**: Functions can execute and terminate rapidly, necessitating real-time telemetry capture to ensure data is not lost.

- **Distributed Execution**: Functions might be distributed across various geographies or services, making it difficult to trace a request end-to-end.

- **Resource Constraints**: Serverless functions typically have limited execution time and memory constraints, so telemetry instrumentation must be lightweight.

OpenTelemetry addresses these challenges by integrating with serverless environments, providing real-time insight into function behavior and execution dynamics.

Integrating OpenTelemetry with Serverless Functions

Effective use of OpenTelemetry in serverless architectures involves embedding OpenTelemetry SDKs within functions to generate trace and metric data. Here, we will explore OpenTelemetry instrumentation within an AWS Lambda function using Node.js:

```
// Import OpenTelemetry modules
const { NodeTracerProvider } = require('@opentelemetry/sdk-trace-node');
const { registerInstrumentations } = require('@opentelemetry/instrumentation');
const { AwsLambdaInstrumentation } = require('@opentelemetry/instrumentation-aws-
    lambda');

// Set up a tracer provider
const tracerProvider = new NodeTracerProvider();

// Initialize instrumentation for AWS Lambda
registerInstrumentations({
  tracerProvider,
  instrumentations: [
    new AwsLambdaInstrumentation(),
  ],
```

```
});

// Lambda handler function
exports.handler = async (event, context) => {
  const tracer = tracerProvider.getTracer('example-lambda-tracer');
  const span = tracer.startSpan('process-incoming-request');

  try {
    const response = {
      statusCode: 200,
      body: JSON.stringify({ message: 'Hello from lambda!' }),
    };
    span.setAttribute('responseCode', response.statusCode);
    return response;

  } catch (error) {
    span.setAttribute('error', true);
    throw error;

  } finally {
    span.end();
  }
};
```

In this example, the OpenTelemetry Node.js SDK with AWS Lambda instrumentation is used to automatically capture and propagate trace context, recording spans for function invocations. The span records essential data such as execution time, outcome, and any associated errors.

Distributed Tracing in Serverless Architectures

One of the primary goals in serverless observability is achieving seamless traceability across diverse services and functions. Tracing allows understanding how events flow through various functions, even when distributed across different platforms or clouds.

Consider a serverless architecture where a function receives an HTTP request, processes data, and calls an external API. With OpenTelemetry, trace data would reveal the sequence and duration of each step, enabling pinpointing of bottlenecks or failures in the execution flow.

```
import json
import boto3
from opentelemetry import trace
from opentelemetry.instrumentation.botocore import BotocoreInstrumentor
from aws_lambda_powertools import Tracer

# Initialize tracer
tracer = Tracer()

# Configure AWS SDK instrumentation
```

```
BotocoreInstrumentor().instrument()

@tracer.capture_lambda_handler
def lambda_handler(event, context):
    with tracer.start_as_current_span("step1-process-input") as span:
        data = process_input(event["data"])
        span.set_attribute("processed_data", json.dumps(data))

    with tracer.start_as_current_span("step2-call-external-api"):
        external_response = call_external_service(data)
        tracer.put_annotation("external_response_status", external_response.
            status_code)

    return {"status": "completed", "data": data}
```

In this Python-based AWS Lambda example, OpenTelemetry tracks
each logical step with specific spans, adding meaningful context and
metadata to the trace for comprehensive analysis. This context is invaluable for identifying performance discrepancies and failed execu-
tions.

Capturing Metrics for Function Performance

While tracing provides detailed contextual information, capturing metrics is central to understanding broader performance patterns and resource utilization. OpenTelemetry allows developers to define custom
metrics capturing invocation counts, latencies, and error rates, instru-
mental for operational insight and optimization.

Implementation of metrics with OpenTelemetry and AWS CloudWatch
can follow a pattern like this:

```
from opentelemetry import metrics
from opentelemetry.sdk.metrics import MeterProvider
from opentelemetry.sdk.metrics.export import ConsoleMetricExporter,
    PeriodicExportingMetricReader

# Initialize meter provider
metrics.set_meter_provider(MeterProvider())

# Create a meter
meter = metrics.get_meter(__name__)

# Define a counter for invocations
invocations_counter = meter.create_counter(
    "serverless_function_invocations",
    description="Counts the number of function invocations",
)

def lambda_handler(event, context):
    invocations_counter.add(1, {"function_name": context.function_name})
```

146

```
# Function logic...
return {"status": "success"}
```

In this script, a counter metric is defined to count function invocations, assisting in analyzing patterns over time to optimize resource allocation and determine periods of high load or irregular activity.

Integration with Observability Tools

Accumulated OpenTelemetry data often needs analysis through purpose-built observability platforms. Transmitting trace and metric data from serverless functions to such platforms can reveal operations at scale in graphical detail, facilitating easier diagnostics and performance tuning.

Popular back-end observability services include:

- **AWS X-Ray**: AWS-specific platform, excellent for tracing requests through AWS services and Lambda functions.

- **Grafana**: Offers dashboards to visualize metrics captured from various sources, including serverless functions.

- **New Relic & DataDog**: Provide centralized views of telemetry data, integrating with OpenTelemetry to monitor serverless application health.

Integration ensures data collected by OpenTelemetry is easily accessible, promoting actionable insights.

Security and Compliance Considerations

Securing telemetry data is paramount, especially in serverless applications handling sensitive information. OpenTelemetry agents and collectors need careful configuration to minimize data exposure and enforce secure transmission.

Basic security practices include:

- **Data Encryption**: Ensure telemetry data is encrypted in transit using protocols like TLS.

- **Access Control**: Use IAM roles and policies to limit access to telemetry data flows and back-end systems.

- **Data Anonymization**: Remove Personally Identifiable Information (PII) from telemetry streams to maintain privacy compliance.

- **Audit Logging**: Record changes in telemetry configurations to maintain accountability.

Cost-Management of Observability in Serverless

Serverless cost models charge for execution time and resource allocation. Added telemetry logic can contribute to cost, so efficient instrumentation is essential to prevent unnecessary spending.

- **Optimize Metrics and Traces**: Capture only essential data points necessary for performance insights.

- **Adjust Sampling Rates**: Balance the need for detailed data against cost by tuning sampling rates; process full traces at critical periods only.

- **Off-load Processing**: Use cost-effective external systems for processing telemetry data, like dedicated OpenTelemetry Collectors outside of high-cost environments.

Through strategic instrumentation and data handling, organizations can efficiently integrate OpenTelemetry in serverless systems while controlling associated costs.

OpenTelemetry provides the means to achieve profound insight into serverless systems, overcoming traditional challenges of ephemeral and stateless execution environments. By embedding unobtrusive instrumentation, unifying trace and metric data, and integrating with rich visualization platforms, organizations can ensure their serverless architectures remain visible, performant, and scalable, thereby leveraging the full potential of serverless computing paradigms.

148

5.7 Optimizing for Cloud-Native Performance

In the rapidly evolving landscape of cloud-native applications, performance optimization is essential for maintaining efficient, scalable, and responsive systems. The characteristics of cloud-native environments, such as microservices architectures, containerization, and orchestration, offer significant benefits but also introduce complexities in achieving optimal performance. This section explores strategies for optimizing performance in cloud-native applications, leveraging tools like OpenTelemetry to gain insights and make data-driven optimizations.

Characteristics Impacting Performance

Cloud-native applications are designed for high scalability, elasticity, and resilience. However, these features introduce specific challenges in performance optimization:

- Microservices Complexity: The decomposition of applications into independent services increases the interaction between components, requiring careful management of network latency, service discovery, and load balancing.

- Resource Overheads: Containers encapsulate applications with their dependencies, which can lead to increased resource utilization if not managed efficiently.

- Dynamic Environments: Continuous integration and deployment pipelines result in frequent changes that can impact performance stability.

- Distributed Systems: Cloud-native applications often span multiple infrastructure layers, including on-premises and cloud services, adding layers of complexity in data flow and bottleneck identification.

Understanding these characteristics is imperative to formulating effective performance optimization strategies.

Strategies for Performance Optimization

To achieve optimal performance in cloud-native environments, developers can employ several strategies:

- Efficient Resource Utilization: Ensure that containers and services are configured to use appropriate CPU and memory resources without overprovisioning. Tools like Kubernetes' resource requests and limits facilitate this.

- Minimizing Latency in Microservices: Since microservices communicate over a network, optimizing API calls, reducing payload sizes, and employing caching mechanisms can significantly improve response times.

- Load Balancing and Traffic Management: Utilize service mesh technologies like Istio to route traffic intelligently based on service load and health, enhancing both performance and reliability.

- Profiling and Bottleneck Identification: Use profiling tools to monitor performance at runtime and identify code-level bottlenecks or inefficient processes.

Leveraging OpenTelemetry for Performance Insights

OpenTelemetry allows for detailed collection and analysis of telemetry data, providing insights necessary for performance enhancements. By instrumenting applications to collect traces, metrics, and logs, developers can achieve full observability, which is critical for understanding and optimizing cloud-native performance.

- Trace Collection: Analyze end-to-end request flows to identify latency sources and service dependencies. Visualizations help pinpoint bottlenecks requiring optimization.

- Metrics Analysis: Collect detailed metrics on CPU, memory usage, request rates, and error rates across services.

- Log Aggregation and Analysis: Analyze logs in conjunction with traces and metrics for a comprehensive understanding of system behavior under load.

Example Code for Instrumenting Performance Metrics

To illustrate how performance data can be collected using OpenTelemetry, consider a Node.js application using an Express.js server:

```
// OpenTelemetry dependencies
const opentelemetry = require('@opentelemetry/api');
const { MeterProvider } = require('@opentelemetry/sdk-metrics-base');
const { collectDefaultMetrics } = require('@opentelemetry/sdk-metrics-defaults');

// Set up the MeterProvider
const meterProvider = new MeterProvider();
collectDefaultMetrics({ meterProvider });

// Create a Meter instance
const meter = meterProvider.getMeter('performance-meter');

// Define custom metrics
const requestCounter = meter.createCounter('request_counter', {
  description: 'Counts number of requests received',
});

// Initialize the Express application
const express = require('express');
const app = express();

// Middleware to record request metrics
app.use((req, res, next) => {
  requestCounter.add(1, { route: req.path });
  next();
});

app.get('/api/data', (req, res) => {
  res.send('Data response');
});

app.listen(3000, () => {
  console.log('Server is running on port 3000');
});
```

In this example, OpenTelemetry is set to collect performance metrics from an Express.js server, recording each incoming request. The request counter metric provides insights into traffic patterns that can help determine potential scaling requirements or recurrent slow endpoints.

Continuous Performance Testing

Continuous performance testing is integral to ensuring that changes do not degrade application performance. By integrating OpenTelemetry with continuous performance testing tools, developers can simulate load and evaluate the impact of application changes:

151

- Automated Test Execution: Configure CI/CD pipelines to execute performance tests automatically. Tools like Apache JMeter
  or Gatling can be used to generate simulated traffic against service endpoints.

- Baseline Comparison: Use historical telemetry data to establish
  baseline performance metrics, against which new changes can be
  compared.

- Alerting and Notification: Integrate alerting mechanisms to no-
  tify developers when performance thresholds are breached.

Implementing Performance Testing in a CI/CD Pipeline

Leveraging OpenTelemetry alongside performance testing in a GitHub
Actions pipeline might look as follows:

```yaml
name: Performance Testing

on:
  push:
    branches:
      - main

jobs:
  test-and-measure:
    runs-on: ubuntu-latest

    steps:
      - name: Checkout repository
        uses: actions/checkout@v2

      - name: Set up Node.js
        uses: actions/setup-node@v2
        with:
          node-version: '14'

      - name: Install dependencies
        run: npm install

      - name: Run performance tests
        run: |
          node performance-test.js
        env:
          OTEL_EXPORTER_OTLP_ENDPOINT: http://localhost:4317

      - name: Analyze performance data
        run: |
          curl -X GET http://localhost:9090/metrics
```

In this setup, after checking out the application code and installing dependencies, a performance-test script runs simulated tests, transmit-

ting telemetry data to an OTLP endpoint. This provides rich performance data for analysis.

Tuning of Application Components

Fine-tuning individual components of a cloud-native application architecture can significantly impact performance. Some common areas for performance tuning include:

- Database Optimization: Indexing, query optimization, and caching improve data retrieval speeds.

- Cache Management: Use distributed caching mechanisms like Redis to reduce database load and enhance data access speeds.

- Concurrency and Thread Management: For high-throughput, consider adjusting thread pools and concurrency levels in service runtimes.

- Container Image Optimization: Ensure container images are lightweight by removing unnecessary dependencies and layers.

In conjunction with OpenTelemetry, telemetry can help identify precisely which areas of the application should be targeted for such optimizations, thereby improving overall system efficiency.

Optimizing cloud-native application performance requires multifaceted strategies, from efficient resource management and minimizing network latency to leveraging profiling tools and performance testing. By utilizing OpenTelemetry to achieve comprehensive visibility into application behavior, developers can make informed decisions to enhance performance, ensuring the adaptive and reliable operation of their applications. Through strategic instrumentation, continuous testing, and application component tuning, cloud-native systems can achieve high levels of performance while meeting modern demands for scalability and reliability.

Chapter 6

Advanced OpenTelemetry Concepts and Techniques

This chapter explores advanced methodologies within OpenTelemetry, focusing on enhancing observability through sophisticated implementations. It provides an in-depth look at context propagation, custom sampler creation, and the construction of span and metric processing pipelines. The chapter also covers instrumentation of asynchronous operations, management of high-cardinality attributes, and integration with legacy systems. By providing strategies for evolving schemas and ensuring robust interoperability, this chapter equips readers with the techniques necessary to tailor OpenTelemetry implementations to complex, enterprise-level applications.

6.1 Context Propagation in Depth

In distributed systems, efficient context propagation is vital for maintaining cohesiveness across various services and applications. This section delves into the advanced techniques of context propagation within OpenTelemetry, a framework designed to capture and report metrics, logs, and traces. Accurate context propagation ensures continuity and reliability of tracing information across asynchronous and network-bound operations.

In OpenTelemetry, context propagation is built upon the *Context API* which is a language-agnostic specification that provides propagation of trace context through system boundaries.

The Context object in OpenTelemetry stores metadata that is passed through call chains and across process boundaries. Specifically, it holds span properties, and it can be critical to preserve this context throughout distributed transactions for accurate end-to-end tracing.

```
from opentelemetry import trace
from opentelemetry.sdk.trace import TracerProvider
from opentelemetry.propagate import extract

# Install the tracing provider
trace.set_tracer_provider(TracerProvider())

# Example function using context
def example_function():
    existing_context = extract()
    with trace.use_span(existing_context) as span:
        span.set_attribute("operation", "example")
        # Additional logic

example_function()
```

The code above initializes a tracer, an essential aspect of extracting and injecting trace data into the current context. The OpenTelemetry extract method gathers context from incoming requests, allowing spans to be correlated appropriately.

- Context in OpenTelemetry must be propagated across process and network boundaries. Typically, this entails context injection into HTTP headers or message attributes for queues or RPC systems. OpenTelemetry supports this through various propagation schemes, including W3C Trace Context and B3 propagation protocols.

```
from opentelemetry.propagators.b3 import B3Format
from opentelemetry.trace.propagation.tracecontext import
    TraceContextTextMapPropagator

# Use B3 propagation format
propagator = B3Format()

# Inject context into an HTTP request
def make_request():
    headers = {}
    propagator.inject(headers)
    # Perform HTTP request with injected headers

make_request()
```

The example demonstrates using the B3 format to propagate context through HTTP headers via the inject method. This allows downstream services to extract the context upon receipt.

- Handling context in asynchronous operations necessitates careful management to preserve the integrity of span contexts across asynchronous boundaries. This can be achieved using inbuilt context managers and ensuring continuity of context within asynchronous tasks.

```
import asyncio
from opentelemetry.context import get_current

async def async_task():
    current_context = get_current()
    with trace.use_span(current_context):
        # Perform asynchronous task
        await asyncio.sleep(1)

asyncio.run(async_task())
```

In the above code, the current context is retrieved and applied with use_span, thereby maintaining the context during the asynchronous task execution, which is critical in environments where concurrency is significant.

- OpenTelemetry supports a variety of context propagation protocols for integration with existing systems or adhering to specific organizational standards.

157

- **W3C Trace Context:** The W3C Trace Context standard provides a framework for interoperability across tracing vendors, making it easier to correlate spans.

```
from opentelemetry.trace.propagation.tracecontext import
    TraceContextTextMapPropagator

propagator = TraceContextTextMapPropagator()

# Inject for W3C context
def inject_w3c_context():
    headers = {}
    propagator.inject(headers)
    return headers

# Extract a received trace context
def extract_context(headers):
    return propagator.extract(headers)

request_headers = inject_w3c_context()
extracted_context = extract_context(request_headers)
```

The W3C Trace Context ensures trace continuity across different languages and tracing services, leveraging standard headers for traceparent and tracestate.

- **B3 Propagation:** B3 Propagation, used widely in Zipkin systems, passes tracing information via HTTP headers. It is crucial for maintaining backward compatibility with existing infrastructure.

- **Challenges in Context Propagation:** Handling network-based propagation comes with challenges such as data encoding, network boundaries, and managing state over time. Encoding context as headers is prone to truncations and variations across diverse systems, potentially leading to loss of tracing fidelity.

To mitigate these concerns, it is vital to employ robust error analysis and validation mechanisms, ensuring headers are correctly formed and utilized across system interfaces. Additionally, monitoring tools should be implemented to audit propagation effectiveness and identify discrepancies in trace data.

- **Advanced Techniques:** Beyond synchronous propagation, advanced techniques can capture contextual changes and forward these in batch jobs, stream processing platforms, and serverless functions. Utilizing distributed task queues and message brokers also requires transforming and adapting context information to suit message-driven architectures.

Worker processes should explicitly manage extraction and injection of context for each message processed, ensuring continuation of tracing information. This approach requires tight integration between application logic and propagation utilities.

```
from opentelemetry.propagators import extract, inject

def worker_task(message):
    context = extract(message.headers)
    with trace.use_span(context):
        # Process task message

def enqueue_task(message):
    headers = {}
    inject(headers)
    message.headers = headers
    # Add message to queue

enqueue_task(QueueMessage())
```

This example demonstrates a systematic approach to context propagation in a worker queue, which is critical for maintaining the integrity of distributed operation tracing.

Achieving effective and reliable context propagation requires a comprehensive understanding of both the underlying distributed system architecture and OpenTelemetry's capabilities. Developers and system architects must incorporate practices such as:

- Consistent usage of context propagation libraries and protocols.

- Routinely testing context propagation boundaries.

- Designing audit trails and logs to track and rectify propagation errors.

Organizations need to establish standardized protocols for context management, enforcing consistent practices across development teams to optimize observability and traceability across their distributed networks. These steps ensure a robust, streamlined, and maintainable tracing strategy in line with evolving user and system demands.

6.2 Span and Metric Processing Pipelines

In distributed observability systems, efficient span and metric processing pipelines are crucial for enabling detailed analysis and monitoring. OpenTelemetry provides a comprehensive framework for creating customized processing pipelines, allowing for tailored data manipulations that suit specific enterprise-level application needs.

To build sophisticated span and metric pipelines, a developer must understand the components involved, including data collection, processing, transformation, and export. The pipeline configuration not only affects performance but also the depth of insight available from the collected traces and metrics.

- **Data Collection**: Initial stage where data is captured through instrumented code. Spans represent individual operations, while metrics quantify specific application behaviors.

- **Data Processing**: Involves filtering, sampling, aggregation, and enriching collected data based on defined criteria.

- **Data Transformation**: Conversion or enhancement of raw data into a more useful format, often to match the target analytics or monitoring system's requirements.

- **Data Export**: The final step where processed data is sent to storage systems or monitoring platforms for analysis and visualization.

Configuring Trace Processing Pipelines

The trace processing pipeline is responsible for handling span data throughout its lifecycle—from generation to export. Its performance and configuration directly influence the system's observability and the granularity of available insights.

```
from opentelemetry.sdk.trace import TracerProvider
from opentelemetry.sdk.trace.export import BatchSpanProcessor, ConsoleSpanExporter


trace_provider = TracerProvider()
processor = BatchSpanProcessor(ConsoleSpanExporter())

trace_provider.add_span_processor(processor)
```

In this example, we initialize a TracerProvider along with a batch span processor paired with a console exporter, demonstrating the foundation of a trace processing pipeline that outputs spans to the console. This configuration can be extended to integrate with other exporters such as Jaeger or Zipkin.

Processing Span Data

Efficient processing is crucial to managing trace data volume, which can grow significantly in high-throughput environments. Key techniques include:

- **Sampling**: Reducing the volume of trace data by selecting a subset of spans for export and analysis. Sampling strategies may vary from always sampling certain critical paths to probabilistically sampling a percentage of all spans.

- **Filtering and Enrichment**: Applying rules to focus on specific spans or enrich span data with additional metadata before exportation. Filtering removes noise from non-essential spans, while enrichment provides context for trace analysis.

- **Batching**: Grouping multiple spans for transmission in a single operation, reducing the overhead associated with sending each span individually.

```
from opentelemetry.sdk.trace import SpanProcessor
from opentelemetry.sdk.trace.export import SpanExporter

class CustomSpanProcessor(SpanProcessor):
    def __init__(self, span_exporter: SpanExporter):
        self.span_exporter = span_exporter

    def on_start(self, span):
        pass # Logic when a span starts

    def on_end(self, span):
```

161

```
    if self.should_process(span):
        enriched_span = self.enrich_span(span)
        self.span_exporter.export([enriched_span])

def shutdown(self):
    self.span_exporter.shutdown()

def force_flush(self):
    self.span_exporter.force_flush()

def should_process(self, span):
    # Custom filtering logic
    return True

def enrich_span(self, span):
    # Custom enrichment logic
    return span
```

This configuration showcases a custom span processor implementation, which includes methods to determine whether to process a span and enrich it prior to export, enhancing the trace pipeline's effectiveness.

Metric Processing Pipelines

Metric processing pipelines, similar to spans, involve capturing, aggregating, and exporting metric data. Metrics provide quantitative insights measuring how applications are performing over time and are vital for ongoing system health checks.

Configuring Metric Processors

Metric processors aggregate and transform metric data before export. The aggregation can range from simple counts to complex statistical combinations that provide a broader view of application performance.

```
from opentelemetry.sdk.metrics import MeterProvider
from opentelemetry.sdk.metrics.export import ConsoleMetricExporter,
    PeriodicExportingMetricReader

meter_provider = MeterProvider()

reader = PeriodicExportingMetricReader(ConsoleMetricExporter())

meter_provider.register_metric_reader(reader)
```

The above setup registers a metric reader that periodically collects and exports metrics using a console exporter. Like the span processor, this setup can be customized to utilize diverse metric exporters, such as Prometheus, Datadog, or other similar services.

162

Advanced Metric Aggregations

Advanced aggregation techniques allow for powerful metric analytics that can lead to actionable insights. Aggregations like histograms, summaries, or custom-defined aggregates are invaluable for performance monitoring.

```
from opentelemetry.sdk.metrics import MeterProvider
from opentelemetry.sdk.metrics.view import View
from opentelemetry.sdk.metrics.export import HistogramAggregation

meter_provider.add_view(View(
    instrument_type=float,
    instrument_name="response_time",
    aggregation=HistogramAggregation(async_boundaries=[0, 10, 100])
))
```

In this example, advanced histogram aggregation is configured for a metric named "response_time" to categorize response times into different buckets, facilitating deeper performance analysis.

Optimizing Pipelines for Performance

Performance optimization is critical for processing pipelines, especially as the scale of applications grows. Essential practices include:

- **Minimizing Overhead**: Customize the pipeline components to limit processing time and resource consumption. Limit excessive logging and prefer batch operations over individual span handling.

- **Asynchronous Processing**: Utilize non-blocking, asynchronous operations where appropriate to enhance throughput and allow the system to handle more data simultaneously.

- **Scalable Architectures**: Design pipelines to be distributed and fault-tolerant, handling spikes in data volume without deteriorating system performance.

- **Efficient Resource Utilization**: Monitor and manage resource consumption by employing lightweight data models and minimizing in-memory data retention.

Exporting Processed Data

The final stage in the processing pipeline involves exporting data to external systems for storage, analysis, and visualization. Choice of exporter directly impacts analytics capability and integration scope with other observability tools.

```
from opentelemetry.exporter.jaeger.thrift import JaegerExporter
from opentelemetry.sdk.trace import TracerProvider
from opentelemetry.sdk.trace.export import BatchSpanProcessor

jaeger_exporter = JaegerExporter(
    agent_host_name="localhost",
    agent_port=6831,
)

trace_provider = TracerProvider()
span_processor = BatchSpanProcessor(jaeger_exporter)
trace_provider.add_span_processor(span_processor)
```

Employing a Jaeger exporter is illustrated above, representing a commonly used exporter in distributed tracing systems. Other exporters can be configured similarly to target compatible storage and visualization backends.

Challenges and Best Practices

Developing efficient span and metric processing pipelines comes with challenges such as managing system resource constraints, maintaining pipeline latency, and balancing data fidelity with performance.

Best practices include:

- **Regular Pipeline Audits**: Perform regular audits and improvements based on monitoring logs and metrics from the pipeline to ensure continual optimization.

- **Load Testing**: Simulate varying loads to test pipeline robustness and responsiveness, ensuring it handles peak scenarios effectively without loss of data fidelity.

- **Comprehensive Error Handling**: Implement holistic error handling mechanisms to capture, log, and address errors without blocking the pipeline's operational flow.

- **Security and Compliance**: Ensure that data handling within pipelines meets regulatory standards and security protocols, protecting sensitive information and adhering to data governance policies.

Implementing these components, strategies, and best practices will equip developers and organizations with the tools necessary to construct robust and efficient span and metric processing pipelines in OpenTelemetry, fostering greater observability and decision-making insights in complex, distributed application landscapes.

6.3   Custom Sampler Implementations

Sampling in distributed tracing is a mechanism used to control the amount of data sent and stored by the system, optimizing resource usage while still retaining critical insights. OpenTelemetry provides a flexible interface for implementing custom samplers, allowing for adjustments tailored to specific application requirements and infrastructural constraints.

- **Resource Management**: By reducing the volume of trace data, sampling helps conserve bandwidth, storage, and processing capacities.

- **Focused Observability**: Allows key transactions to be prioritized for tracing, enhancing focus on critical application parts requiring monitoring.

- **Cost Efficiency**: Helps mitigate costs associated with data storage and analysis in environments with economic constraints for cloud-based services.

In OpenTelemetry, the Sampler interface is foundational for defining sampling logic. Custom samplers can be devised to determine whether a specific trace should be sampled based on criteria such as service demands, trace attributes, and dynamic thresholds.

A sampler's primary role is to decide whether to sample a new trace, returning either RecordAndSample, Drop, or Record, which dictate the fate of the trace.

```
from opentelemetry.sdk.trace import Sampler, Decision

class AlwaysOnSampler(Sampler):
    def should_sample(self, parent_context, trace_id, name, kind, attributes, links):
```

```
    return Decision.RECORD_AND_SAMPLE

def get_description(self):
    return "AlwaysOnSampler"
```

The AlwaysOnSampler ensures that all traces are sampled and recorded. Conversely, other strategies like AlwaysOffSampler or ProbabilityBasedSampler utilize different logic. Custom samplers can extend this interface to implement complex sampling decisions tailored to specific needs.

Probabilistic sampling is a widely used mechanism where a fixed probability determines whether a trace should be sampled. This method effectively reduces data volume while statistically retaining a representative set of trace data.

```
import random
from opentelemetry.sdk.trace import Sampler, Decision

class ProbabilisticSampler(Sampler):
    def __init__(self, probability):
        self.probability = probability

    def should_sample(self, parent_context, trace_id, name, kind, attributes, links):
        return Decision.RECORD_AND_SAMPLE if random.random() < self.
            probability else Decision.DROP

    def get_description(self):
        return f"ProbabilisticSampler({self.probability*100:.1f}%)"
```

In this example, the ProbabilisticSampler generates a random number and compares it against a predefined probability, effectively sampling the desired percentage of traces.

Attribute-based sampling involves making sampling decisions based on specific span attributes. This approach can target specific types of requests or trace characteristics, promoting focused visibility into defined business operations.

```
from opentelemetry.sdk.trace import Sampler, Decision

class AttributeBasedSampler(Sampler):
    def __init__(self, key, value):
        self.key = key
        self.value = value

    def should_sample(self, parent_context, trace_id, name, kind, attributes, links):
        if attributes.get(self.key) == self.value:
            return Decision.RECORD_AND_SAMPLE
        return Decision.DROP
```

```
def get_description(self):
    return f"AttributeBasedSampler({self.key}={self.value})"
```

In the AttributeBasedSampler, traces are sampled based on whether they include specified attributes, allowing emphasis on critical operations known to affect performance or compliance.

Dynamic sampling adapts according to traffic patterns, allowing systems to maintain performance under varying load conditions. This technique can offer real-time configurability by scaling sampling rates depending on traffic volume.

```
from opentelemetry.sdk.trace import Sampler, Decision

class DynamicSampler(Sampler):
    def __init__(self, base_rate, load_threshold):
        self.base_rate = base_rate
        self.load_threshold = load_threshold

    def evaluate_load(self):
        # Custom logic to determine current system load
        return 0.5 # Placeholder for actual load value

    def should_sample(self, parent_context, trace_id, name, kind, attributes, links):
        load = self.evaluate_load()
        current_rate = self.base_rate * (1 - load / self.load_threshold)
        if random.random() < max(0.0, current_rate):
            return Decision.RECORD_AND_SAMPLE
        return Decision.DROP

    def get_description(self):
        return f"DynamicSampler(Base rate={self.base_rate}, Threshold={self.
            load_threshold})"
```

This DynamicSampler adjusts the sampling rate dynamically based on system load, decreasing the propensity to sample as load approaches a specified threshold. It is critical to ensure that evaluate_load returns an accurate representation of the system's state.

Complex business logic samplers are designed to address intricate business requirements, potentially considering a mixture of attributes, real-time events, and contextual insights to optimize sampling strategies.

Integrating these samplers requires defining logic that aligns with system objectives, often involving multiple conditional checks and state evaluations.

```
from opentelemetry.sdk.trace import Sampler, Decision
```

```
class ComplexBusinessSampler(Sampler):
    def __init__(self, important_rate, high_value_attributes):
        self.important_rate = important_rate
        self.high_value_attributes = high_value_attributes

    def is_high_value_trace(self, attributes):
        # Determine if trace holds high business value
        return any(attributes.get(k) == v for k, v in self.high_value_attributes.items()
        )

    def should_sample(self, parent_context, trace_id, name, kind, attributes, links):
        if self.is_high_value_trace(attributes):
            return Decision.RECORD_AND_SAMPLE
        return Decision.RECORD_AND_SAMPLE if random.random() < self.
            important_rate else Decision.DROP

    def get_description(self):
        return f"ComplexBusinessSampler(Rate: {self.important_rate})"
```

The ComplexBusinessSampler uses both probabilistic checks and specific attribute evaluations to determine which traces to sample, aligning with complex business logic that prioritizes certain transactions.

Crafting efficient custom samplers entails balancing performance demands with resource constraints and ensuring the captured sample retains statistical validity. Challenges include:

- **Overhead Management**: Samplers must implement logic that
  incurs minimal performance overhead, ensuring that decision-
  making is swift and does not impact application throughput.

- **Appropriateness of Sampling Rates**: Selecting the correct
  sampling rate is crucial to ensure a balance between data com-
  prehensiveness and resource utilization.

- **Maintaining Statistical Representation**: Even with customized criteria, it's essential to ensure the sampling process
  maintains a representative view of the application behavior.

Key practices for successful sampler establishment include:

- **Iterative Testing**: Conduct extensive validation to ensure sampling strategies deliver the intended observational insights without adversely impacting performance.

168

- **Adaptive Strategies**: Consider dynamic and adaptive sampling frameworks that automatically respond to system and traffic conditions.

- **Holistic Monitoring**: Combine sampling with real-time monitoring to verify the effectiveness of the strategy and adjust configurations in line with changing needs.

- **Documentation and Configuration**: Clearly document and make configurations accessible, ensuring teams understand sampler behaviors and can make informed adjustments.

By customizing sampler implementations, organizations can optimize observability frameworks to accommodate unique needs and challenges inherent to each system and workload. OpenTelemetry provides a robust foundation for these customizations, thereby supporting the establishment of high-performance, scalable monitoring solutions essential for modern distributed systems.

6.4 Instrumenting Asynchronous Operations

Asynchronous operations are integral to modern computing. They enable efficient execution by allowing higher concurrency in programs, optimizing system utilization, and reducing latency. Instrumenting these operations in OpenTelemetry is crucial for tracing transactions across distributed systems, where asynchronous function calls and event-driven patterns are predominant.

Understanding Asynchronous Programming

Asynchronous programming allows a system to handle other operations while waiting for a particular task to complete, like I/O-bound processes, file reading/writing, or network requests. This non-blocking execution model increases throughput and responsiveness, especially in distributed systems where multiple services might interact concurrently.

Instrumentation Challenges

Tracing asynchronous operations presents unique challenges:

- **Context Propagation**: Ensuring trace context is correctly passed across asynchronous boundaries so that distributed traces are seamless.

- **Span Continuity**: Maintaining the correct linkage and sequence of spans, despite the non-linear execution flow.

- **Event Loop Handling**: Properly managing event loop integrations without interfering with the native behavior.

Basic Asynchronous Control Flow

A basic asynchronous function in Python utilizes the `async/await` syntax to define non-blocking operations. Instrumentation involves creating and managing spans around these calls.

```
import asyncio
from opentelemetry import trace

async def sample_async_task(duration):
    tracer = trace.get_tracer(__name__)
    with tracer.start_as_current_span("sample_async_task"):
        await asyncio.sleep(duration)

asyncio.run(sample_async_task(1))
```

Context Propagation in Asynchronous Systems

Context propagation for asynchronous tasks involves ensuring that the context, critical for tracing, is passed through asynchronous control flows accurately. This requires setting a shared context across asynchronous boundaries.

Propagation with Context Managers

Context managers allow us to capture and re-establish the tracing context in asynchronous tasks.

```
import asyncio
from opentelemetry import trace
from opentelemetry.context import attach, detach

async def context_aware_task():
    tracer = trace.get_tracer(__name__)
    context = tracer.start_as_current_span("context_aware_task")
    token = attach(context)
    try:
```

170

```
      await asyncio.sleep(2)
   finally:
      detach(token)

asyncio.run(context_aware_task())
```

In this example, the context is attached when a span starts and subsequently detached once completed, ensuring that any asynchronous operation retains awareness of its tracing context.

Span Management in Asynchronous Operations

Managing spans in asynchronous operations ensures each span aligns correctly with its parent, regardless of task completion order. This involves explicit handling of span lifecycle events such as start and end in relation to asynchronous function execution.

Managing Child Span Relations

```
import asyncio
from opentelemetry import trace

async def parent_async_task():
    tracer = trace.get_tracer(___name___)
    with tracer.start_as_current_span("parent_async_task") as parent_span:
        await asyncio.gather(
            child_async_task(parent_span),
            child_async_task(parent_span)
        )

async def child_async_task(parent_span):
    tracer = trace.get_tracer(___name___)
    with tracer.start_as_current_span("child_async_task", parent=parent_span):
        await asyncio.sleep(1)

asyncio.run(parent_async_task())
```

Child spans are initiated with awareness of their parent spans, maintaining the trace sequence and hierarchy.

Event-Driven Asynchronous Operations

In distributed systems, asynchronous operations frequently use event-driven paradigms. Instrumenting such models necessitates capturing event trigger contexts and subsequent asynchronous task invocations.

Using Callbacks for Event Tracing

```
from threading import Timer
from opentelemetry import trace
```

```
tracer = trace.get_tracer(__name__)

def on_event_callback():
    with tracer.start_as_current_span("event_callback"):
        print("Asynchronous event occurred!")

def trigger_event(delay):
    Timer(delay, on_event_callback).start()

trigger_event(2)
```

By leveraging callback functions, asynchronous event handling can be instrumented to ensure that events and callbacks are well-traced within the system.

Integrating with Message Queues

Message queues are pivotal in asynchronous execution in distributed environments. Here, context propagation across message consumption ensures continuity in observability.

Context Propagation Via Message Attributes

```
import json
from opentelemetry import trace
from opentelemetry.context import attach, detach

async def process_queue_message(message):
    tracer = trace.get_tracer(__name__)
    context_token = attach(message.get("context", trace.INVALID_SPAN))
    try:
        with tracer.start_as_current_span("process_queue_message"):
            # Process message here
            await asyncio.sleep(1)
    finally:
        detach(context_token)

# Simulate message receipt
mock_message = {"context": "trace-id-example"}
asyncio.run(process_queue_message(mock_message))
```

This ensures that when a message is consumed, it carries the context needed for accurate tracking through asynchronous operations across distributed infrastructure.

Leveraging Advanced Patterns

Advanced asynchronous patterns such as futures, coroutines, and non-blocking I/O can further enhance application performance. Instrumenting these patterns involves understanding their execution flow and ensuring spans and contexts are accurately managed.

Future-Based Asynchronous Operations

Futures, which represent a placeholder for a result that is initially unknown, can be particularly tricky to instrument due to their concurrent nature.

Instrumenting Futures

```
from concurrent.futures import Future
from opentelemetry import trace

def future_callback(fut):
    tracer = trace.get_tracer(__name__)
    with tracer.start_as_current_span(f"future_completion_{fut.result()}"):
        print("Future completed with result:", fut.result())

fut = Future()
fut.add_done_callback(future_callback)
fut.set_result("success")
```

This setup ensures spans are initiated when futures complete, and their execution results can influence further asynchronous tracing decisions.

Best Practices for Instrumenting Asynchronous Operations

To ensure robust and seamless instrumentation of asynchronous operations:

- **Consistent Context Management**: Adopt a standardized approach to context handling using context libraries provided by OpenTelemetry.

- **Contextual Awareness**: Consider the scope and lifespan of spans and context functions—ensure integrity is preserved across all possible asynchronous call paths.

- **Concurrency Considerations**: Ensure threads or event loops do not interfere with the sequence or continuity of spans, meaning careful design of instrumented structures is essential for coherence.

- **Scalability**: Design instrumentation to be lightweight to avoid overhead that may impact the efficiency gains intended by asynchronous programming.

Instrumenting asynchronous operations in OpenTelemetry involves harmonizing context propagation, span management, and trace continuity across asynchronous and distributed systems. With careful design, these extensions provide a holistic view of application performance, ensuring detailed insights regardless of transaction complexity or execution model. By mastering these techniques, practitioners can ensure that observability does not sacrifice performance or flexibility inherent in asynchronous architectures.

6.5 Handling High-Cardinality Attributes

High-cardinality attributes are a significant concern in observability systems like OpenTelemetry. These attributes, containing a vast number of unique values, can lead to performance bottlenecks, excessive resource consumption, and data storage challenges. Properly managing and instrumenting high-cardinality data is crucial for maintaining a system's reliability and efficacy in monitoring and analysis.

Understanding High-Cardinality Attributes

In the context of distributed systems, cardinality refers to the number of unique values a particular field can assume. High-cardinality fields might include user IDs, IP addresses, transaction IDs, or UUIDs—fields with distinct values for each unique interaction or event.

Implications of High Cardinality

While these attributes provide valuable granularity and insights, they pose several challenges:

- Data Volume: High-cardinality attributes can exponentially increase the amount of data captured, stored, and processed, leading to scalability issues.

- Query Performance: The granularity comes at the cost of decreased query and aggregation performance, as more unique values require extensive computation.

- Resource Utilization: The additional overhead in storage and processing can strain computational resources and telemetry infrastructure.

Strategies for Managing High Cardinality

To mitigate the challenges posed by high-cardinality attributes, strategic implementations in OpenTelemetry can be adopted, facilitating a balance between data fidelity and system performance.

Cardinality Reduction

Reducing cardinality by aggregation or approximation can effectively manage data volume while retaining meaningful insights.

```
from opentelemetry import trace

def record_transaction(user_id, transaction_value):
    tracer = trace.get_tracer(__name__)
    aggregated_value = aggregate_transaction_value(user_id)
    with tracer.start_as_current_span("record_transaction") as span:
        span.set_attribute("aggregated_transaction_value", aggregated_value)

def aggregate_transaction_value(user_id):
    # Implement domain-specific aggregation logic, e.g., sum last hour transactions
    return 1000

record_transaction("user123", 500)
```

Aggregation transforms high-frequency measurements into batch insights, reducing cardinality while providing a holistic view of events.

Sampling Techniques

Leveraging sampling strategies to decimate the data from high-cardinality sources allows the system to focus on a representative subset of data.

- Random Sampling: Select a random subset of items for analysis, providing a statistical overview without capturing exhaustive details.

- Conditional Sampling: Focus sampling on events meeting specific conditions, like errors or thresholds surpassing certain values.

```
from opentelemetry.sdk.trace import Sampler, Decision
```

175

```
class TransactionValueSampler(Sampler):
    def __init__(self, threshold):
        self.threshold = threshold

    def should_sample(self, parent_context, trace_id, name, kind, attributes, links):
        value = attributes.get('transaction_value', 0)
        return Decision.RECORD_AND_SAMPLE if value > self.threshold else
            Decision.DROP

    def get_description(self):
        return f"TransactionValueSampler(threshold={self.threshold})"
```

The 'TransactionValueSampler' ensures sampling only when a transaction value exceeds a set threshold, maintaining focus on significant operations while omitting less impactful data.

Attribute Tagging and Slicing

- Tagging: Segmenting data into tagged subsets or slices enables focused analysis while circumventing the breadth usually associated with high-cardinality values.

- Slicing: Adopting schemes to reduce processing during queries can substantially lower performance demands.

Downsampling and Aggregation

- Downsampling: Strategically reduces the granularity of data points collected. It serves to optimize storage and analytical workloads.

- Approximation Algorithms: Algorithms like HyperLogLog can be integrated to estimate unique interactions, providing cardinality approximations without complete data retention.

```
import random
from opentelemetry import trace

def downsampling_aggregator(event_id):
    tracer = trace.get_tracer(__name__)
    if random.random() < 0.1:  # 10% downsampling rate
        with tracer.start_as_current_span("downsampled_event"):
            pass  # Event recording logic for downsampled events

downsampling_aggregator("event3456")
```

176

In this example, downsampling reduces the metrics that are literally stored and processed, helping tackle memory and processing limitations inherent to high-cardinality attributes.

Enhancing Performance with Indexing and Caching

To address the performance hit from high-cardinality queries, leveraging database indexing strategies and utilizing caching frameworks can optimize data retrieval times.

- Indexing: Proper indexing schemas on high-cardinality fields improve query efficiency by minimizing data scanning overhead.

- Caching: Frequent query results can be cached to reduce load times during subsequent accesses, thus enhancing the system's responsiveness.

Utilizing Machine Learning for Pattern Recognition

Incorporating machine learning techniques to identify patterns within high-cardinality data can alleviate manual overhead and aid in deriving actionable insights.

- Clustering Algorithms: Determine natural groupings within high-cardinality data for more focused analysis.

- Anomaly Detection: Discover outlier behaviors within cardinal data, drawing attention to potentially suspicious activities or bottlenecks.

```
from sklearn.cluster import KMeans
import numpy as np

def cluster_high_cardinality_data(data):
    kmeans = KMeans(n_clusters=5, random_state=0).fit(data)
    return kmeans.labels_

data_samples = np.random.rand(100, 3)
labels = cluster_high_cardinality_data(data_samples)
print("Clustering Result:", labels)
```

By employing clustering algorithms like KMeans, the inherent complexity within high-cardinality datasets can be distilled into tangible categories, facilitating a more digestible analysis.

Contextual Reporting and Visual Analytics

High-cardinality data demands advanced visualization techniques to aid analytics, such as heatmaps and multi-dimensional plots, for effective comprehension of data distributions.

Using timeline representations or dashboards that offer dynamic data slicing can spotlight trends and outliers otherwise embedded within dense datasets.

These methodologies make the daunting task of analyzing high-cardinality data manageable by aligning visual simplifications with underlying distribution patterns.

Tailoring OpenTelemetry Instrumentation

Besides technical strategies, effective handling of high-cardinality attributes involves precise instrumentation of OpenTelemetry, ensuring that only necessary data points are captured, and the observability framework is tuned for performance.

- Minimalist Instrumentation: Limit instrumented spans and metrics to essential data points, reducing storage and query load from high-cardinality attributes.

- Dynamic Configuration: Allow runtime adjustments for sampling rates or attribute selections, making the telemetry system agile to changes in application behavior.

High-cardinality attributes present opportunities for detailed insights and potential challenges in terms of resource and performance constraints. By employing a judicious mix of reduction strategies, intelligent sampling, effective indexing, and machine learning enhancements, organizations can robustly manage and utilize high-cardinality data within OpenTelemetry setups, driving more informed decision-making and sustaining system operability in the face of burgeoning data scales.

6.6 Integrating with Legacy Systems

Integrating modern observability tools like OpenTelemetry with legacy systems is a critical step toward achieving comprehensive visibility across your infrastructure. Legacy systems, often entrenched in organizational operations, can present unique challenges due to outdated architectures, limited extensibility, and heterogeneous technology stacks. Nevertheless, with careful planning and thoughtful execution, these integrations can provide valuable insights while preserving the continuity of the existing system landscape.

Understanding Legacy System Constraints

Legacy systems are typically characterized by older technologies, bespoke solutions, and a lack of inherent support for modern observability practices. These constraints can manifest in several ways:

- Incompatibility with Modern Protocols: Legacy systems may not support contemporary data formats or communication protocols, necessitating bespoke interfaces.

- Limited Extensibility: Closed or monolithic architectures can hinder integration, requiring non-intrusive instrumentation approaches.

- Performance Sensitivity: Many legacy systems operate with limited hardware resources, so integration must minimize additional processing load.

Recognizing these constraints is foundational when endeavoring to integrate OpenTelemetry or any modern tooling with such systems.

Assessing Integration Opportunities

Before embarking on integration, it is essential to conduct a thorough assessment of the legacy systems in question, identifying factors that influence integration feasibility:

- System Interfacing Capabilities: Assess whether the system provides extensible interfaces, such as APIs, message queues, or logging facilities, which can be leveraged for data extraction and instrumentation.

- Data and Communication Protocols: Determine supported data formats, such as JSON, XML, or CSV, and communication protocols, whether HTTP, RPC, or custom protocols.

- Historical Data Collection: Evaluate existing logging or monitoring mechanisms that can serve as starting points for introducing observability practices.

Leveraging Adapter Patterns

Adapter patterns can bridge the gap between legacy systems and modern frameworks by converting incompatible interfaces into operable ones. This approach encapsulates the disparities and establishes a conduit for data exchange.

```python
class LegacyLogAdapter:
    def __init__(self, legacy_system):
        self.legacy_system = legacy_system

    def fetch_logs(self):
        return self.legacy_system.get_legacy_logs()

    def parse_logs(self, raw_logs):
        # Implement parsing logic to transform raw logs into desired format
        parsed_logs = []
        for log in raw_logs:
            parsed_logs.append(self.transform_log(log))
        return parsed_logs

    def integrate(self):
        raw_logs = self.fetch_logs()
        return self.parse_logs(raw_logs)
```

In this example, a 'LegacyLogAdapter' class interfaces with a legacy log subsystem, converting raw log data into a format compliant with modern observability frameworks via a parse_logs method.

Instrumentation Techniques for Legacy Systems

Instrumentation in legacy systems requires non-intrusiveness and minimal disruption to existing operations. Two approaches often used are:

- Sidecar or Proxy Mechanisms: Deploy sidecar containers or proxy components to intercept and augment traffic to and from the legacy system, adding observability data without altering the primary application.

180

- Log Scraping and Transformation: Extract valuable data from existing log files by applying parsing and enrichment techniques to convert data into trace and metrics-friendly formats.

```python
import re

class LogScraper:
    def __init__(self, file_path):
        self.file_path = file_path

    def scrape_logs(self):
        records = []
        with open(self.file_path, 'r') as logfile:
            for line in logfile:
                log_record = self.extract_log_record(line)
                if log_record:
                    records.append(log_record)
        return records

    def extract_log_record(self, log_line):
        match = re.search(r'(?P<timestamp>\d+-\d+-\d+ \d+:\d+:\d+).*?level=(?P
            <level>\w+).*?msg=(?P<message>.*)', log_line)
        return match.groupdict() if match else None

scraper = LogScraper("legacy_system.log")
parsed_records = scraper.scrape_logs()
```

This 'LogScraper' employs regular expressions to extract structured information from unstructured legacy log data, integrating it into an observability pipeline.

Bridging Communication Protocols

Communication discrepancies between legacy systems and modern architectures can be handled by introducing intermediary translation layers, acting as a bridge to standardize interactions.

Custom Protocol Converters

Implement converters to translate legacy protocols to standard ones, such as HTTP/REST or gRPC, thereby making the data accessible to OpenTelemetry collectors.

```python
class CustomProtocolConverter:
    def __init__(self, legacy_protocol):
        self.legacy_protocol = legacy_protocol

    def convert_to_http(self, message):
        # Convert legacy protocol message to an HTTP request
        return {
            "url": "http://modern-system.endpoint",
            "headers": {
```

```
            "Content-Type": "application/json"
        },
        "data": self.transform_message(message)
    }

def transform_message(self, message):
    # Implement conversion logic
    return {
        "id": message.legacy_id,
        "body": message.legacy_body
    }
```

This 'CustomProtocolConverter' can encapsulate business logic to convert messages from a legacy protocol into technology-agnostic formats, aiding in the system's integration into broader monitoring solutions.

Maintaining Performance and Stability

Integration should prioritize minimal intervention, ensuring high performance and reliability of legacy systems. Solutions must be stress-tested to prevent introducing performance bottlenecks that could degrade the system's operability.

- Load Testing: Conduct performance testing to assess the system's behavior under various loads, ensuring observability instrumentation does not negatively impact performance.

- Fault Tolerance: Design integrations with fail-safes to handle unavailable services gracefully, preventing telemetry failures from cascading into primary system failures.

```
import time

def mock_legacy_integration_task():
    start_time = time.time()
    # Simulated task workload
    time.sleep(0.1)
    return time.time() - start_time

def run_load_test(iterations, task):
    total_time = 0
    for _ in range(iterations):
        total_time += task()
    return total_time / iterations

average_time_per_task = run_load_test(100, mock_legacy_integration_task)
print("Average time per task:", average_time_per_task)
```

Monitoring and Continuous Improvement

Establish feedback loops to monitor integration health and iteratively improve performance. Continuously analyze telemetry data to detect anomalies, optimize integration paths, and refine observability coverage.

- Observability Dashboards: Implement comprehensive dashboards to visualize key metrics and system performance indicators, enabling timely intervention and improvement opportunities.

- Anomaly Detection: Use machine learning techniques to identify patterns or behavior changes that might signify issues requiring remediation.

6.7 Evolving Schemas and Versioning

In the dynamic landscape of distributed systems and observability frameworks like OpenTelemetry, evolving schemas and maintaining versioning continuity is paramount. Schema evolution and versioning address the changes in data models over time, allowing systems to adapt without sacrificing stability and compatibility. As systems evolve, the need to ensure backward compatibility, robust data representation, and minimal disruption becomes critical.

Understanding Schema Evolution

Schema evolution refers to the process of adapting the structure of data over time without disrupting the consuming applications. As business needs evolve, so must the schemas that represent the underlying data. This evolution includes changes such as adding new fields, deprecating obsolete attributes, or restructuring the logical data model.

Key Principles of Schema Evolution

- Backward Compatibility: Changes made should not break existing consumers of the data. New structures should remain operable with old versions to ensure seamless integration.

183

- Forward Compatibility: The ability of newer systems to read and process data written by older versions, enabling smoother rollouts and upgrades.

- Schema Versioning: Explicitly versioning schemas helps in managing changes effectively, where each schema version provides clarity on the data structure and expected fields.

The main advantage of schema evolution lies in its ability to keep systems flexible and adaptable, promoting continuous delivery and deployment in fast-paced development environments.

Techniques for Schema Evolution

Implementing schema evolution involves a blend of strategies to ensure that new versions of data structures can coexist and interoperate with older versions.

Open Telemetry Semantic Conventions

OpenTelemetry utilizes semantic conventions to ensure uniformity and interpretability across telemetry data. These conventions provide predefined attributes and structures to standardize schema implementations across different telemetry signals.

- Attribute Naming Consistency: Consistent naming conventions help prevent conflicts and confusion during schema evolution.

- Uniform Data Types: Standardizing data types across different attributes enhances compatibility and coherence as schemas evolve.

Schema Evolution Patterns

Adopting strategic patterns can streamline schema changes and maintain compatibility:

- Addition of New Optional Fields: Introducing new fields as optional ensures that existing data remains valid, while new consumers can benefit from the added information without immediate disruption.

```
{
  "trace_id": "abc123",
  "span_id": "def456",
  "optional_field": "new information" // Newly added, optional for continued
      backward compatibility
}
```

- Field Deprecation and Migration: Marking fields as deprecated before removal can provide consumers with a transition period to adapt to schema changes, gradually phasing out obsolete structures.

- Use of Translators and Adapters: Develop middleware or translation layers to handle interactions between old and new schemas, providing dynamic translation at runtime.

```
class SchemaTranslator:
    def __init__(self, data):
        self.data = data

    def translate_to_new_schema(self):
        if 'old_field' in self.data:
            self.data['new_field'] = self.data.pop('old_field')
        # Handle other translation operations as required
        return self.data

old_data = {"trace_id": "xyz789", "old_field": "legacy data"}
translator = SchemaTranslator(old_data)
new_schema_data = translator.translate_to_new_schema()
```

The 'SchemaTranslator' facilitates on-the-fly schema transformations, providing smooth transitions without disrupting the existing data flow.

Implementing Versioning Strategies

Effective versioning is fundamental to managing changes in schemas over time, allowing multiple versions to coexist and ensuring system stability.

Versioning Best Practices

- Semantic Versioning: Employ semantic versioning conventions (e.g., major.minor.patch) to communicate the impact and scale of changes clearly, where:

  - Major changes introduce breaking changes.
  - Minor changes add new features without breaking existing functionality.
  - Patch changes involve backward-compatible bug fixes.

```
version_info = {
    "major": 1,
    "minor": 2,
    "patch": 0,
    "metadata": "Initial version with new optional fields"
}
```

- Version Headers in APIs: Include version information in API headers to identify and route requests accordingly, supporting backward and forward compatibility.

```
import requests

headers = {"Accept": "application/vnd.myapp.v2+json"}
response = requests.get("https://api.example.com/resource", headers=headers)
response_data = response.json()
```

By embedding the API version within the request headers, systems can manage routing to the appropriate version handlers, ensuring compatibility with client expectations.

- Deprecation Announcements: Clearly announce deprecated versions and specify end-of-support timelines, allowing consumers to update and adapt smoothly.

Challenges and Solutions in Schema Evolution

While evolving schemas provide benefits, they also introduce challenges that need to be addressed via thoughtful considerations and strategic solutions.

Dealing with Breakages

Breakages, often the result of changes in attributes or structure, can be mitigated by providing comprehensive documentation, change logs, and adequate communication channels with stakeholders to ensure awareness and preparedness.

Complexity Management

In cases where numerous service interactions are affected by schema changes, managing complexity through microservices architecture and modular design becomes essential. This modular approach limits the impact of changes within contained boundaries.

Automated Testing

Continuous integration and automated testing frameworks should enforce schema validation against multiple versions to detect and prevent regressions in schema compatibility.

```python
import json
import jsonschema
from jsonschema import validate

def validate_json_schema(data, schema):
    try:
        validate(instance=data, schema=schema)
    except jsonschema.exceptions.ValidationError as err:
        return False
    return True

json_data = {"span_id": "s12345", "trace_id": "t67890"}
schema = {
    "type": "object",
    "properties": {
        "span_id": {"type": "string"},
        "trace_id": {"type": "string"}
    }
}

is_valid = validate_json_schema(json_data, schema)
```

This sample code illustrates automatic schema validation to ensure compliance with predefined structures, minimizing chances for erroneous data processing.

187

Documentation and Communication Channels

Maintain accurate and comprehensive documentation to support developers and users in understanding schema changes, providing migration guides, exemplifying deprecated fields, and elucidating version impacts.

Engage communication channels, including developer forums and technical support, to facilitate open dialogue that enables quick adaptation and resolution of issues encountered in schema evolutions.

Chapter 7

Integrating OpenTelemetry with Popular Cloud Platforms

This chapter provides a comprehensive guide to integrating OpenTelemetry with leading cloud platforms, including AWS, Google Cloud, Azure, and IBM Cloud. It highlights practical strategies for leveraging native services and tools within these environments to enhance observability. The chapter also addresses integration with Red Hat OpenShift and explores challenges associated with multi-cloud and hybrid cloud deployments. Readers will learn to navigate these platforms' specific nuances to achieve seamless interoperability, ensuring efficient data collection and monitoring across diverse cloud infrastructures.

7.1 AWS Integration with OpenTelemetry

Integrating OpenTelemetry with Amazon Web Services (AWS) provides a robust framework for monitoring and debugging applications running in the cloud. By leveraging AWS's rich suite of services integrated with the instrumentation capabilities of OpenTelemetry, developers and system administrators can ensure high observability across distributed systems. This section will elucidate the methods and practices for seamlessly integrating OpenTelemetry with AWS services such as Amazon CloudWatch and AWS X-Ray.

Throughout this section, we will cover essential concepts, detailed procedural steps, and illustrative examples to facilitate a comprehensive understanding of how to implement this integration effectively.

AWS provides a wide array of tools and services that can be utilized in tandem with OpenTelemetry to collect, process, and visualize telemetry data. At the core of this integration lies the ability to automatically gather instrumentation data such as traces, metrics, and logs which can be sent to services like CloudWatch and X-Ray for analysis and visualization. OpenTelemetry functions as a bridge between your application and these AWS services, collecting telemetry data and exporting it in formats compatible with AWS tools.

One of the key motivations for integrating OpenTelemetry with AWS is to leverage the scalability and native capabilities of AWS services to monitor and debug production workloads with minimal operational overhead. This integration can enhance the observability of applications by providing deeper insight and enabling finer granularity in monitoring—all vital for maintaining system reliability and performance at scale.

Before any data can be analyzed via AWS services, it must first be gathered. Instrumentation is the process of adding code to an application to collect telemetry data. OpenTelemetry provides language-specific SDKs that can be used to instrument applications. By using these SDKs, developers can capture critical telemetry data seamlessly.

To illustrate, consider a sample application written in Python. In this application, we'll use the OpenTelemetry Python SDK to perform in-

190

strumentation:

```
from opentelemetry import trace
from opentelemetry.instrumentation.django import DjangoInstrumentor
from opentelemetry.sdk.trace import TracerProvider
from opentelemetry.sdk.trace.export import BatchSpanProcessor, ConsoleSpanExporter


# Set up a trace provider
trace.set_tracer_provider(TracerProvider())

# Instrument Django framework
DjangoInstrumentor().instrument()

# Configure the export of telemetry data
span_processor = BatchSpanProcessor(ConsoleSpanExporter())
trace.get_tracer_provider().add_span_processor(span_processor)
```

In this example, the DjangoInstrumentor is used to automatically instrument a Django application. The BatchSpanProcessor and ConsoleSpanExporter are configured to process and export telemetry data locally to the console. For AWS integration, the console exporter can be replaced with AWS-specific exporters that send data to CloudWatch or X-Ray.

CloudWatch acts as a central hub for monitoring and observability on AWS, providing data insights necessary to maintain application operability and performance. Utilizing OpenTelemetry for exporting data to CloudWatch involves setting up appropriate exporters within your application code.

Consider an example in which telemetry data is exported directly to CloudWatch:

```
from opentelemetry.exporter.awscloudwatch.metrics import
    CloudWatchMetricsExporter

# Configure CloudWatch Metrics Exporter
cw_exporter = CloudWatchMetricsExporter(namespace="MyApplicationNamespace",
    region_name="us-west-2")

# Set the exporter in the provider
trace.get_tracer_provider().add_metric_exporter(cw_exporter)
```

Here, the CloudWatchMetricsExporter configuration specifies a namespace for metrics and directs data to a particular AWS region. This data can then be visualized within CloudWatch, where it can be monitored and analyzed through dashboards and alarms.

191

AWS X-Ray is another key service used to provide insights into application performance via request tracing. It offers built-in analytics to track requests as they travel through an application, providing a detailed view of service execution patterns.

To integrate OpenTelemetry with AWS X-Ray, you can configure an Exporter that directly sends trace data to X-Ray:

```
from opentelemetry.exporter.aws.xray import XRaySpanExporter

# Configure the X-Ray Span Exporter
xray_exporter = XRaySpanExporter()

# Add the X-Ray exporter to the trace provider
trace.get_tracer_provider().add_span_processor(BatchSpanProcessor(xray_exporter))
```

In this setup, the XRaySpanExporter is used to send span data directly to AWS X-Ray. By integrating with OpenTelemetry, developers can achieve a uniform method to monitor distributed systems, whether they're hosted on AWS or another platform.

For OpenTelemetry to successfully send data to AWS services such as CloudWatch and X-Ray, it requires valid AWS credentials and appropriate permissions. AWS provides IAM (Identity and Access Management) which can be used to create roles and policies that define what resources OpenTelemetry can access.

Below is an IAM policy that grants permissions to send data to CloudWatch and X-Ray:

Key	Value
Version	"2012-10-17"
Statement	{Effect: Allow}
Action	{cloudwatch:PutMetricData, xray:PutTraceSegments, xray:PutTelemetryRecords}
Resource	"*"

This JSON policy allows necessary actions to be performed by OpenTelemetry on both CloudWatch and X-Ray. It is essential that this policy is attached to an IAM role used by the application instance or container running the instrumented application.

The successful integration of OpenTelemetry with AWS services enhances the ability to capture and process telemetry data effectively. The monitoring system's efficacy should be continuously assessed to ensure it meets the operational requirements.

Key evaluation metrics include:

- **Data Latency:** Measure the time taken for data to appear in AWS CloudWatch/X-Ray after being generated by the application.

- **Data Accuracy:** Ensure that the data relayed accurately reflects the application's state and performance without loss.

- **System Overhead:** Monitor the resources consumed by the instrumentation and exporting processes to avoid performance degradation.

Integrating OpenTelemetry with AWS services also opens avenues for advanced monitoring capabilities. It includes leveraging AWS's additional features like anomaly detection, alarm generation, and embedding telemetry data with contextual metadata for richer insights.

The use of custom metrics, dynamically tagging telemetry data with resource-specific identifiers, or tracking contextual data such as correlation IDs across distributed systems can provide added dimensions for observability.

Using AWS X-Ray integrated with Amazon CloudWatch Logs also offers comprehensive analytics—which can be extended by using AWS Lambda functions to analyze trace data in near real time, or integrating with Amazon Elasticsearch Service for intricate search and visualization capabilities.

This complex architecture requires an understanding of both OpenTelemetry and AWS services, allowing for the creation of a robust telemetry ecosystem that adapts to evolving application environments and scaling needs.

Developers and system architects are encouraged to continually iterate over the instrumentation and data export processes, tuning the configurations based on operational insights gathered from the AWS monitoring services to enhance application observability systematically.

7.2 Google Cloud Platform Integration

Integrating OpenTelemetry with Google Cloud Platform (GCP) allows the harnessing of GCP's comprehensive service offerings to gather, analyze, and visualize telemetry data from applications. This integration enables enhanced monitoring and observability through Google Cloud Monitoring and Google Cloud Trace, aligning performance metrics with business objectives and ensuring smooth operation of cloud-native applications.

This section explains the processes involved in integrating OpenTelemetry with GCP, providing in-depth insight into the tools, steps, and methodologies for a successful setup. By the end of this section, readers will possess the knowledge needed to implement OpenTelemetry for their application stacks hosted on GCP, using the best practices and examples provided.

- Google Cloud Platform offers an extensive range of services for deploying, managing, and scaling applications. Two critical observability services within GCP are Google Cloud Monitoring and Google Cloud Trace. Cloud Monitoring provides visibility into performance metrics, while Cloud Trace offers insights into application latency and request tracing. Together with OpenTelemetry, these services contribute to a cohesive monitoring ecosystem.

- OpenTelemetry functions as the base layer, extracting telemetry data from your applications—complementing GCP's capabilities by offering a standard interface to capture this data. The integration is especially useful for leveraging GCP's machine learning-based anomaly detection and high-fidelity application performance monitoring.

To begin integrating OpenTelemetry with GCP, you must first instrument your application to output the desired telemetry data. Open-Telemetry offers SDKs for multiple languages that facilitate this step. This section will explore a Java application example to showcase instrumentation and exporting capabilities to GCP.

The following example sets up OpenTelemetry for a Java application:

```
import io.opentelemetry.api.OpenTelemetry;
import io.opentelemetry.sdk.OpenTelemetrySdk;
import io.opentelemetry.sdk.trace.SdkTracerProvider;
import io.opentelemetry.sdk.trace.export.SimpleSpanProcessor;
import io.opentelemetry.exporter.logging.LoggingSpanExporter;

public class OpenTelemetryExample {
    public static void main(String[] args) {
        // Set up the tracer provider
        SdkTracerProvider tracerProvider = SdkTracerProvider.builder()
            .addSpanProcessor(SimpleSpanProcessor.create(new LoggingSpanExporter()
                ))
            .build();

        OpenTelemetry openTelemetry = OpenTelemetrySdk.builder()
            .setTracerProvider(tracerProvider)
            .build();

        // Use the OpenTelemetry instrumentation here
    }
}
```

In this Java example, a LoggingSpanExporter is initially configured to verify the instrumentation locally. This can subsequently be replaced with a GCP-compatible exporter to send data to Cloud Monitoring or Cloud Trace.

Google Cloud Monitoring is GCP's primary service for collecting and visualizing metrics—providing real-time insight into the status and health of your cloud resources. To export telemetry data to this service, OpenTelemetry provides exporters aligned with Cloud Monitoring's API.

Below is a sample integration flow to send metrics to Cloud Monitoring:

```
import io.opentelemetry.exporter.logging.LoggingMetricExporter;
import io.opentelemetry.sdk.metrics.SdkMeterProvider;
import io.opentelemetry.sdk.metrics.export.IntervalMetricReader;
import com.google.cloud.opentelemetry.metric.MetricExporter;

public class GCPTelemetryExample {
    public static void main(String[] args) {
        MetricExporter metricExporter = MetricExporter.
            createWithDefaultConfiguration();

        SdkMeterProvider meterProvider = SdkMeterProvider.builder()
            .registerMetricReader(IntervalMetricReader.builder()
            .setMetricExporter(metricExporter)
            .build())
            .build();
```

```
    // Application logic with metric recording
    }
}
```

In this setup, the MetricExporter from the Google Cloud OpenTelemetry Java library is used to configure and send metrics to Cloud Monitoring efficiently. The IntervalMetricReader continually pushes metrics at
specified intervals, ensuring data consistency in Cloud Monitoring.

Google Cloud Trace provides distributed tracing capabilities essential
for understanding performance issues, tracing request paths, and diagnosing latencies in distributed systems. By integrating OpenTelemetry
with Cloud Trace, developers gain valuable insights into request flows,
enhancing their ability to optimize applications.

To export OpenTelemetry traces to Cloud Trace, you can configure the
following:

```
import com.google.cloud.opentelemetry.trace.TraceExporter;
import io.opentelemetry.sdk.OpenTelemetrySdk;
import io.opentelemetry.sdk.trace.SdkTracerProvider;
import io.opentelemetry.sdk.trace.export.BatchSpanProcessor;

public class GCPTraceExample {
    public static void main(String[] args) {
        TraceExporter traceExporter = TraceExporter.createWithDefaultConfiguration
            ();

        SdkTracerProvider tracerProvider = SdkTracerProvider.builder()
            .addSpanProcessor(BatchSpanProcessor.builder(traceExporter).build())
            .build();

        OpenTelemetrySdk.builder().setTracerProvider(tracerProvider).build();

        // Application logic that starts spans and emits traces
    }
}
```

Here, the TraceExporter directly interfaces with Google Cloud Trace,
exporting span data that depicts detailed execution timelines. This
capability is vital for tracing complex distributed transactions within
GCP-hosted architectures.

For OpenTelemetry to interact seamlessly with GCP services, appropriate credentials and permissions must be established. This entails
creating a service account with roles that permit writing to Cloud Monitoring and Cloud Trace.

A sample IAM role policy allowing necessary GCP actions is as follows:

Role	Members
roles/monitoring.metricWriter	serviceAccount:YOUR_SA_EMAIL
roles/cloudtrace.agent	serviceAccount:YOUR_SA_EMAIL

The service account designated by YOUR_SA_EMAIL must be authenticated within the application environment, ensuring it has sufficient privileges to dispatch metrics and traces to GCP services.

Effectively utilizing OpenTelemetry with GCP entails continuous evaluation to calibrate performance monitoring and tracing setups. Key performance metrics for consideration include:

- **Instrumentation Overhead:** Monitor CPU and memory usage to ensure that telemetry collection does not degrade application performance.

- **Data Fidelity:** Validate that metrics and trace data within Google Cloud accurately mirror the application's state.

- **Alert Sensitivity:** Tweak alert thresholds in Cloud Monitoring to avoid noise or missed anomalies, ensuring timely alerting for critical system events.

Integrating OpenTelemetry with GCP's ecosystem paves the way for sophisticated observability by exploiting GCP's multi-dimensional analytics and machine learning frameworks. Advanced strategies include:

1. **Dynamic Resource Tagging:** Tagging telemetry data dynamically with resource identifiers facilitates correlation with specific GCP resources, enabling precise diagnostics and targeted optimizations.

2. **Custom Metric Synthesis:** Crafting nuanced custom metrics to capture application-specific performance characteristics supplements default monitoring suites, offering tailored insights.

3. **Real-time Anomaly Detection:** Leverage Cloud Monitoring's anomaly detection to automatically unearth irregular patterns, using ML models to rapidly flag performance deviations with minimal manual intervention.

4. **Integrated Dashboards and Reporting:** Create cohesive dashboards in Cloud Monitoring that consolidate data sources, visually encapsulating service health across microservices architectures.

5. **Latent Issue Forecasting:** Utilize Google Cloud's predictive analytics tools to extrapolate trends from existing data, preemptively addressing potential application bottlenecks.

Developers and architects must adapt the telemetry infrastructure iteratively, implementing learnings from monitored data to refine application architecture and elevate operational excellence mutually leveraging OpenTelemetry and GCP.

7.3 Microsoft Azure Integration Strategies

Integrating OpenTelemetry with Microsoft Azure enhances the observability of cloud-based applications by utilizing Azure's suite of monitoring and diagnostics tools. By leveraging OpenTelemetry's capabilities to instrument applications and gather telemetry data, developers and system administrators can take advantage of Azure's built-in analytics to ensure seamless application performance and resilience.

This section provides a comprehensive examination of integrating OpenTelemetry with Azure services, detailing practical steps, coding examples, and insights to guide practitioners in making informed decisions. The goal is to empower users to fully exploit Azure's monitoring offerings, such as Azure Monitor, Azure Application Insights, and Azure Log Analytics, to achieve robust observability for their applications.

- Microsoft Azure provides multiple services to monitor applications and infrastructure. Azure Monitor is the umbrella service that captures metrics and logs, offering deep insights into system health. Azure Application Insights focuses on application-specific data, enabling request tracing and performance monitoring. Azure Log Analytics allows for sophisticated query-based investigation and data aggregation from various sources.

- These services, when integrated with OpenTelemetry, provide a unified view of application performance, fostering effective monitoring of distributed applications running on Azure. The integration enables developers to track applications' performance dynamically across different environments, supporting optimal resource allocation and operational efficiency.

The initial step in the integration is instrumenting the application. OpenTelemetry offers SDKs specific to various programming languages. For example, we can use the .NET SDK to instrument a .NET Core application. The following example demonstrates setting up OpenTelemetry in a .NET application:

```
using Microsoft.Extensions.DependencyInjection;
using OpenTelemetry;
using OpenTelemetry.Trace;
using OpenTelemetry.Resources;

public class OpenTelemetrySetup
{
    public void ConfigureServices(IServiceCollection services)
    {
        services.AddOpenTelemetryTracing(builder =>
        {
            builder
                .SetResourceBuilder(ResourceBuilder.CreateDefault().AddService("
                    MyService"))
                .AddAspNetCoreInstrumentation()
                .AddHttpClientInstrumentation()
                .AddConsoleExporter() // Use console exporter for local debugging
                .AddAzureMonitorTraceExporter(); // Integrate with Azure Monitor
        });
    }
}
```

In this example, we add the OpenTelemetry tracing capabilities to a .NET application and utilize the Azure Monitor Trace Exporter to send telemetry data to Azure Monitor.

Azure Monitor serves as a central repository for collecting and analyzing metrics. By using Azure Monitor's powerful analytics engine, developers can generate insights into application health and performance. For OpenTelemetry to send metrics data to Azure Monitor, an exporter is configured as depicted below:

```
using OpenTelemetry.Metrics;
using OpenTelemetry.Exporter.AzureMonitor;
using OpenTelemetry.Resources;

public class OpenTelemetryMetricsSetup
{
    public void ConfigureServices(IServiceCollection services)
    {
        services.AddOpenTelemetryMetrics(builder =>
        {
            builder
                .SetResourceBuilder(ResourceBuilder.CreateDefault().AddService("
                    MetricService"))
                .AddMeter("MyMetrics")
                .AddAspNetCoreInstrumentation()
                .AddAzureMonitorMetricExporter(options =>
                {
                    options.ConnectionString = "InstrumentationKey=<your-
                        instrumentation-key>";
                });
        });
    }
}
```

The Azure Monitor Metric Exporter is configured to send metrics to Azure, utilizing an instrumentation key to authenticate and identify the data source for the collected metrics.

Azure Application Insights offers advanced tracing functionality necessary to monitor complex application environments. It enables developers to trace requests, investigate errors, and analyze user interactions with applications hosted on Azure. OpenTelemetry integrates with Application Insights using a seamless trace exporting process.

```
using OpenTelemetry.Trace;
using OpenTelemetry.Exporter.AzureMonitor;

public class ApplicationInsightsSetup
{
    public void ConfigureServices(IServiceCollection services)
    {
        services.AddOpenTelemetryTracing(builder =>
        {
            builder
                .AddAspNetCoreInstrumentation()
                .AddHttpClientInstrumentation()
                .SetSampler(new AlwaysOnSampler())
                .AddAzureMonitorTraceExporter(options =>
                {
                    options.ConnectionString = "InstrumentationKey=<your-
                        instrumentation-key>";
                });
        });
```

```
        }
    }
```

Through such an integration, spans and traces created throughout the application lifecycle are exported to Application Insights. These traces are then accessed via the Application Insights interface, where rich analytics and visualizations enable precise performance assessments and troubleshooting.

For OpenTelemetry to export data to Azure monitoring services securely, appropriate credentials and permissions must be established. Generally, a service principal with permissions to write data to Azure Monitor and Application Insights is utilized. Below is an example of setting up a service principal using Azure CLI:

```
az ad sp create-for-rbac --name OTelIntegrationSp --role Contributor \
--scopes /subscriptions/{subscription-id}/resourceGroups/{resource-group}
```

This command creates a service principal with contributor rights on a specified resource group, allowing it to send telemetry data to Azure services.

When employing OpenTelemetry with Azure, evaluating integration efficiency and the quality of telemetry data collected is pivotal. Key considerations include:

- **Latency Analysis:** Monitor the delay between telemetry generation in your application and its appearance in Azure Monitor.

- **Data Completeness:** Ensure comprehensive metrics and traces are accurately captured and not truncated or lost during exportation.

- **Performance Impact:** Measure the overhead introduced by telemetry instrumentation on the application's response time and resource usage.

The combination of OpenTelemetry with Microsoft's Azure services offers an extensive range of advanced observability strategies:

1. **Custom Dimensions and Telemetry Enrichment:** Enhance telemetry metadata with custom dimensions, adding con-

textual information such as release version, user demographics, and feature flags, to enable nuanced analysis.

2. **Centralized Log Analytics:** Leverage Azure Log Analytics to create Kusto Query Language (KQL)-based queries aggregating logs and metrics for real-time monitoring and cross-resource correlation.

3. **Predictive Maintenance and Anomaly Detection:** Utilize Azure Monitor's predictive capabilities for forecasting resource usage trends and proactively alerting on deviations or anticipated bottlenecks.

4. **Integration with Azure DevOps:** Automate telemetry collection and data correlation processes as part of the CI/CD pipeline in Azure DevOps, utilizing observed anomalies to improve code quality and deployment strategies.

5. **Azure Functions as Data Processors:** Implement Azure Functions to process telemetry data in real time, transforming and rerouting it to various Azure services for specialized processing and archiving.

Each of these strategic integrations requires a deep understanding of both OpenTelemetry configurations and Azure ecosystem intricacies, enabling comprehensive observability that aligns with specific application architectures and operational goals.

By employing these strategies, systems architects and developers can harness telemetry data across Azure-hosted services effectively, translating raw data into actionable intelligence that fosters operational resilience and optimization.

Deploying OpenTelemetry alongside Azure monitoring solutions equips businesses with the sophisticated tools necessary for adapting to the dynamic cloud environments, enabling seamless scaling and enhanced end-user experiences. As cloud infrastructures evolve, maintaining rigorous observability through such integrations will remain a cornerstone of competitive cloud strategy alignment.

7.4 Leveraging OpenTelemetry with IBM Cloud

Integrating OpenTelemetry with IBM Cloud empowers organizations to enhance their application observability by exploiting the comprehensive capabilities of IBM's cloud services. OpenTelemetry, acting as a robust framework for instrumenting applications, provides the necessary tools to gather, process, and export telemetry data such as metrics, traces, and logs. This data can be effectively managed and visualized using IBM Cloud's suite of monitoring and diagnostics services, including IBM Cloud Monitoring with Sysdig and IBM Cloud Log Analysis.

This section delves into the methodologies and practices required to integrate OpenTelemetry with IBM Cloud, providing a detailed explanation augmented by examples to ensure a deep understanding. By leveraging OpenTelemetry on IBM Cloud, developers and administrators can achieve a cohesive monitoring environment, enabling them to maintain application performance, troubleshoot issues, and optimize resource utilization.

- **Understanding IBM Cloud Services for Observability:**

  IBM Cloud offers various services aimed at providing end-to-end visibility into application performance. IBM Cloud Monitoring with Sysdig is designed to collect and monitor system metrics, offering dashboards and alarm functionality to keep applications running smoothly. IBM Cloud Log Analysis, on the other hand, is used for log collection, aggregation, and real-time analytics, enabling deep insights into application and infrastructure events.

  These services, when combined with OpenTelemetry's instrumentation capabilities, facilitate a comprehensive observability strategy that is essential for managing cloud-native and hybrid environments. By marrying OpenTelemetry with IBM Cloud services, one can analyze telemetry data in context, supported by intuitive visualization and alert mechanisms.

- **Instrumenting Applications with OpenTelemetry:**

  Instrumenting your application is the first step in capturing telemetry data. OpenTelemetry provides language-specific SDKs to help embed instrumentation seamlessly within your application codebase. Let's explore an example in JavaScript for a Node.js application:

```
const opentelemetry = require('@opentelemetry/api');
const { NodeTracerProvider } = require('@opentelemetry/node');
const { SimpleSpanProcessor } = require('@opentelemetry/tracing');
const { ConsoleSpanExporter } = require('@opentelemetry/tracing');

const provider = new NodeTracerProvider();
provider.addSpanProcessor(new SimpleSpanProcessor(new
    ConsoleSpanExporter()));
provider.register();

const tracer = opentelemetry.trace.getTracer('example-tracer');
// Application code that utilizes tracing
```

In this example, the basic setup includes a console exporter for local testing. However, to leverage IBM Cloud's capabilities, one must configure appropriate export mechanisms to direct the data into IBM's monitoring infrastructure.

- **Exporting Metrics to IBM Cloud Monitoring with Sysdig:**

  To export metrics from OpenTelemetry to IBM Cloud Monitoring, you need to configure a Sysdig-compatible exporter. Sysdig collects and visualizes metrics, providing real-time insights across IBM's cloud infrastructure. Though OpenTelemetry does not have a specific exporter for Sysdig, custom exporters can be implemented or configured to push metrics via HTTP(S) to the Sysdig API.

  Here's a hypothetical example of setting up such integration using a custom HTTP(S) exporter (note: actual implementation may vary):

```
// Pseudocode for a custom exporter setup
class SysdigExporter {

  constructor(apiUrl, apiKey) {
    this.apiUrl = apiUrl;
    this.apiKey = apiKey;
  }

  export(metrics) {
    // Convert metrics to the format accepted by Sysdig
    const formattedMetrics = convertToSysdigFormat(metrics);
```

```
// Send metrics to Sysdig API
sendToSysdigAPI(this.apiUrl, this.apiKey, formattedMetrics);
  }
}

// Use the exporter in the provider
provider.addMetricProcessor(new SysdigExporter('https://api.sysdigcloud.com',
    '<API_KEY>'));
```

This demonstrates a pattern where an exporter is configured with Sysdig API credentials, formatted according to their accepted schema, and subsequently transmitted for visualization and alerting.

- **Tracing with IBM Cloud Log Analysis:**

  IBM Cloud Log Analysis provides robust tracing and logging capabilities that integrate with OpenTelemetry to provide distributed tracing solutions. Tracing involves capturing the execution flow within an application—critical for debugging and performance monitoring.

  Below is an example of setting up OpenTelemetry tracing for export to IBM Cloud Log Analysis:

```
const { CollectorTraceExporter } = require('@opentelemetry/exporter-collector
    ');
const { SimpleSpanProcessor } = require('@opentelemetry/tracing');

// Configure the Collector Exporter for IBM Cloud Log Analysis
const collectorOptions = {
  serviceName: 'example-service',
  url: 'https://logs.ng.bluemix.net/collect',
  headers: {
    'apiKey': '<YOUR_API_KEY>',
    'Content-Type': 'application/json'
  }
};

const exporter = new CollectorTraceExporter(collectorOptions);
provider.addSpanProcessor(new SimpleSpanProcessor(exporter));
provider.register();

// Further application logic goes here
```

In this integration, spans generated within the execution path are transmitted to IBM Cloud Log Analysis via the Collector Trace Exporter, offering robust logging functionalities designed to handle diverse client logs in real-time while maintaining scalability.

205

- **Setting Up IBM Cloud Authentication and Permissions:**

  Operating with IBM Cloud services necessitates configuring the necessary authentication and permissions to interact with its APIs. Access mechanisms generally involve API keys, detailed in the following example for setting up IBM service keys:

  ```
  ibmcloud resource service-key-create my-service-key Writer --instance-name
      MyInstance
  ```

  This command creates a service key with action "Writer" on a specific service instance, which can be utilized to authenticate API requests when sending telemetry data to IBM Cloud services.

- **Assessing Integration Effectiveness:**

  To ensure that OpenTelemetry integrated with IBM Cloud adds the expected observability benefits, you must evaluate several performance metrics:

  - Telemetry Transmission Latency: Measure the time delay between telemetry data generation and its appearance in IBM Cloud Monitoring.

  - Data Integrity: Validate that all expected traces and metrics are accurately captured and exported without loss.

  - Performance Overhead: Continuous assessment of application performance to ensure that the integration of instrumentation does not adversely impact application responsiveness or resource consumption.

- **Advanced Strategies for IBM Cloud Observability:**

  Integrating OpenTelemetry with IBM Cloud enables adopting advanced observability frameworks. Consider the following advanced strategies:

  - Dynamic Alerts and Dashboards: Design dynamic dashboards and alerts within IBM Cloud Monitoring to keep track of critical performance metrics. Implement real-time notifications to alert teams about threshold breaches or unexpected application behavior.

206

– Synchronous Log Integration: Develop seamless integration with IBM's Log Analysis service for enhanced insight into interop across application components, enabling real-time log aggregation and correlation with tracing data.

– Predictive Insights with AI: Leverage IBM Watson's AI capabilities alongside monitoring data to predict anomalies before they impact production environments. This involves using historical telemetry data to train models for pattern recognition and anomaly detection.

– Integrated Security Monitoring: Implement a multi-faceted security observability framework combining IBM Cloud's security services with telemetry data, detecting vulnerabilities through behavior analysis and auditing.

– Resource Allocation Optimization: Utilize telemetry data patterns to inform horizontal and vertical scaling decisions. Predictive capacity planning ensures optimal resource utilization aligning with application demand.

Adapting to these strategies requires investing in extensive development and architectural skills to understand the rich intricacies of both OpenTelemetry instrumentation and IBM Cloud's monitoring ecosystem, enabling innovative and effective problem-solving.

By strategically operationalizing these observability frameworks, organizations strengthen the resilience of their cloud-hosted applications, supporting operational excellence and superior user experiences. As technologies advance and cloud infrastructure becomes more intricate, establishing effective partnerships between telemetry and cloud monitoring platforms will be crucial in maintaining observability as a core component of cloud architecture.

7.5   Integration with Red Hat OpenShift

Integrating OpenTelemetry with Red Hat OpenShift provides unparalleled insights into Kubernetes-based deployments by combining OpenTelemetry's observability capabilities with OpenShift's comprehensive container orchestration and management functionalities. OpenShift, as an enterprise Kubernetes platform, offers powerful tools for building, deploying, and managing containerized applications at scale. By incorporating OpenTelemetry, developers can achieve robust monitoring and tracing, enhancing application reliability and performance through detailed analytics and visualization.

This section explores the processes and strategies needed to effectively integrate OpenTelemetry with OpenShift. It offers a step-by-step guide, coding examples, and strategic insights designed to equip practitioners with the necessary tools and knowledge to fully harness OpenShift's capabilities for a cohesive observability ecosystem.

Understanding OpenShift for Container Management

Red Hat OpenShift is a Kubernetes-powered platform designed to facilitate the deployment and management of containerized applications. OpenShift enhances Kubernetes's core capabilities by providing additional features such as integrated development tools, CI/CD pipelines, and a robust security framework. These features contribute to a streamlined development workflow and operational efficiency within cloud-native environments.

Integrated with OpenTelemetry, OpenShift becomes a powerful observability platform, offering visibility into the dynamic interactions and behaviors of complex, distributed application components running within containers. OpenTelemetry serves as the instrumentation layer, capturing telemetry data that OpenShift can consume to drive insights and optimizations across the application lifecycle.

Instrumenting Applications on OpenShift

The initial step in integrating OpenTelemetry and OpenShift involves instrumenting applications to capture necessary telemetry data. OpenTelemetry provides SDKs for various languages to facilitate this process. Below is a Python example demonstrating OpenTelemetry instrumentation for a Flask application deployed on OpenShift:

```
from flask import Flask, jsonify
from opentelemetry import trace
from opentelemetry.instrumentation.flask import FlaskInstrumentor
from opentelemetry.sdk.trace import TracerProvider
from opentelemetry.sdk.trace.export import BatchSpanProcessor, ConsoleSpanExporter
```

```
app = Flask(___name___)

# Set up OpenTelemetry Tracer
trace.set_tracer_provider(TracerProvider())
tracer = trace.get_tracer(___name___)

# Instrument Flask application
FlaskInstrumentor().instrument_app(app)

# Configure Console Exporter for testing
span_processor = BatchSpanProcessor(ConsoleSpanExporter())
trace.get_tracer_provider().add_span_processor(span_processor)

@app.route('/')
def hello_world():
    return jsonify(message='Hello, OpenShift with OpenTelemetry!')

if ___name___ == '___main___':
    app.run()
```

In this example, the Flask application is instrumented using the Open-Telemetry Python SDK. A console exporter is used for initial testing to verify instrumentation correctness. For integration with OpenShift, more suitable exporters can be employed to transmit telemetry data effectively.

Exporting Telemetry to OpenShift Compatible Systems

With the application instrumented, the next step is to export telemetry data to relevant systems compatible with OpenShift's ecosystem. OpenShift can integrate with observability solutions like Prometheus, Grafana, and Jaeger for metrics tracking and trace visualization, supporting a wide array of exporters designed to interoperate within the Kubernetes environment.

Here is an example of configuring an exporter for Prometheus metrics collection:

```
from opentelemetry.sdk.metrics import PushController
from opentelemetry.sdk.metrics.export import MetricExportResult, MetricsExporter
from prometheus_client import start_http_server, Summary

class PrometheusMetricsExporter(MetricsExporter):
    def export(self, metrics):
        # Logic to export the metrics in Prometheus format
        return MetricExportResult.SUCCESS

# Start Prometheus metrics HTTP server
start_http_server(8000)

# Set up metrics with the PushController
metrics_exporter = PrometheusMetricsExporter()
```

```
controller = PushController(metrics_exporter, interval=10)

@app.route('/metrics')
def metrics_endpoint():
    # Metrics logic
    pass
```

This pseudocode demonstrates setting up a custom exporter to output metrics in the Prometheus format, exposing an endpoint for Prometheus to scrape and visualize within Grafana dashboards.

Tracing via Jaeger in OpenShift

Jaeger, an open-source distributed tracing system, is often utilized within Kubernetes environments, including OpenShift, for tracing complex service interactions. Configuring OpenTelemetry to export traces to Jaeger provides deep insights into application performance.

The following demonstrates configuring OpenTelemetry to work with Jaeger:

```
from opentelemetry.exporter.jaeger.thrift import JaegerExporter

# Create Jaeger Exporter
jaeger_exporter = JaegerExporter(
    agent_host_name='jaeger-agent.istio-system.svc.cluster.local',
    agent_port=6831,
)

# Set up the span processor with the Jaeger exporter
span_processor = BatchSpanProcessor(jaeger_exporter)
trace.get_tracer_provider().add_span_processor(span_processor)
```

In this coding example, the Jaeger exporter is set to transmit traces to the Jaeger agent deployed within the OpenShift cluster, utilizing the Istio service mesh's capabilities to streamline inter-service communication and trace handling.

OpenShift Cluster Configuration for OpenTelemetry

Proper integration also requires appropriate configuration of the Open-Shift cluster to manage telemetry data routing and consumption efficiently. OpenShift's flexible architecture allows for custom configurations and resource definitions that streamline observability workflows.

Deploying operators such as the OpenTelemetry Operator simplifies OpenTelemetry configuration within a Kubernetes namespace, managing the instrumentation components through custom resources.

Here's an example using OpenShift YAML configuration for deploying an OpenTelemetry Collector:

Key	Value
apiVersion	opentelemetry.io/v1alpha1
kind	OpenTelemetryCollector
metadata.name	my-otel-collector
spec.config	|
	receivers:
	otlp:
	protocols:
	grpc:
	exporters:
	prometheus:
	jaeger:
	endpoint: jaeger-all-in-one-collector:14250
	processors:
	batch:
	service:
	pipelines:
	traces:
	receivers: [otlp]
	processors: [batch]
	exporters: [jaeger]
	metrics:
	receivers: [otlp]
	processors: [batch]
	exporters: [prometheus]

This configuration file outlines the deployment of an OpenTelemetry Collector in an OpenShift environment, utilizing both Jaeger and Prometheus exporters for traces and metrics, respectively.

Evaluating Integration Success with OpenShift

Ensuring a successful integration requires assessing the observability setup's functionality. Key indicators include:

- **Latency in Trace Reporting:** Evaluate the delay from trace creation within applications to their appearance in tools like Jaeger.

- **Metrics Fidelity:** Validate that metrics collected and displayed accurately represent real-time application states.

- **Resource Consumption Efficiency:** Observe the performance impact of the instrumentation on the cluster's resources, ensuring that observability does not hinder application workloads.

Advanced Observability Strategies in OpenShift

With the foundational integration in place, organizations can explore advanced observability strategies to fully leverage OpenTelemetry with OpenShift:

- **Automated Analysis with AI/ML:** Incorporate machine learning models within observability frameworks for predictive analytics, utilizing telemetry data to forecast system performance and detect anomalies.

- **Service Dependency Mapping:** Use telemetry data to map dependencies across microservices, identifying critical interaction pathways and bottlenecks in complex applications.

- **SLO and SLA Compliance Monitoring:** Define and monitor service level objectives and agreements through real-time telemetry data analysis, ensuring contractual performance targets are met.

- **Root Cause Analysis and Incident Response:** Deploy telemetry-enhanced automation to accelerate root cause analysis during incidents, integrating alerting systems that orchestrate remediation workflows.

- **Multi-Cluster Observability:** Extend observability systems to encompass multi-cluster environments, leveraging OpenTelemetry to aggregate cross-cluster data streams and analytical outputs.

To maximize efficacy, organizations should continually refine their OpenTelemetry setups within OpenShift, iterating over telemetry preferences based on empirical data outcomes and evolving infrastructure complexities. By embedding these strategies, enterprises enhance the resilience, scalability, and reliability of their cloud-native applications on OpenShift, supporting sustained competitive advantage through operational excellence.

7.6 Challenges and Solutions in Multi-Cloud Environments

The evolution of cloud computing has led organizations to adopt multi-cloud strategies, allowing them to leverage the best features of different cloud service providers. This approach provides increased flexibility, resilience, and optimization opportunities but also introduces a set of unique challenges, particularly in observability and telemetry. Integrating OpenTelemetry in such environments can overcome these challenges, enabling improved visibility and management across diverse cloud platforms.

This section discusses the complexities of operating within multi-cloud infrastructures, identifies key challenges, and explores OpenTelemetry-based solutions and strategies to ensure optimal observability and performance across different cloud platforms.

Complexities of Multi-Cloud Adoption

Multi-cloud environments often consist of disparate cloud service providers like AWS, Google Cloud Platform, Azure, IBM Cloud, etc. These environments might involve diverse geographic locations, various service offerings, and different architectural frameworks. Organizations adopt multi-cloud strategies to avoid vendor lock-in, enhance disaster recovery, ensure compliance, and exploit competitive pricing models.

Despite these benefits, multi-cloud adoption complicates several operational aspects:

1. **Visibility:** Achieving end-to-end visibility across various clouds is challenging due to differing logging, monitoring, and tracing protocols, rendering unified observability difficult.

2. **Data Integration and Correlation:** Aggregating and correlating data drawn from different clouds requires harmonization to facilitate meaningful insights.

3. **Latency and Performance Fluctuations:** Network latency and variable performance characteristics across clouds can hinder applica-

tion performance stability.

4. Security and Compliance: Ensuring consistent security policies and compliance standards across multiple clouds adds complexity.

5. Cost Management: Managing and optimizing costs across several billing models and pricing schemas is complex.

Addressing these complexities necessitates a thorough understanding and application of cross-cloud observability tools and strategies.

The Role of OpenTelemetry in Multi-Cloud Setups

OpenTelemetry offers a vendor-agnostic observability framework that can address many issues inherent to multi-cloud platforms. By standardizing the collection and export of telemetry data, it serves as a unifying layer that simplifies monitoring across disparate environments.

Unified Instrumentation: The first step is the uniform instrumentation of applications using OpenTelemetry SDKs, which covers distributed tracing, application metrics, and logging. These SDKs provide consistent data formats and protocols, allowing a seamless integration with various cloud-powered monitoring services.

```
from opentelemetry import metrics
from opentelemetry.sdk.metrics import MeterProvider

# Standardized setup across multi-cloud
metrics.set_meter_provider(MeterProvider())
meter = metrics.get_meter(__name__)
http_requests_counter = meter.create_counter(
    "http_requests",
    description="Number of HTTP requests",
    unit="1"
)

def on_request():
    http_requests_counter.add(1)
```

This Python example demonstrates how to utilize OpenTelemetry for creating consistent metric instrumentation, applicable uniformly across different cloud environments.

Integrating Observability Across Multiple Clouds

The next step is adapting OpenTelemetry exporters to the specific monitoring and logging services of the respective cloud providers. This includes configuring suitable exporters to ensure telemetry data is appropriately directed and visualized across different platforms.

```java
// Java example for AWS and Google Cloud integration
import io.opentelemetry.exporter.trace.aws.AwsXrayExporter;
import io.opentelemetry.exporter.trace.cloudtrace.CloudTraceExporter;
import io.opentelemetry.sdk.trace.SdkTracerProvider;
import io.opentelemetry.sdk.trace.export.BatchSpanProcessor;

// AWS X-Ray Exporter Setup
AwsXrayExporter awsExporter = AwsXrayExporter.builder().build();
SdkTracerProvider awsTracerProvider = SdkTracerProvider.builder()
    .addSpanProcessor(BatchSpanProcessor.builder(awsExporter).build())
    .build();

// Google Cloud Trace Exporter Setup
CloudTraceExporter gcpExporter = CloudTraceExporter.builder().build();
SdkTracerProvider gcpTracerProvider = SdkTracerProvider.builder()
    .addSpanProcessor(BatchSpanProcessor.builder(gcpExporter).build())
    .build();
```

This Java code provides an illustration of configuring application tracing for both AWS X-Ray and Google Cloud Trace simultaneously, leveraging OpenTelemetry's exporter interfaces.

Data Aggregation and Correlation Solutions

Data collected from various clouds via OpenTelemetry often needs aggregation into centralized platforms to provide holistic insights. Two main strategies are:

1. **Centralized Data Lakes:** Establish unified data repositories, such as Azure Data Lake or AWS S3, to store telemetry data uniformly. Tools like Apache Kafka can be used to buffer data streams before writing to the data lake.

2. **Federated Observability Frameworks:** Deploy centralized monitoring systems that ingest, process, and correlate data from multicloud sources; Prometheus federations or OpenTelemetry Collector pipelines are common practices.

For example, establishing a unified dashboard in Kibana that visualizes logs from different cloud environments using Elasticsearch allows a single-glance review of multi-cloud operations:

```
# Setup Logstash for multi-cloud log unification
input {
  cloudwatch {
    # AWS CloudWatch Input
  }
  google_cloud_logging {
    # Google Cloud Input
  }
}

output {
  elasticsearch {
    hosts => "http://elasticsearch:9200"
  }
}
```

Addressing Latency and Performance Issues

Latency-sensitive applications in multi-cloud environments require strategies that minimize the impact of geographic distribution. These strategies include:

- **Edge Computing:** Deploy applications closer to users by using cloud-native edge solutions, handling latency-sensitive tasks at the cloud periphery.

- **Multi-Region Clustering:** Configure multi-cloud deployments with regional clusters to limit cross-region traffic.

- **Network Optimization Tools:** Leverage Content Delivery Networks (CDNs) and Network Optimization tools like AWS Global Accelerator to enhance global performance.

Ensuring Security and Compliance

Maintaining consistent security and compliance standards across multi-cloud environments requires cross-cutting strategies:

- **Unified Identity and Access Management:** Implement IAM solutions like Google Identity Platform, AWS IAM, or Azure Active Directory, ensuring uniform access policies.

- **Encryption and Key Management:** Use platform-neutral encryption standards and coordinate key management across cloud services using tools like HashiCorp Vault.

- **Regulatory Compliance Management:** Employ multi-cloud compliance frameworks like Evident.io or Prisma Cloud to automate compliance checks against regulatory standards across cloud services.

Multi-Cloud Cost Optimization

Cost management in multi-cloud setups involves effective resource and billing strategies:

- **Cost Monitoring and Analysis Tools:** Use services like Cloud-Health, Spot.io, or AWS Cost Explorer along with telemetry data for expense tracking and prediction.

- **Resource Optimization Algorithms:** Apply scheduling and load prediction models to optimize resource allocations and billing agreements.

By employing these optimized solutions, organizations can ensure consistent observability, performance, security, and cost efficiency across multi-cloud deployments, thus maintaining operational excellence. OpenTelemetry serves as the critical binding factor, ensuring that telemetry data supports informed decision-making spanning multiple cloud environments. As cloud architectures continue to scale and evolve, mastering multi-cloud observability will be essential for realizing competitive business advantages in the cloud domain.

7.7 Maximizing Observability in Hybrid Cloud Systems

Hybrid cloud systems, which blend public cloud services with private cloud or on-premises infrastructure, offer substantial flexibility, scalability, and cost benefits. However, achieving comprehensive observability within these arrangements involves overcoming unique challenges associated with disparate environments, heterogeneous infrastructure, and varying technology stacks. Leveraging OpenTelemetry can significantly improve observability by providing a unified framework for monitoring and tracing across hybrid cloud configurations.

This section explores the strategies and methodologies necessary to maximize observability in hybrid cloud environments. It focuses on understanding the architectural considerations, integrating OpenTelemetry, setting up data pipelines, and employing sophisticated analytics to ensure seamless operation and management of hybrid cloud systems.

- **The Complexities of Hybrid Cloud Environments**

  Hybrid cloud solutions inherently introduce complexities due to the integration of on-premises systems with public cloud resources. These complexities manifest in several ways:

  - **Infrastructure Heterogeneity:** Different hardware and software configurations across public and private environments complicate unified monitoring.

  - **Data Movement and Consistency:** Ensuring consistent and secure data movement between environments is challenging due to differing data protocols and formats.

  - **Network Latency and Availability:** Data transfer over public networks introduces latency, impacting performance predictability.

  - **Security and Compliance:** Enforcing consistent security policies and adhering to compliance standards across hybrid configurations require meticulous orchestration.

  - **Operational and Management Complexity:** Coordinating management interfaces and operational processes across disparate systems necessitates standardization and automation.

  Addressing these challenges effectively ensures organizations gain the full advantage of their hybrid cloud investments.

- **Integrating OpenTelemetry in Hybrid Cloud Systems**

  OpenTelemetry provides a cross-cutting solution for collecting, exporting, and analyzing telemetry data, which is essential across hybrid environments. By instrumenting applications

218

using OpenTelemetry SDKs, organizations can capture and standardize telemetry data uniformly.

```go
// Go example for hybrid cloud instrumentation
package main

import (
    "log"

    "go.opentelemetry.io/otel"
    "go.opentelemetry.io/otel/metric/global"
    sdktrace "go.opentelemetry.io/otel/sdk/trace"
    "go.opentelemetry.io/otel/exporters/stdout"
)

func main() {
    // Initialize a trace exporter
    exp, err := stdout.NewExporter(stdout.WithPrettyPrint())
    if err != nil {
        log.Fatalf("Failed to create stdout exporter: %v", err)
    }

    // Create a trace provider
    tp := sdktrace.NewTracerProvider(sdktrace.WithBatcher(exp))
    otel.SetTracerProvider(tp)

    // Use the global meter provider
    meter := global.GetMeterProvider().Meter("example-metric")

    // Application logic with tracing and metrics
}
```

This Go example demonstrates setting up a trace exporter, providing a consistent method for collecting telemetry data across different environments within a hybrid cloud setup.

- **Data Aggregation and Pipeline Configuration**

  A significant aspect of hybrid cloud observability is configuring data pipelines that efficiently manage the flow of telemetry data between on-premises infrastructure and cloud environments. This involves setting up collectors and exporters tailored to specific workloads.

```yaml
# OpenTelemetry Collector Pipeline Configuration
receivers:
  otlp:
    protocols:
      grpc:
exporters:
  logging:
  jaeger:
    endpoint: my-jaeger-instance:14268
processors:
```

219

```
  batch:
service:
  pipelines:
    traces:
      receivers: [otlp]
      processors: [batch]
      exporters: [logging, jaeger]
```

This YAML configuration file outlines an OpenTelemetry Collector setup designed to receive telemetry data using gRPC, process the data, and export it to different backends such as a centralized log server or a Jaeger instance for trace visualization.

- **Ensuring Security and Compliance Across Hybrid Cloud Systems**

  Consistent security measures and compliance protocols are mandatory across hybrid cloud systems. Data encryption, access controls, and identity management must reflect an organization's security policies across all infrastructure components.

  - **End-to-End Encryption:** Utilize Transport Layer Security (TLS) or IPsec to secure data in transit across hybrid connections.

  - **Identity Federation and Access Management:** Implement identity federation to manage user credentials and access control policies uniformly across environments using solutions like Azure AD or AWS IAM.

  - **Compliance Automation:** Regular audits and compliance automation using tools tailored for hybrid environments, such as Open Policy Agent and HashiCorp Sentinel, ensure adherence to standards such as GDPR, PCI-DSS, etc.

- **Minimizing Latency and Optimizing Performance**

  Reducing latency and maintaining optimal performance is a critical challenge for hybrid cloud systems due to inherent differences in infrastructure and network characteristics. Strategies to address these include:

  - **Edge Computing Adoption:** Employ edge computing capabilities to process data closer to the source, reducing the amount of data transported across network boundaries.

– **Hybrid Network Architectures:** Design hybrid architectures utilizing dedicated connections like AWS Direct Connect or Azure ExpressRoute to minimize latency and improve data throughput.

– **Performance-Centric Resource Allocation:** Use OpenTelemetry data to inform dynamic resource allocation policies that adapt to shifting workload demands, optimizing cost-efficiency and performance.

- **Advanced Observability Techniques and Strategies**

  Maximizing observability in hybrid cloud systems also involves employing advanced techniques that extend beyond basic telemetry:

  – **Synthetic Monitoring:** Deploy synthetic monitoring tools that simulate user transactions across hybrid environments, detecting anomalies and performance degradation proactively.

  – **Machine Learning for Anomaly Detection:** Harness machine learning models to analyze telemetry data for anomaly detection and predictive alerting, providing foresight into potential system issues.

  – **Unified Dashboards and Reporting:** Implement dashboards that merge data from both on-premises and cloud environments, providing holistic insights and enhancing situational awareness.

  – **Holistic Incident Management:** Enhance incident response workflows by integrating telemetry-derived insights, facilitating rapid root-cause analysis and orchestrated remediation actions.

  – **Dynamic Telemetry Data Management:** Apply context-driven telemetry filtering and aggregation techniques to reduce data volume, focusing on priority metrics and traces to streamline observability resource usage.

Incorporating these methodologies elevates hybrid cloud observability, equipping organizations with robust tools for monitoring, troubleshooting, and optimizing their environment.

221

By employing OpenTelemetry as a core component of hybrid observability strategies, businesses create a unified data-driven ecosystem that enhances visibility, improves operational efficiencies, and ensures sustainability through tailored approaches to observability. The advanced analytics and cross-environment insights gained from these strategies empower organizations to make informed decisions that support innovation, compliance, and performance in increasingly complex hybrid cloud landscapes.

Chapter 8

Analyzing and Visualizing Data Collected by OpenTelemetry

This chapter delves into the methods and tools for effectively analyzing and visualizing data collected by OpenTelemetry. It examines various data storage solutions and provides guidance on querying telemetry data to extract actionable insights. Readers will learn to create compelling visualizations using tools like Grafana and Prometheus, as well as leverage Kibana within the Elastic Stack for enhanced data exploration. The chapter also covers the setup of real-time monitoring dashboards and offers best practices for designing visualizations that facilitate quick and accurate decision-making.

8.1 Data Storage Options for Open-Telemetry

The deployment of OpenTelemetry within cloud-native environments often necessitates efficient and effective data storage solutions to manage vast volumes of telemetry data, ensuring rapid querying, seamless integration, and reliable persistence. Storage options differ widely in their architectures, capabilities, and suitability for various use cases. This section examines several predominant data storage solutions, delving into their architecture, the advantages they offer, the challenges encountered, and how they can be effectively utilized within an OpenTelemetry ecosystem.

- **Relational Databases**

  Relational databases, such as MySQL and PostgreSQL, are traditional choices for numerous applications due to their robustness and ability to enforce strict data schema. These systems utilize structured query language (SQL) for data manipulation, providing high consistency and the ability to perform complex analytical queries.

  Advantages:

  - ACID Properties: Relational databases uphold atomicity, consistency, isolation, and durability, which ensures reliable transaction processing.
  - Query Complexity: SQL enables complex queries that can aggregate and join multiple tables, which is beneficial for extracting advanced insights from telemetry data.
  - Integration: Many orchestration tools and monitoring dashboards can easily integrate with relational databases, providing straightforward access to telemetry data.

  Challenges:

  - Scalability: As data volumes grow, scaling relational databases to efficiently handle large-scale telemetry data can be challenging and typically requires vertical scaling or sharding.

- Rigid Schema: Altering the schema can be non-trivial, especially as telemetry data types evolve over time.

```
SELECT host, AVG(cpu_usage) as avg_cpu FROM telemetry_data
WHERE timestamp >= NOW() - INTERVAL '1 day'
GROUP BY host;
```

This query demonstrates the power of SQL in computing the average CPU usage per host over the past day, a common necessity in performance monitoring scenarios.

- **NoSQL Databases**

  The rise of cloud-native applications has seen NoSQL databases become preferred due to their flexibility and scalability. Systems such as MongoDB, Cassandra, and Couchbase allow for the storage of semi-structured data, making them fitting in dynamic environments where telemetry data structures are non-static.

  Advantages:

  - Scalability: These databases are inherently designed to scale horizontally by distributing data across many nodes, thereby accommodating large volumes of telemetry data.
  - Flexibility: Given that telemetry data schemas can frequently change, the flexible data models of NoSQL databases allow easy adaptation.

  Challenges:

  - Consistency: Many NoSQL databases prioritize availability and partition tolerance over immediate consistency, which might necessitate additional logic in the application layer to manage eventual consistency.
  - Limited Complex Queries: Unlike SQL, complex query capabilities are limited, though this is improving as these systems evolve.

```
{
  "timestamp": "2023-10-25T13:45:00Z",
  "service_name": "auth_service",
  "metrics": {
    "latency_ms": 123,
    "throughput": 450
  }
}
```

In this MongoDB example, telemetry data is stored flexibly, allowing fields to be added as needed without altering the structure of the entire dataset.

- **Time-Series Databases**

  For telemetry data that is inherently time-series in nature, databases like InfluxDB and TimescaleDB are particularly well-suited because they are optimized for storing and querying sequences of data points, each associated with a timestamp.

  Advantages:

  - Efficiency: Time-Series databases are optimized for handling sequential data, enabling performant reads and writes tailored for telemetry data.
  - Built-in Aggregation: They frequently provide native functions for downsampling and aggregating data over time, reducing the need for complex queries in analysis.

  Challenges:

  - Specialization: These systems are highly specialized, which can lead to inefficiencies when used for data types that do not fit the time-series model.
  - Complexity: Understanding and utilizing the full capabilities of these systems often requires a learning curve different from that of more general-purpose databases.

```
SELECT mean("latency"), max("latency") FROM telemetry
WHERE time > now() - 1h GROUP BY time(1m)
```

  This query in InfluxDB syntax efficiently calculates mean and maximum latencies over rolling one-minute windows for the last hour.

- **Object Storage Systems**

  Object storage systems such as Amazon S3, Google Cloud Storage, and Azure Blob storage provide an alternative that is increasingly popular for telemetry data due to their cost-effectiveness and scalability.

  Advantages:

226

- Scalability: Object storage architectures are inherently scalable, supporting petabytes and even exabytes of data, suitable for high-throughput telemetry.

- Cost-Effectiveness: As a pay-as-you-go model without the need to preload capacity, object storage can be more economical for large datasets.

Challenges:

- Query Performance: Unlike databases, most object storage systems are not optimized for querying, requiring additional tools or frameworks to extract insights.

- Latency: Access and retrieval latency from object storage can be higher than more traditional databases.

```
import boto3

s3_client = boto3.client('s3')
s3_client.put_object(
    Bucket='telemetry-data-bucket',
    Key='2023-10-25/telemetry_data.json',
    Body=json.dumps(telemetry_data)
)
```

This Python snippet illustrates using the Boto3 library to store telemetry data as JSON in an Amazon S3 bucket, highlighting the simplicity and power of object storage solutions in a cloud-native context.

- **Hybrid Approaches**

  In practical deployments, combining multiple storage solutions often yields the most effective results. A hybrid approach harnesses the strengths of different systems to address a diverse set of requirements associated with telemetry data.

  For instance, telemetry data might be initially ingested and processed in a time-series database such as InfluxDB for real-time analysis and dashboarding. Subsequently, the data can be periodically archived to object storage systems to minimize costs while retaining the ability to perform retrospective analysis on historical datasets.

Such architectures are designed to be dynamically adaptable, taking advantage of cloud-native capabilities to optimize both performance and cost.

Overall, the choice of data storage for OpenTelemetry depends on several factors including scale, data structure flexibility, query performance requirements, and total cost of ownership. Moving forward with any of these options necessitates a thorough understanding of their individual and collective capabilities in relation to the specific needs of the enterprise's telemetry landscape.

8.2   Querying and Analyzing Telemetry Data

In the context of large-scale systems and cloud-native applications, telemetry data plays a crucial role in diagnosing performance issues, understanding customer behavior, and ensuring the smooth operation of services. Querying and analyzing this data effectively is fundamental to derive actionable insights that enhance system performance and availability. This section offers an extensive exploration of methodologies and tools available for querying and analyzing telemetry data collected by OpenTelemetry, emphasizing both quantitative and qualitative approaches.

Essentials of Telemetry Data Querying

OpenTelemetry captures a wide array of telemetry data, including metrics, logs, and traces. Understanding the specific needs of your data analysis goals is essential to utilize appropriate querying techniques. Metrics offer quantitative measurements over time, logs provide contextual information on specific events, and traces give insights into requests as they traverse distributed systems.

When querying telemetry data, consider the following components:

- Data Granularity: Determine the level of detail required based on analysis objectives, such as high-level summaries versus detailed event trails.

228

- Time-Bound Analysis: Telemetry data is inherently temporal, thus enabling time-based queries is essential for trend analysis and anomaly detection.

- Aggregation Needs: Depending on the analysis, aggregation functions (such as sum, average, max) are often necessary to synthesize meaningful summaries from raw data.

- Dimensional Analysis: Employ dimensions, such as service name or region, to filter and categorize the telemetry data effectively.

```
import pandas as pd

# Load telemetry data
telemetry_df = pd.read_csv('telemetry_data.csv')

# Filter data for last 24 hours
filtered_data = telemetry_df[
    telemetry_df['timestamp'] >= (pd.Timestamp.now() - pd.Timedelta(days=1))
]

# Aggregate CPU usage
aggregated_data = filtered_data.groupby('host')['cpu_usage'].mean()
```

The above Python code sample demonstrates the use of Pandas to filter telemetry data for the last 24 hours and compute the average CPU usage per host, showcasing time filtering and aggregation.

Tools and Languages for Telemetry Data Querying

Various tools and languages are at the disposal of data analysts to query telemetry data efficiently. SQL, as a standard language for data manipulation, retains its relevance, especially when telemetry data is stored in relational databases or SQL-compatible engines.

In addition, several purpose-built languages have emerged:

PromQL: Used with Prometheus, PromQL is a powerful querying language that excels at expressing Prometheus' multidimensional data model and is tailor-made for working with time-series data.

```
node_cpu_seconds_total{job="node-exporter"}[5m]
```

This PromQL query retrieves CPU utilization metrics for a node over the last five minutes, illustrating PromQL's capability to handle time range selection and dimensional filtering elegantly.

229

Elasticsearch Query DSL: If using the Elastic Stack, Elasticsearch Query DSL provides a rich, JSON-based approach to execute full-text search and structured queries.

```json
{
  "query": {
    "bool": {
      "must": [
        { "match": { "service": "auth_service" }},
        { "range": { "@timestamp": { "gte": "now-1h", "lt": "now" }}}
      ]
    }
  }
}
```

Here, Elasticsearch's DSL is used to query logs for the auth_service from the last hour, demonstrating how to combine multiple conditions into a query.

Data Processing and Analysis Techniques

Once data is retrieved through querying, several analytical techniques can be applied to extract insights. These techniques vary in complexity and are suited to different types of telemetry datasets.

Descriptive Analysis: This involves summarization of historical telemetry data through measures such as average latency, error rates, and service uptime.

Anomaly Detection: Key in identifying unusual patterns that deviate from expected behavior, such as spike detection in response time or throughput.

```python
from scipy import stats

# Calculate z-scores
z_scores = stats.zscore(filtered_data['latency'])

# Identify anomalies
anomalies = filtered_data[abs(z_scores) > 2.0]
```

This Python script uses z-scores to detect anomalies in latency, where scores greater than two standard deviations from the mean are flagged as anomalies.

Predictive Analysis: Involves creating models to forecast future telemetry data trends, which can aid in resource planning and capacity management.

Correlational Analysis: This can uncover relationships between different telemetry metrics, such as the correlation between request load and latency.

Machine Learning Approaches to Telemetry Analysis

Machine learning (ML) techniques are becoming increasingly integral in sophisticated telemetry data analysis, facilitating automation in pattern recognition, prediction, and anomaly detection.

Clustering Algorithms: These algorithms, such as K-Means, are used for segmenting telemetry data into similar groups based on selected features, helping in identifying patterns or common characteristics within the data.

Supervised Learning: Techniques like regression and classification can be employed to model relationships between input feature sets and specific system outcomes.

```
from sklearn.linear_model import LinearRegression
import numpy as np

# Prepare data
X = filtered_data[['request_rate']].values
y = filtered_data['latency'].values

# Fit model
model = LinearRegression().fit(X, y)

# Predict latency given new request rates
predicted_latency = model.predict(np.array([[100], [200]]))
```

In the above example, a linear regression model is trained to predict latency based on the request rate, demonstrating one of the many applications of supervised learning in telemetry data.

Deep Learning Models: In complex systems, deep learning approaches such as recurrent neural networks (RNNs) and TensorFlow models can be leveraged to handle nuanced temporal patterns within telemetry data for advanced prediction applications.

Challenges in Telemetry Data Analysis

Analyzing telemetry data is not without its challenges. With the scale and velocity of data generated by contemporary systems, achieving continuous insights with low processing latency is a significant technical challenge.

231

- Data Volume: Telemetry data is typically voluminous; thus, efficient storage and retrieval techniques are necessary to ensure analysis can be performed in a timely manner.

- Noise: Telemetry data can contain noise and irrelevant data points, necessitating effective filtering and cleaning techniques.

- Data Integration: It may become essential to correlate telemetry data across different sources or systems requiring effective join operations and holistic integrations.

While overcoming these challenges requires strategic infrastructure design and computational resource management, the outcome is an enhanced capability to facilitate intelligent, data-driven decisions that improve service reliability and performance.

With these detailed explorations, one can effectively query and analyze telemetry data gathered by OpenTelemetry, steering it towards actionable insights that not only pinpoint existing problems but also illuminate paths towards enhanced system robustness and user experience.

8.3 Creating Visualizations with Grafana

Grafana is a powerful open-source platform designed for analytics and interactive visualization of monitoring data and is particularly adept at creating dynamic, informative dashboards for an array of data sources including systems metrics, logs, and traces. This section provides a comprehensive examination of how Grafana can be utilized to create compelling visualizations of telemetry data gathered via OpenTelemetry, facilitating quick understanding and actionable insights.

Understanding Grafana Data Sources

Grafana supports a wide range of data sources to accommodate diverse data storage methodologies in use across modern systems. By understanding how to effectively configure these data sources, users can unlock the full potential of Grafana's flexible visualization capabilities:

- Prometheus: As a widely used time-series database, Prometheus integrates seamlessly with Grafana, offering excellent performance for metrics data visualization.

- Elasticsearch: This enables visualization of logs and events data, optimizing the exploration and analysis of textual telemetry data.

- Graphite: Provides a real-time graphing system to visualize metric data effectively.

- InfluxDB: Known for its high retrieval speed and performance, suitable for environments with high telemetric data throughput demands.

Each data source connector comes with its configuration process, typically involving setting the database URL, access credentials, and selecting the default query language if multiple options are supported by the source.

```
curl -X POST -H "Content-Type: application/json" -d '{
   "name":"Prometheus",
   "type":"prometheus",
   "url":"http://localhost:9090",
   "access":"proxy",
   "basicAuth":false
}' http://admin:admin@localhost:3000/api/datasources
```

The above command uses Grafana's HTTP API to add Prometheus as a data source, showing how integrations can be performed programmatically, crucial for automated deployment setups.

Creating Dashboards in Grafana

The core of Grafana's utility lies in its capacity to synthesize multiple data sources into coherent, interactive dashboards. A dashboard in Grafana is a collection of organized panels, with each panel representing a specific query and visualization.

Panels are the building blocks of Grafana dashboards. They support various visualization types such as:

- Graphs: Show metrics over time.

- Stat: Display a panel with aggregate data (e.g., single values indicating current CPU usage).

233

- Heatmaps: Represent data intensity as colors.

- Tables: Present data in a structured tabular format.

To create a panel, users must define a data source, construct a query, and select an appropriate visualization type. Grafana's query editor provides an intuitive interface to write and test these queries, catering comprehensively to each specific data source's syntax.

```
http_requests_total{job="webserver"}[1m]
```

This PromQL query can be used within a Grafana panel to visualize the HTTP request rate over the past minute, highlighting its dynamic data polling ability using Prometheus as a data source.

Advanced Visualization Techniques in Grafana

Grafana's versatility extends beyond basic charting with advanced visualization capabilities that transform data into actionable insights:

- Thresholds and Alerts: Vital for anticipating performance issues; thresholds can be defined on panels to trigger color changes or alert notifications when conditions are met.

```
"thresholds": [
    { "value": 80, "color": "orange" },
    { "value": 90, "color": "red" }
]
```

- Annotations: Add contextual information to charts by marking significant events on the timeline, great for correlating visible patterns with known occurrences.

- Templating: Through the use of template variables, users can create dynamic dashboards that adjust in real time. Templates can encapsulate data sources, timeframes, and queries, allowing one dashboard to adapt to various servers or data metrics without editing the underlying queries.

- Transformations: Enable further manipulation of data post-retrieval, such as renaming fields, calculating new data series, or rearranging table data. This increases the applicability and precision of visualization queries and provides easier interpretations.

234

- Custom Visualizations: While Grafana contains many built-in visualizations, it also supports plugins, which allow for custom and complex solutions tailored to specific visualization requirements.

```
{
  "type": "graph",
  "title": "Service Latency",
  "dataSource": "Prometheus",
  "targets": [
    {
      "expr": "histogram_quantile(0.9, sum(rate(latency_bucket[5m])) by (le))",
      "format": "time_series"
    }
  ],
  "yaxes": [
    {
      "show": true,
      "label": "Latency (ms)"
    }
  ]
}
```

This JSON configuration exemplifies a Grafana graph panel setup for monitoring latency, illustrating the integration of parameters and metadata for capturing complex data analyses.

Interactivity and User Engagement in Dashboards

Grafana dashboards are highly interactive, designed to promote user engagement. Among features enhancing interactivity are:

- Zooming and Panning: Users can focus on specific time periods or dataset portions by zooming and panning, which recalibrates data ranges dynamically.

- Drilldown Links: Enable transitions from aggregated data views to specific details by clicking on chart elements, significantly aiding root-cause analysis processes.

- Hover Tooltips: Providing context and data details on hover actions, these tooltips enhance user interaction by supplying immediate, concise insights.

Developing proficiency in Grafana's interactive features helps users not only glean insights but also derive correlations and patterns from telemetry data efficiently.

Real-World Use Cases of Grafana Visualizations

Grafana is deployed across numerous real-world scenarios, making it invaluable wherever telemetry data visualization aids operational intelligence. Examples include:

- Service Health Monitoring: Real-time dashboards that monitor system-wide health metrics, such as latency and throughput, can preemptively alert teams to deviations from operational norms.

- Capacity Planning: Analyzing resource usage across distributed systems helps forecast future demands, guiding resource allocation and scaling decisions.

- Incident Response: Visualizations aid in pinpointing the root cause of system failures, improving mean time to resolution by correlating logs, traces, and metrics in one cohesive view.

```
"notifications": [
  {
    "uid": "T5B865DHq",
    "name": "SlackChannel",
    "isDefault": true
  }
],
"alert": {
  "alertRule": {
    "conditions": [
      { "evaluator": { "type": "gt", "params": [500] } }
    ],
    "for": "5m"
  }
}
```

The JSON snippet above integrates Grafana's alerting infrastructure with a notification channel, demonstrating how users can receive timely alerts, enhancing proactive monitoring.

Optimizing Grafana Dashboards for Performance

For extensive deployments, optimizing Grafana dashboards ensures efficiency in data visualization and query response, necessitating:

- Efficient Queries: Structuring queries to limit data retrieval only to the necessary metrics reduces load and accelerates panel rendering times.

- Caching: Using data caching and downsampling techniques to handle large datasets, enhancing dashboard responsiveness.

- Panel Organization: Aggregating similar or interrelated metrics within the same dashboard reduces cross-panel loading times and improves cognitive load.

Grafana's impact in visualizing telemetry data from OpenTelemetry is profound. Its ability to transform voluminous and diverse datasets into real-time insights empowers teams to understand their systems in depth, foster proactive management, and ultimately drive operational excellence across complex distributed environments.

8.4 Integrating with Prometheus for Visualization

Prometheus has emerged as a leading open-source systems monitoring and alerting toolkit, renowned for its powerful time-series database capability. Integrating Prometheus with OpenTelemetry facilitates robust metrics collection and visualization solutions, leveraging Prometheus's query language (PromQL) and its well-architected ecosystem for monitoring cloud-native environments. This section explores the intricacies of integrating Prometheus with OpenTelemetry, encompassing setup, data ingestion, querying, and visualization, alongside providing illustrative examples to fully demonstrate its capabilities.

Prometheus excels in capturing numeric time-series data, stored with dimensional labels, making it an ideal partner for OpenTelemetry, which generates telemetry data from distributed systems. This integration facilitates seamless data collection, allowing for enhanced monitoring and analytics of system health, performance, and operations.

The integration process involves:

- Instrumentation: Adding OpenTelemetry SDK and APIs to your application collects metrics, logs, and traces.

237

- Exporter Configuration: OpenTelemetry leverages exporters, such as the Prometheus exporter, to transmit collected data to Prometheus.

- Prometheus Configuration: Configuring Prometheus to scrape, process, and store the metrics provided by OpenTelemetry.

```
scrape_configs:
 - job_name: 'service-metrics'
   scrape_interval: 10s
   static_configs:
     - targets: ['localhost:9464']
```

This Prometheus configuration example specifies scraping metrics from an endpoint ('localhost:9464') every 10 seconds, illustrating the foundational step in connecting Prometheus with OpenTelemetry.

Integrating OpenTelemetry involves setting up the OpenTelemetry SDK within the application to emit data, after which the Prometheus exporter is configured to make the collected metrics accessible to Prometheus.

- Instrumentation: Applications need to be instrumented to generate telemetry data. This involves integrating the appropriate OpenTelemetry client libraries supported by your programming language.

- Prometheus Exporter: This component enables OpenTelemetry to expose collected metrics in a format that can be scraped by Prometheus.

```
import (
    "go.opentelemetry.io/otel"
    "go.opentelemetry.io/otel/exporters/prometheus"
    "go.opentelemetry.io/otel/sdk/metric"
    "go.opentelemetry.io/otel/sdk/resource"
)

func initOpenTelemetry() {
    cfg := prometheus.Config{}
    exp, err := prometheus.New(cfg)
    if err != nil {
        log.Fatalf("failed to initialize prometheus exporter %v", err)
    }

    meterProvider := metric.NewMeterProvider(
```

238

```
        metric.WithResource(resource.NewWithAttributes()),
        metric.WithReader(exp),
    )

    otel.SetMeterProvider(meterProvider)
}
```

The Go language example sets up OpenTelemetry instrumentation with a Prometheus exporter, capable of collecting and exposing metrics to Prometheus.

PromQL is Prometheus's powerful query language, designed to retrieve and manipulate time-series data. It's utilized extensively within Prometheus for both ad-hoc queries on historical data and for configuring alerting rules.

- Basic Terminology:

  - Instant Vector: A snapshot of time-series data at a single instant.
  - Range Vector: A sequence of time-series data over a range of time.
  - Scalar: A simple numeric value.
  - String: A simple textual value.

Examples of PromQL queries:

- Retrieve CPU Usage:

```
rate(node_cpu_seconds_total[5m]) * 100
```

This query calculates the percentage of CPU usage over the last five minutes.

- Memory Utilization:

```
node_memory_Active_bytes / node_memory_MemTotal_bytes * 100
```

Retrieves the memory utilization proportion.

These expressions highlight PromQL's ability to perform rate calculations and derive percentages, supporting comprehensive monitoring analytics.

Prometheus itself offers a simple web UI, primarily useful for testing queries. However, most production setups integrate Prometheus with Grafana for advanced visualization capabilities.

- Adding Prometheus as a Data Source in Grafana: By configuring Prometheus as a data source, Grafana can execute PromQL queries, enabling the creation of interactive dashboards.

```
{
  "datasource": {
    "name": "Prometheus",
    "type": "prometheus"
  },
  "panels": [
    {
      "type": "graph",
      "title": "HTTP Request Rate",
      "targets": [
        { "expr": "rate(http_requests_total[1m])" }
      ]
    }
  ]
}
```

This JSON snippet illustrates how to configure a Grafana panel to use PromQL for visualizing HTTP request rates from Prometheus metrics.

- Dashboard Creation: With Grafana, dashboards that complement Prometheus data are created, featuring various panels that offer multi-dimensional views of telemetry data, spanning real-time and historical analyses.

- Thresholds and Anomalies: Configuring dashboards to visually signal metric values that exceed certain thresholds is vital for quick, intuitive anomaly detection.

- Alerting Integration: Setup alerts in Grafana that leverage Prometheus metrics, such as incident notifications to operations teams, ensuring proactive problem resolution.

Prometheus facilitates alerting through its Alertmanager component, allowing users to define alert rules based on Prometheus expressions and manage notification delivery.

- Defining Alerts: Alerts are defined based on PromQL expressions, triggering notifications under predefined conditions.

```
groups:
  - name: example
    rules:
      - alert: HighCPUUsage
        expr: avg by (instance) (rate(node_cpu_seconds_total[5m])) > 0.8
        for: 5m
        labels:
          severity: critical
          job: node
        annotations:
          summary: "Instance {{ $labels.instance }} high CPU usage"
```

This rule alerts when average CPU usage across an instance exceeds 80

- Alertmanager Configuration: Specify routing, grouping, and notification rules to determine how alerts are managed and delivered.

- Silencing: Temporarily mute notifications, crucial during maintenance.

- Grouping and Routing: Group similar alerts to minimize noise and route them to specific teams based on labels such as service or severity.

Managing Prometheus in large environments requires an understanding of scaling approaches to ensure performance and reliability.

- Federation: Prometheus supports data federation, segmenting the monitoring workload across multiple Prometheus servers and federating data to a central server for unified queries.

- Sharding and Intermittent Scraping: Distribute targets across multiple servers and adjust scrape intervals to balance the load and ensure lag-free data collection.

- Retention and Storage Considerations: Configure retention policies for time-series data to balance between data availability for analysis and storage efficiency.

- Remote Storage Integrations: Utilize long-term storage solutions, like Thanos or Cortex, to persist telemetry data indefinitely while keeping Prometheus lean.

By delving into these configurations and optimizations, gathering accurate, actionable insights from telemetry through Prometheus can transform operational strategies and facilitate data-driven decision-making across technology ecosystems.

Through adept utilization of Prometheus and its integration with OpenTelemetry, robust system monitoring transforms potentially overwhelming telemetry data volumes into streamlined, actionable intelligence, enabling more effective management and continuous system improvement.

8.5 Using Kibana with Elastic Stack

The Elastic Stack, also known as ELK Stack, is an integrated collection of open-source tools composed primarily of Elasticsearch, Logstash, and Kibana, designed for real-time data search, analysis, and visualization. Kibana serves as the powerful visualization layer within this stack, enabling users to create dynamic and interactive dashboards out of the vast telemetry data indexed in Elasticsearch. This section delves deep into utilizing Kibana within the Elastic Stack to explore and visualize telemetry data collected via OpenTelemetry, emphasizing practical setups, configurations, and advanced visualization techniques.

Understanding the Elastic Stack components work synergistically to process, store, and visualize data as follows:

- **Elasticsearch**: A NoSQL distributed search and analytics engine that provides full-text search capabilities, scalability, and near-real-time data analysis. It stores the telemetry data ingested from OpenTelemetry and makes it searchable.

- **Logstash**: This data processing pipeline ingests data from diverse sources, transforms it, and then sends it to a configured output, e.g., Elasticsearch. It acts as a bridge managing data ingestion from OpenTelemetry exporters.

- **Kibana**: Primarily the front-end that reads data from Elasticsearch and provides the user interface for dashboarding, advanced querying, and data visualization in diverse formats.

The capture, orchestration, and visualization pipelines facilitate intricate data exploration and insight extraction, integral for operational monitoring and business intelligence.

```
input {
    http {
        port => "5044"
    }
}
filter {
    json {
        source => "message"
    }
}
output {
    elasticsearch {
        hosts => ["http://localhost:9200"]
        index => "telemetry-index"
    }
}
```

This Logstash pipeline configuration accepts telemetry data over HTTP, transforms the JSON payload, and indexes it into Elasticsearch under 'telemetry-index'.

The integration of OpenTelemetry with the Elastic Stack involves several steps, from configuring data ingestion to setting up Kibana for visualization:

- **Data Ingestion through Logstash**: OpenTelemetry exports telemetry in structured formats such as JSON which Logstash can ingest, transform, and ship to Elasticsearch. Filters can manipulate data, enrich metadata, or handle nesting intricacies before indexing.

- **Data Indexing with Elasticsearch**: Elasticsearch handles indexing tasks, enabling rapid search, querying, and aggregation functions.

- **Visualization Setup in Kibana**: With data organized in Elasticsearch, Kibana can configure index patterns that describe data

243

schemas, allowing for the creation of various visualization panels.

```
Index Patterns in Kibana:
- telemetry-index          # Pattern for telemetry data
- logs-*                   # Pattern for general logs
```

The above index patterns define how data in 'telemetry-index' is recognized, building a foundation for aggregation tasks required for visualizations.

Kibana supports a wide array of visualizations, each enabling unique insights and serving specific analytical needs:

- **Pie Charts**: Ideal for showing proportions and segment distributions within a dataset.

- **Histograms**: Useful for analyzing data frequency distributions over specified intervals.

- **Line and Area Charts**: Perfect for visualizing trends across time-series datasets, emphasizing changes over periods.

- **Data Tables**: Provide granular data exploration, summarizing key metrics in tabular form for easy interpretation.

- **Heat Maps**: Highlight distributed intensity across matrices, often used for correlation exploration.

These examples demonstrate Kibana's capabilities to break down complex data structures visually, supporting both granular inspections and holistic overviews.

```
Example Visualization:
- Name: CPU Usage Over Time
- Type: Area Chart
- Axes: Time (X), CPU Usage % (Y)
- Filters: host.keyword="server1"
```

This specific setup helps in visualizing how CPU usage on 'server1' fluctuates over time, leveraging area charts to showcase variability and trends along temporal dimensions.

Kibana's power grows exponentially through dashboard functionalities, enabling integrative analysis that combines multiple visualizations into one coherent interface. Dashboards can link multiple indices and facilitate cross-referencing metrics with logs and traces:

- **Dashboard Panels**: Each panel can be set to reflect a unique visualization, such as maps for geographic data, and provide a unified monitoring view.

- **Interactivity and Filters**: Interactive goal-driven filters allow users to slice and dice data along different dimensions or apply drill-down paths.

```
GET /telemetry-index/_search
{
  "query": {
    "range": {
      "response_time": {
        "gte": 500
      }
    }
  }
}
```

This KQL example retrieves records where response time exceeds 500ms, facilitating identification of high-latency occurrences for further investigation.

For proactive monitoring, Kibana can integrate with the Elastic Stack's Watcher utility, providing real-time alerting based on telemetry data conditions:

- **Define Watches**: A Watch contains a trigger, criteria, and an action executed when the criteria are met. It allows users to automate responses to anomalies.

```
{
  "trigger": {
    "schedule": {
      "interval": "5m"
    }
  },
  "input": {
    "search": {
      "request": {
```

```
    "indices": ["telemetry-index"],
    "body": {
      "query": {
        "range": {
          "latency": { "gte": 400 }
        }
      }
    }
  }
},
"condition": {
  "compare": {
    "ctx.payload.hits.total.value": { "gte": 10 }
  }
},
"actions": {
  "log": {
    "logging": {
      "text": "High latency detected over threshold in last 5 minutes"
    }
  }
}
}
```

This watch logs a warning message when latency above 400ms is detected more than ten times in the past five minutes, aiding proactive management.

Managing Elastic Stack deployments effectively is crucial as data volume surges and teams scale:

- **Data Rollups and Aging**: Manage index size and performance via rollup jobs and data lifecycle policies, reducing storage requirements while retaining analytical capabilities.

- **Cluster Management**: Adjust Elasticsearch shard allocation and node handling, addressing resource bottlenecks and ensuring high availability.

- **Resource Configuration**: Tune JVM settings and thread pool allocations for Elasticsearch nodes to handle peak loads, maximizing throughput and response times.

Through these optimization techniques, the Elastic Stack scales gracefully, enabling continuous and efficient telemetry data management while maintaining optimal performance.

Kibana, when used in conjunction with Elasticsearch and the broader Elastic Stack, enables rich, real-time insights from telemetry data, empowering users to enhance systems observability and operational intelligence. By effectively employing its visualization and monitoring capabilities, teams can ensure both reliable system performance and intelligent, data-driven decision-making practices that embrace the complexities of modern cloud-native applications.

8.6 Real-Time Monitoring with OpenTelemetry Dashboards

The integration of real-time monitoring solutions within distributed systems is a pivotal practice that enhances operational visibility, facilitates stringent performance management, and empowers teams to swiftly adapt to fluctuations in system behavior. OpenTelemetry, with its multi-faceted capabilities in collecting and exposing telemetry data, serves as the backbone for developing these comprehensive monitoring frameworks. This section thoroughly investigates real-time monitoring using OpenTelemetry dashboards, highlighting setup, configuration optimizations, and practical demonstrations of monitoring strategies.

Real-time monitoring enables the continuous observation of system metrics, logs, and traces, offering immediate insights into the current state of an application. Key principles include:

- Proactive Problem Detection: Identifying anomalies or threshold breaches before they escalate into user-facing problems.

- Immediate Feedback Loops: Providing stakeholders with timely alerts, enabling rapid response and resolution.

- Visualization: Leveraging dashboards to present telemetry data in an accessible and coherent manner, allowing stakeholders to quickly grasp system health.

OpenTelemetry facilitates instrumentation of distributed applications, automatically capturing detailed telemetry data such as metrics, traces, and logs:

247

- Instrumentation: OpenTelemetry SDKs are integrated within the application, enabling automatic or manual telemetry generation across diverse components.

- Telemetry Exporters: These components ship telemetry data to analysis and visualization backends like Prometheus, Grafana, or Elastic Stack for real-time monitoring.

- Setup of a Data Retrieval Pipeline: Defining a fluent telemetry flow from data generation to analysis dashboards, considering factors such as data fidelity, network overhead, and response time.

```python
from opentelemetry import trace

# Setup OpenTelemetry tracing
trace.set_tracer_provider(TracerProvider())
tracer = trace.get_tracer(__name__)

# Example trace in an application operation
with tracer.start_as_current_span("operation_name"):
    # Logic within the traced operation
    process_data()
```

The Python snippet exemplifies how to integrate OpenTelemetry tracing into an application using automatic capture and visualization targets to create open streams of actionable insights.

Dashboards serve as the visualization layer, aggregating telemetry data for efficient interpretation and decision-making. They typically consist of panels that translate raw telemetry data into visually insightful layouts:

- Dynamic Dashboards Configuration: Enabling dynamic update capabilities to refresh displayed data in alignment with near-real-time telemetry refresh rates.

- Data Aggregation: Using queries to consolidate data streams, juxtaposing real-time metrics and historical data for deep analytical context.

- Thresholds and Alert Visualizations: Configuring visual markers and alerts within dashboards for threshold breaches enhance quick recognition of issues.

248

```
{
  "title": "Real-Time System Monitoring",
  "panels": [
    {
      "type": "graph",
      "title": "CPU Usage",
      "targets": [
        { "expr": "avg_over_time(node_cpu_seconds_total[1m])" }
      ],
      "yaxes": [
        { "label": "Percentage", "format": "percent" }
      ],
      "refresh": "5s"
    },
    {
      "type": "stat",
      "title": "Current Active Sessions",
      "targets": [
        { "expr": "sum(current_sessions)" }
      ],
      "refresh": "10s"
    }
  ]
}
```

The JSON showcases a multi-panel Grafana dashboard setup, visualizing CPU usage and active session counts with rapid refresh intervals, underscoring real-time data projection.

Advanced techniques extend beyond basic data visualization, incorporating more challenging scenarios and deeper capability sets:

- Correlation and Contextualization: Achieving observability that encapsulates cross-cutting concerns of metrics, traces, and logs, aiming to triangulate root causes through correlation capabilities.

- Anomaly Detection: Implementing predictive models within the telemetry pipeline to auto-detect anomalies (e.g., spikes or drops in traffic/usage metrics).

- Distributed Tracing: Real-time tracing across distributed service boundaries, revealing performance bottlenecks or latencies in service calls.

```
absent_over_time(rate(http_requests_total[5m]) > 100)[1h:5m]
```

The PromQL example detects high traffic anomalies by evaluating request patterns over time, allowing for distinguishing anomalies from expected behavior patterns.

Real-time monitoring is exponentially more potent when integrated with automated alerting systems. These systems utilize telemetry signals to trigger responses or notifications based on predefined or predictive metrics:

- Dynamic Alerting: Configuring threshold-based alerts that predictively scale in response to changes in historical baseline patterns.

- Integrated Notification Channels: Leverage integrations such as email, Slack, or pager alerts, ensuring multiple channels for delivering urgent alerts to stakeholders.

```
alert: HighMemoryUsage
expr: avg by (service) (rate(container_memory_usage_bytes[5m])) > 0.9
for: 10m
labels:
  severity: critical
annotations:
  summary: "High Memory Usage in {{ $labels.service }}"
receivers:
- name: 'slack-channel'
  slack_configs:
  - channel: '#alerts'
```

The YAML configuration shows an alerting rule using Alertmanager, targeting elevated memory usages over 90% in critical systems, with alerts routed to a Slack channel.

Dashboard performance optimization ensures visibility without undue lag or resource drain on systems:

- Efficient Query Design: Use aggregated queries and downsample data to reduce payloads without sacrificing crucial visual insights.

- Caching and Preloading: Employ data caching strategies or preloaded data to improve visualization speed.

- Modular Panel Organization: Streamline information by arranging panels logically and hierarchically, minimizing cognitive load and maximizing clear visualization benefits.

```
import redis

# Connect to Redis
r = redis.StrictRedis(host='localhost', port=6379, db=0)

# Fetch latest summary data
summary = r.hgetall("system:stats")

# If no current cache, compute and store
if not summary:
    summary = compute_current_summary()
    r.hmset("system:stats", summary)
```

This Python script demonstrates a basic methodology for caching computed statistical summaries leveraging Redis, underpinning improved dashboard response times.

Implementing real-time monitoring with OpenTelemetry dashboards evolves comprehensive surveillance over systems, embedding predictive insights and fostering environments equipped to preemptively address challenges before they escalate. Robust real-time dashboards bolster operational resilience, empower data-centric strategies, and augment observability, thereby leading to more informed decision-making and sustained service excellence.

8.7 Best Practices for Data Visualization

Effective data visualization transforms raw data into understandable and actionable insights. It is a crucial element of data analysis, offering a visual framework to comprehend complex patterns, trends, and outliers within datasets. This section delves into the best practices for data visualization, emphasizing principles of clarity, design, accuracy, and accessibility. It also explores technical implementations, fostering enhanced communication of data insights to stakeholders across various disciplines.

Good data visualization practices are anchored in a set of fundamental principles designed to ensure clarity and precision:

- Clarity: The design should convey the intended message clearly, avoiding unnecessary complexity or embellishments that can obscure the data's meaning.

- Consistency: Use consistent colors, symbols, and iconography across visualizations to avoid confusion, particularly in comparative analyses or longitudinal studies.

- Relevance: Only include elements that directly aid in the comprehension of the data. Superfluous information should be avoided to maintain focus on key insights.

Choosing the right type of visualization is paramount to effectively communicating particular data aspects. Various types of visualizations serve different purposes depending on the data's story:

- Bar Charts: Ideal for comparing quantities across different categories. Suitable for displaying discrete data and categorical comparisons.

- Line Graphs: Best used for showing trends over time, particularly continuous data to observe trends and projections.

- Pie Charts: Useful for showing part-to-whole relationships, though they should be used sparingly due to issues with interpreting angles and areas.

The choice of visualization type influences not only user engagement but also the accuracy of data interpretation.

```
import matplotlib.pyplot as plt

# Sample data
years = [2018, 2019, 2020, 2021]
values = [120, 130, 125, 135]

# Create line graph
plt.plot(years, values, marker='o')
plt.title('Annual Revenue Growth')
plt.xlabel('Year')
plt.ylabel('Revenue (in million)')
plt.grid(True)
plt.show()
```

In this script, a simple line graph created using Matplotlib demonstrates trends in annual revenue growth, emphasizing the use of line graphs for temporal data.

Maintaining the integrity and accuracy of data visualizations is critical for trustworthy communication:

- Avoiding Distortion: Ensure scales are consistent and do not misrepresent the data. Avoid truncated axes or inappropriate scaling that can exaggerate or understate findings.

- Data Validation: Cross-check data inputs and transformations employed during the preparation stages to avoid introducing errors.

- Precision and Significant Figures: Display figures with precision levels that reflect the data's accuracy, without causing clutter or overprecision.

```
import matplotlib.pyplot as plt
import numpy as np

# Generate data
data = np.random.normal(loc=0, scale=1, size=1000)

# Create histogram
plt.hist(data, bins=30, alpha=0.7, color='blue', edgecolor='black')
plt.title('Normal Distribution Histogram')
plt.xlabel('Value')
plt.ylabel('Frequency')
plt.show()
```

This histogram setup ensures clarity and precision by employing consistently scaled bins and well-defined edges, avoiding data misrepresentation.

Ensuring visualizations are accessible to a wider audience enhances inclusivity:

- Color Accessibility: Use color palettes that are distinguishable by individuals with color vision deficiencies. Tools like Color Brewer provide colorblind-friendly palettes.

- Interactive Elements: Incorporate interactive elements like zoom, tooltip, or drill-down features to make complex data more navigable and engaging for users with varied literacy levels.

- Descriptive Annotations: Utilize annotations and callouts to highlight key data points or provide context, aiding in understanding significant insights without overwhelming the viewer.

```
library(ggplot2)

# Sample data
df <- data.frame(
    category = c("A", "B", "C"),
    value = c(4, 3, 9)
)

# Create plot with colorblind-friendly palette
ggplot(data = df, aes(x = category, y = value, fill = category)) +
  geom_bar(stat="identity", width=0.7) +
  scale_fill_manual(values=c("#E69F00", "#56B4E9", "#009E73")) +
  theme_minimal()
```

This bar plot demonstrates the use of ggplot2 with a color palette suitable for viewers with color vision deficiencies, showcasing data inclusivity.

Dashboards consolidate multiple visualizations into coherent presentations that communicate overarching trends and insights:

- Storytelling with Data: Order visualizations logically to guide the viewer through the data narrative, layering information complexity progressively.

- Balance and Layout: Ensure visual elements are balanced within the available space, maintaining a non-cluttered, intuitive layout that enhances readability.

- Highlighting Important Metrics: Use visual hierarchy to draw attention to critical metrics, employing font, color, or size variations to emphasize importance.

```
const svg = d3.select("svg").attr("width", 800).attr("height", 600);

// Sample data and real-time update mechanism here...

svg.append("circle")
   .attr("cx", 200)
   .attr("cy", 100)
   .attr("r", 50)
   .style("fill", "teal");

// More real-time updates and dashboard elements here...
```

The JavaScript example outlines the structure of a D3.js-based dashboard, showcasing flexibility and interactive capabilities in dynamic data environments.

Various tools and libraries assist in crafting exceptional data visualizations:

- D3.js: A powerful JavaScript library for producing dynamic and interactive data visualizations in web browsers, offering flexibility with a steep learning curve.

- Tableau: A business intelligence tool providing extensive GUI functionalities for building interactive and shareable dashboards.

- Matplotlib & Seaborn (Python): Popular for static visualization in scripts and reports, offering comprehensive charting options with ease of use.

These tools deliver robust capabilities for varied visualization goals, facilitating both static and interactive content creation tailored to audience needs.

Finally, consider the following when presenting visualizations to stakeholders:

- Audience Understanding: Know the audience's background and data literacy levels. Tailor visual complexity accordingly.

- Concise Messaging: Communicate insights directly and clearly. Avoid over-explaining or adding unnecessary commentary, focusing on the data story.

- Iterative Feedback and Refinements: Use feedback loops to refine visualizations, ensuring they remain relevant and useful.

```
library(shiny)

# Define UI
ui <- fluidPage(
  sliderInput("bins", "Number of Bins:", 1, 50, 30),
  plotOutput("distPlot")
)

# Define server logic
server <- function(input, output) {
  output$distPlot <- renderPlot({
    x <- faithful[, 2]
```

```
   bins <- seq(min(x), max(x), length.out = input$bins + 1)

   hist(x, breaks = bins, col = 'darkgray', border = 'white')
 })
}

# Run app
shinyApp(ui = ui, server = server)
```

In this Shiny app example, interactive sliders allow users to manipulate a histogram, contributing to accessible and engaging presentation of data insights.

Adhering to these best practices in data visualization ensures that complex datasets are communicated in a manner that is both accessible and actionable, fostering informed decision-making and deeper insights across numerous disciplines and applications.

Chapter 9

Security and Compliance in Observability

This chapter addresses the critical aspects of security and compliance in observability systems, focusing on safeguarding telemetry data and ensuring adherence to regulatory standards. It outlines strategies for implementing secure data pipelines, maintaining data privacy, and meeting compliance frameworks like GDPR and HIPAA. Additionally, the chapter discusses the role of access controls, methods for auditing telemetry systems, and best practices for incident response to security breaches, equipping readers with the tools to protect observability infrastructure from vulnerabilities.

9.1 Security Challenges in Observability

In the domain of complex distributed systems, observability has emerged as a critical mechanism for maintaining and enhancing system performance and reliability. Observability involves the systematic collection, analysis, and visualization of data from various system components to gain insights into their behavior. However, integrating observability solutions into modern infrastructures introduces a myriad of security challenges that need thoughtful consideration and robust solutions.

One substantial challenge concerns the risk of data exposure. Observability systems continually gather extensive data sets from across the network, including logs, metrics, traces, and events. This data often contains sensitive information, such as system configurations, environment variables, or even user data, which is susceptible to exposure if not adequately protected. The sheer volume and variety of data collected can obscure insecure practices, making it difficult to enforce consistent security controls across all data streams.

The subsequent challenge is unauthorized access. As observability systems require visibility into numerous interconnected components, they necessitate communication across several endpoints and services. This connectivity can introduce vulnerabilities, presenting opportunities for unauthorized individuals or entities to gain access to sensitive information. Ensuring that access controls are appropriately enforced across wide-ranging environments — such as hybrid clouds, multi-clouds, and on-premises deployments — becomes a formidable task.

One effective way to underscore these security concerns is through practical coding examples. The following example demonstrates a basic setup for securing access to an observability system using API keys. The idea is to highlight how sensitive data could be attracted by inadequate security practices:

```
import requests

# Example of an unsecured API request
response = requests.get('http://observability-system.example.com/api/v1/data')
print(response.json())
```

Even an ostensibly simple API call to an observability endpoint, if unsecured, can result in unintended data exposure. Implementing secured pipelines wherein communications and data access require authentication tokens or API keys is critical:

```
import requests

# Example of secured API request with a token
```

```
headers = {'Authorization': 'Bearer YOUR_API_TOKEN'}
response = requests.get('http://observability-system.example.com/api/v1/data',
    headers=headers)
print(response.json())
```

Observability poses another challenge: the potential for data breaches through misconfigured systems. Configuration errors, often stemming from human oversight, can inadvertently expose systems to external threats. Moreover, managing configurations across different environments and technology stacks exacerbates this issue. Effective observability requires not only that configurations are correct but that they are maintained consistently across dynamic environments.

To address this, configuration management must be automated and adhere to best practices. Tools such as Terraform or Ansible can standardize configurations and ensure that security settings are uniformly applied across all environments. The following Terraform example demonstrates a simple infrastructure setup that includes network security considerations:

```
provider "aws" {
  region = "us-west-2"
}

resource "aws_security_group" "observability_security" {
  name = "observability-security-group"
  description = "Security group for observability system."

  ingress {
    from_port = 443
    to_port = 443
    protocol = "tcp"
    cidr_blocks = ["0.0.0.0/0"]
  }

  egress {
    from_port = 0
    to_port = 0
    protocol = "-1"
    cidr_blocks = ["0.0.0.0/0"]
  }
}
```

Visibility and control over data flow across these systems are imperative to ensuring that observability doesn't inadvertently become a vulnerability. This necessity extends to adversarial threats where attackers aim to exploit observability mechanisms to map system topologies, identify potential points of attack, or even inject malicious payloads

259

into telemetry data streams.

Advanced adversarial methods can involve exploiting weak cryptography or protocol vulnerabilities to intercept and manipulate observability data. Encryption, both at rest and in transit, using strong cryptographic algorithms is essential to mitigate these threats. The configuration below demonstrates setting up a secure TLS configuration in NGINX for observability data transmission:

```
server {
    listen 443 ssl;
    server_name observability-system.example.com;

    ssl_certificate /etc/ssl/certs/mycert.crt;
    ssl_certificate_key /etc/ssl/private/mykey.key;

    ssl_protocols TLSv1.2 TLSv1.3;
    ssl_ciphers HIGH:!aNULL:!MD5;
    ssl_prefer_server_ciphers on;

    location /api/ {
        proxy_pass http://backend-observability-service;
        proxy_set_header Host $host;
    }
}
```

The design of observability systems must also carefully manage dependencies and third-party integrations, which can introduce additional attack vectors. These dependencies often include external libraries, platforms, or services that extend observability capabilities like dashboards, analytics, or alerting. Each integration must be evaluated for security risks, such as vulnerable dependencies or deprecated technologies. The management of these third-party components should employ a vulnerability management process, regularly scanning for, and remediating, any discovered risks.

Moreover, observability data is subject to inspection by various teams spanning operations, development, and security. This collaborative access, while necessary for effective debugging and system performance monitoring, can also enhance the risk of internal threats. Role-Based Access Control (RBAC) is vital for defining and enforcing roles and permissions that restrict access to observability data according to the principle of least privilege.

Here is an example of implementing RBAC in a hypothetical observability system:

```
def has_access(user_role, required_role):
    # Define roles in hierarchical order
    role_hierarchy = {'viewer': 1, 'developer': 2, 'admin': 3}
    return role_hierarchy.get(user_role, 0) >= role_hierarchy.get(required_role, 0)

# EXAMPLE: Grant access if user's role meets the required level
user_role = 'developer'
required_role = 'viewer'
if has_access(user_role, required_role):
    print("Access granted")
else:
    print("Access denied")
```

Identity and access management (IAM) systems can further be integrated into observability frameworks to streamline user authentication processes and enforce access policies systematically.

Finally, the monitoring and auditing of observability systems play a crucial role in their security posture. Implementing logging and monitoring solutions provides real-time visibility into how these systems are being accessed and used, enabling the detection and deterrence of suspicious activities. Configuring alerts and analysis mechanisms to detect anomalies ensures that potential security incidents are promptly detected and addressed.

A practical example would involve deploying monitoring agents alongside the observability stack to check for security-related anomalies, as exemplified below:

```
#!/bin/bash

# Simple script to monitor for abnormal HTTP requests
tail -f /var/log/nginx/access.log | grep --line-buffered "400\|401\|403\|404" | while
    read line;
do
    echo "Alert: Potential security breach detected: $line"
    # Additional analysis or notification logic
done
```

Through comprehensive auditing, system administrators can assess the overall security of observability implementations, making informed decisions to fortify their environment against emerging threats and vulnerabilities. This practice not only aids in compliance with regulatory standards but also assures organizational stakeholders of the security and integrity of their observability solutions.

Observability provides critical insights into system operations but in-

261

herently bears significant security challenges. Effective management involves implementing security best practices, such as robust authentication, encryption, configuration management, dependency evaluation, access control, and proactive monitoring. Bolstering these systems against threats ensures that observability serves its purpose without compromising the security or integrity of the systems it is meant to improve.

9.2   Implementing   Secure   Telemetry Pipelines

The proliferation of complex distributed systems has driven the need for robust observability solutions capable of providing real-time insights into infrastructure health and performance. A central component of observability is telemetry, which involves the automated collection and transmission of data from various system components. However, telemetric data is sensitive and requires secure transmission mechanisms to protect its integrity and confidentiality. Implementing secure telemetry pipelines is paramount to safeguarding this information from interception, tampering, or unauthorized access.

A telemetry pipeline typically involves several stages: data collection, data transfer, ingestion, processing, storage, and analysis. Securing each component of this pipeline is crucial for maintaining the overall security of the telemetry system. Encryption, authentication, and access control are foundational strategies that, when meticulously applied, fortify these pipelines against potential threats.

At the outset, data collection sources and agents, such as application code, network sensors, or system monitoring agents, should be secured to prevent unauthorized data extraction or manipulation. Securing data at the source ensures that only authorized software processes are able to collect and transmit telemetry data. Agents can leverage authentication tokens or certificates to establish secure communication channels back to centralized telemetry services.

The following example demonstrates a secure setup for a telemetry collection agent using TLS certificates to authenticate its connection to a telemetry server:

```
import ssl
import socket

# Implement SSL context for secure communication
context = ssl.create_default_context(ssl.Purpose.SERVER_AUTH)
context.load_cert_chain(certfile="path/to/client.crt", keyfile="path/to/client.key")
context.load_verify_locations("path/to/server_chain.pem")

# Establish secure TCP connection
with socket.create_connection(('telemetry-server.example.com', 443)) as sock:
    with context.wrap_socket(sock, server_hostname='telemetry-server.example.com')
        as ssock:
        ssock.sendall(b'Telemetry data payload')
```

Data transfer, constituting the movement of data from collection agents to centralized servers, represents a stage replete with interception risks. Secure transmission protocols such as HTTPS or Secure File Transfer Protocol (SFTP) must be employed. These protocols encrypt data in transit, preventing unauthorized eavesdropping.

Given the emphasis on encryption, data must also remain secure once it reaches its destination for ingestion and processing. At this juncture, server endpoints must perform mutual TLS authentication to verify both the authenticity and the origin of incoming data streams. This approach ensures that telemetry data is not unwittingly accepted from malicious or compromised sources.

To enhance security further, telemetry pipelines may incorporate message queuing services like Apache Kafka or Amazon SQS to temporarily store data that can be processed and analyzed asynchronously. Such services are secured through access policies and encrypted topics or queues that prevent unauthorized access due to compromised credentials or service misconfiguration:

```
# Example Kafka topic configuration with encryption
topic.name = "telemetry-topic"
topic.replication.factor = 3
topic.partitions = 6

# Enable encryption for this topic
topic.security.protocol = "SSL"
ssl.endpoint.identification.algorithm = "HTTPS"
ssl.truststore.location = "/etc/security/kafka.client.truststore.jks"
ssl.truststore.password = "your_secure_password"
```

Data processing and storage stages require stringent access controls and encryption at rest, in addition to timely rotation of encryption keys to minimize damage risk in the event of a security breach. Cloud providers and modern data platforms offer encryption solutions where encryption keys are managed (KMS) or where users can bring their own keys (BYOK). This flexibility allows organizations to adapt encryption practices to their specific security policies and requirements while ensuring compliance with regulatory mandates.

Beyond the encryption of telemetry data stored in databases or data warehouses, data integrity checks can be implemented to ensure that processed and analyzed outputs have not been subject to unauthorized changes. Utilizing hashing mechanisms to verify data integrity and maintaining audit logs of data access and processing activities serve as vital components for thwarting data tampering attempts.

At the data analysis and visualization stages, secure handling of telemetry data becomes necessary to preserve both the confidentiality and utility of the data. Access controls embedded within analysis platforms ensure that only authorized users or user groups can view sensitive telemetry data. Furthermore, these platforms often come with audit capabilities that track changes to data and user access patterns, which are indispensable for detecting potential internal threats.

Implementing secure telemetry pipelines requires a balanced approach that addresses the human element. Organizations must foster a culture of security by continually training employees on secure coding practices and the implications of telemetry security. Security awareness and expertise decrease the likelihood of configuration errors or negligent secure programming practices that could jeopardize telemetry data.

In practice, security tools integrate with existing telemetry infrastructures, providing enhanced visibility and control over telemetry data flows. The following example introduces how a security-focused monitoring system might be set up alongside a telemetry pipeline using open-source tools:

```bash
#!/bin/bash

# Example of a script to setup a secure telemetry monitoring pipeline with
    Elasticsearch and Fluentd
# Elasticsearch instance
docker run -d --name elasticsearch -p 9200:9200 -e "discovery.type=single-node" docker.
    elastic.co/elasticsearch/elasticsearch:8.0.0
```

```
# Fluentd instance that forwards logs to Elasticsearch securely
cat << EOF > fluentd.conf
<source>
  @type http
  port 9880
  bind 0.0.0.0
</source>
<match **>
  @type elasticsearch
  host elasticsearch
  logstash_format true
  ssl_verify true
  ssl_version TLSv1_2
</match>
EOF

docker run -d --name fluentd -p 9880:9880 -v $(pwd)/fluentd.conf:/fluentd/etc/fluent.
    conf fluent/fluentd
```

This script provisions a simple secure telemetry monitoring pipeline combining Elasticsearch with Fluentd, demonstrating how popular open-source tools can be integrated for monitoring.

Effective logging and audit trails throughout the telemetry pipeline record who accessed data, when, and for what purpose. Compliance with standards, such as PCI-DSS or HIPAA, often necessitates elaborate audit capabilities and can prompt organizations to incorporate these checks into routine security assessments.

Finally, incident response planning specifically addressing telemetry pipeline vulnerabilities is crucial. This involves implementing mechanisms for rapid detection of anomalies in telemetry patterns that could indicate potential security incidents and establishing protocols for containment and recovery. Incident response must be robust and flexible, delineating clear roles and responsibilities, ensuring that security teams are prepared to respond to breaches quickly and effectively.

Overall, secure telemetry pipelines incorporate multiple layers of security controls, ensuring that data integrity, confidentiality, and availability are maintained from collection to analysis. By using a combination of encryption, access control, secure architecture and infrastructure design, and continuous monitoring and assessment, organizations can implement telemetry pipelines that are both robust and adaptable to the evolving threat landscape.

9.3 Ensuring Data Privacy in Observability

In the contemporary digital landscape, data privacy has become a paramount concern, particularly as systems and networks grow more complex and interconnected. Observability in such environments involves collecting, processing, and analyzing telemetry data to gain insights into system behavior and performance. While invaluable, this process introduces challenges related to maintaining data privacy. The volume and sensitivities involved with telemetry data necessitate a careful and comprehensive approach to privacy at all stages of observability.

Data privacy within observability centers on the protection of sensitive information that telemetry data may inadvertently expose, such as personal identifiers, confidential business data, or system authentication details. Effective data privacy strategies must adhere to applicable legal and regulatory guidelines, such as the General Data Protection Regulation (GDPR) or the California Consumer Privacy Act (CCPA).

A robust privacy strategy for observability accounts for three key stages: data collection, data processing, and data consumption. Each stage requires tailored measures to mitigate privacy risks while maximizing the utility of the telemetry data.

During the data collection stage, only the necessary minimum data should be gathered — a practice often referred to as data minimization. This approach ensures that the telemetry system does not collect excessive information that does not directly contribute to performance and operational insights. Engineers should define clear data collection policies that identify which data points are essential for observability objectives and which remain superfluous.

An example configuration for collecting and filtering data can be expressed using a data collection agent, such as Fluentd with filter plugins that drop sensitive fields:

```
<source>
  @type tail
  path /var/log/app.log
  pos_file /var/log/fluentd/app-log.pos
  tag app.log
```

```
  format json
</source>

<filter app.log>
  @type grep
  <exclude>
    key message
    pattern /sensitive_info/
  </exclude>
</filter>
```

This Fluentd configuration illustrates how logs can be filtered to exclude messages containing sensitive information before further processing.

Data anonymization is another vital practice at the data collection or ingestion stage to bolster privacy. Anonymization ensures that personal data cannot be traced back to an individual, commonly through techniques like pseudonymization or aggregation. This can be particularly necessary when compliance requirements stipulate strict privacy controls.

After collection, the data moves to the processing stage, where it undergoes transformation and analysis. Securing privacy at this stage requires advanced techniques like homomorphic encryption, which allows computations to be performed on encrypted data, or secure multi-party computation (SMPC), where data is processed in a way that conceals sensitive details from any party involved. While computing on encrypted data is resource-intensive, it offers a high degree of confidentiality and privacy.

For privacy-preserving data processing by anonymizing IP addresses using pseudonymization, one could leverage this kind of coding logic:

```
import hashlib

def pseudonymize_ip(ip_address):
    # Hash IP with added salt to create a pseudonymized identifier
    salt = "unique_salt_value"
    pseudonymized_ip = hashlib.sha256((ip_address + salt).encode()).hexdigest()
    return pseudonymized_ip

# Example usage
original_ip = "192.168.1.100"
print("Pseudonymized IP:", pseudonymize_ip(original_ip))
```

This script demonstrates basic pseudonymization by hashing the IP address with additional salt, making it challenging to revert to the original

IP without the salt.

Protecting privacy at the data consumption stage involves controlling access to data visualization and analysis tools. Role-Based Access Control (RBAC) mechanisms limit who can access, modify, and trace historical data within these tools. Techniques like data masking, which obscure portions of sensitive data during presentation, are essential when displaying telemetry data that may inadvertently reveal personal or confidential information.

The following example shows how to mask sensitive fields in Python:

```
def mask_personal_data(data, fields):
    masked_data = data.copy()
    for field in fields:
        if field in masked_data:
            masked_data[field] = '***MASKED***'
    return masked_data

# Usage example
personal_information = {'username': 'john_doe', 'email': 'john.doe@example.com'}
masked_info = mask_personal_data(personal_information, ['email'])
print(masked_info)
```

In this example, the function masks the specified fields within a data structure, ensuring that any sensitive data is concealed from unauthorized view.

Regulations like GDPR mandate that personal data be handled with transparency and accountability. Telemetry systems must include mechanisms for individuals to access their data, request corrections, or demand deletion as necessary. Implementing audit trails and immutable logging within the observability architecture helps demonstrate compliance and support requests for data access or removal.

Establishing a data privacy framework requires a holistic assessment of policies, practices, and technical measures to mitigate risks. An essential practice is conducting privacy impact assessments (PIAs) that identify, assess, and manage privacy risks in the observability schema. Regular security and privacy audits on telemetry architectures ensure continued alignment with evolving regulatory frameworks and threat environments.

Employee awareness and training play fundamental roles in a successful privacy strategy within observability. Organizations must foster an environment of privacy consciousness through regular training sessions, emphasizing the criticality of privacy in observability processes. Training should cover prevalent privacy threats, successful mechanisms for addressing these threats, and the legal implications of data breaches.

Technological advancements and evolving compliance standards necessitate dynamism and adaptability in observability systems. Ensuring data privacy is an ongoing process that requires frequent policies, controls, and technological updates in response to emerging threats or regulatory changes. Automation and the use of artificial intelligence in managing privacy within telemetry pipelines can offer significant optimization opportunities. AI-driven systems can proactively discover and protect sensitive data, dynamically adjust privacy settings based on contextual data processing, and provide real-time privacy alerts and recommendations.

In integrating privacy into observability systems, zero trust architectures can be deeply influential. Zero trust approaches assume breach possibilities at any point, thereby ensuring that continuous verification and validation are enacted as a necessity for all interactions within the telemetry system.

Privacy by design and by default become essential paradigms, embedding privacy considerations across all phases of the telemetry pipeline lifecycle — from initial development through deployment and all subsequent updates or enhancements. Developers and system architects must prioritize privacy principles in the earliest stages of system design.

Data privacy within observability cannot be an afterthought, but rather a core consideration of any telemetry strategy. By employing a mix of data minimization, anonymization, encryption, user access controls, and ongoing policy assessments, organizations can ensure that their observability systems not only yield vital operational insights but do so in a manner that respects and protects the privacy of all involved parties. A privacy-centric approach to observability builds trust, respects legal mandates, and empowers organizations to harness observability insights without compromising on confidentiality or compliance.

9.4 Compliance Requirements and Frameworks

Navigating the intricate landscape of compliance requirements and frameworks is crucial for organizations deploying observability systems. The collation and analysis of telemetry data, while advantageous for operational insight, must align with regulatory mandates to ensure lawful and ethical handling of sensitive information. Compliance frameworks establish a structured approach to managing data privacy, security, and governance, mitigating risks associated with legal breaches and maintaining public trust.

In observability systems, compliance involves addressing a multitude of standards and regulatory requirements across data collection, processing, storage, and sharing. Some of the most pertinent frameworks include the General Data Protection Regulation (GDPR), the Health Insurance Portability and Accountability Act (HIPAA), the Sarbanes-Oxley Act (SOX), and the Payment Card Industry Data Security Standard (PCI-DSS), among others.

GDPR governs the collection and processing of personal data within the European Union, mandating stringent data protection protocols to ensure user privacy rights. Any observability system that processes EU residents' personal data must ensure robust data protection measures, including explicit consent acquisition, data anonymization, and guaranteed rights for data access, correction, and erasure.

To demonstrate GDPR compliance in observability systems, developers can implement consent management modules and data processing audits. Here's a basic implementation example of consent management in Python:

```python
class ConsentManager:
    def __init__(self):
        self.user_consent = {}

    def obtain_consent(self, user_id):
        # Simulate user consent granting process
        consent = input(f"User {user_id}: Do you consent to data collection? (yes/no):
            ").lower()
        self.user_consent[user_id] = (consent == 'yes')

    def has_consent(self, user_id):
        return self.user_consent.get(user_id, False)
```

```
# Example usage
consent_manager = ConsentManager()
consent_manager.obtain_consent('user123')
print(consent_manager.has_consent('user123'))
```

This script exemplifies capturing user consent, an essential compliance action under GDPR when collecting personal data for observability purposes.

HIPAA regulates the protection of health information in the United States, relevant for observability in healthcare sectors. Systems must implement encryption, access controls, and audit mechanisms to secure protected health information (PHI). Logging access to and modifications of PHI is crucial, as demonstrated in the following logging setup:

```
import logging

# Configuring a basic logger for HIPAA-compliant access logging
logging.basicConfig(filename='hipaa_access.log', level=logging.INFO)

def log_access(user_id, action, resource):
    log_entry = f'User: {user_id}, Action: {action}, Resource: {resource}'
    logging.info(log_entry)

# Example usage
log_access('doctor456', 'accessed', 'patient_record_789')
```

This log captures access attempts to sensitive health records, aiding auditability and compliance verification.

PCI-DSS applies to entities handling payment card information and mandates secure transmission and storage practices. Compliance involves implementing robust encryption, maintaining a secure network architecture, and conducting regular vulnerability assessments to ensure data sanctity.

Encryption of payment data within observability systems can be managed with libraries such as PyCrypto:

```
from Crypto.Cipher import AES
import base64

def encrypt_payment_data(data, key):
    cipher = AES.new(key.encode('utf-8'), AES.MODE_EAX)
    nonce = cipher.nonce
    ciphertext, tag = cipher.encrypt_and_digest(data.encode('utf-8'))
    return base64.b64encode(nonce + ciphertext).decode('utf-8')
```

```
# Example usage
secure_key = 'my_secure_key_123'
encrypted_data = encrypt_payment_data('credit_card_info', secure_key)
print(encrypted_data)
```

This example highlights encrypting sensitive payment data to comply with PCI-DSS encryption requirements.

SOX, or the Sarbanes-Oxley Act, demands stringent record-keeping and financial information integrity. Although focused on financial data, observability systems can be utilized to uphold audit trails ensuring compliance with SOX requirements.

Implementing audit trails involves systematic logging of actions, including user access, data changes, and system behaviors:

```
import logging
from datetime import datetime

# Basic SOX-compliant audit trail logging
logging.basicConfig(filename='sox_audit.log', level=logging.INFO)

def audit_record(user_id, action, description):
    audit_entry = f'Timestamp: {datetime.now()}, UserID: {user_id}, Action: {action
        }, Details: {description}'
    logging.info(audit_entry)

# Example usage
audit_record('admin321', 'update', 'Financial statement Q1 2023')
```

These examples demonstrate the foundational practices in observing compliance under key regulatory frameworks. Observability systems must accommodate these to ensure that data both aligns with operational needs and fulfills compliance criteria.

Compliance-driven implementations of observability systems rely on a mixture of technical solutions and procedural policies. These strategies include, among others, data encryption, access management, anonymization, logging, and monitoring.

Data Encryption: Information that flows through an observability system requires encryption both in transit and at rest. As legislation often mandates, encrypted data limits unauthorized access, ensuring data confidentiality and integrity. Encrypting through HTTPS communication channels or employing file system encryption tools, such as LUKS on Linux, are standard practices.

Access Management: Authentication and authorization mechanisms are set in place to enforce access based on organizational roles and responsibilities. Implementations of RBAC or attribute-based access control (ABAC) can enhance security by aligning user permissions with data access policies. The need for such rigor in access management is both a technological and a compliance requirement, mandating that users authenticate successfully before data access.

Anonymization: Removing identifiable personal data from telemetry datasets to protect privacy enables observability activities while complying with data protection laws. This involves applying techniques like data masking and tokenization, which encourage data processing without compromising individual privacy.

Logging and Monitoring: Compliance audits often query verifiable logs to review system activities. Consequently, observability systems must integrate logging mechanisms that generate detailed records of operations over time. Monitoring tools complement these efforts by promptly identifying anomalies, such as unauthorized access or data tampering, providing a robust reporting mechanism.

Data Retention and Deletion Policies: Managing data lifecycle through well-founded retention policies underpins compliance efforts. Storing telemetry data beyond its needed scope can breach data protection laws. Therefore, enforce logical policies to securely delete or archive irrelevant data that no longer adds value to operational insight nor fulfills compliance criteria.

Incident Response Plans: A strong incident response plan addresses unauthorized data access or breaches consistent with compliance requirements. The capabilities of such plans entail rapid detection, efficient breach notification processes, and post-incident reviews to strengthen system defenses.

In summary, the overarching goal of integrating compliance with observability systems is not merely to evade penalties but to create systems that reflect accountability while investing in the cultural ethos of privacy and security. Bridging the demand for regulatory compliance with functional observability requires detailed understanding and integration of policies, technical tools, and processes that build transparency without sacrificing system efficacy or integrity. Organizations stand to benefit from observability systems that meet compliance requirements by building a trust-centric environment that promotes secure innovation and operational excellence.

9.5 Role-Based Access Control in Telemetry

In the arena of observability systems, managing access to sensitive telemetry data is crucial to ensuring both security and regulatory compliance. Role-Based Access Control (RBAC) is a pivotal access management paradigm that assigns permissions to users based on defined organizational roles rather than individual user attributes. This controlled access mechanism provides a scalable and efficient security model for managing permissions in telemetry systems, promoting a least-privilege approach that enhances system security.

RBAC facilities manage and restrict access to telemetry data by establishing roles that correlate with job functions and responsibilities within an organization. Each role is granted specific permissions that determine what data and systems users within that role can access. This model is advantageous for its simplicity and its ability to cater to organizations with dynamic and structured role definitions.

The RBAC model consists of several components:

- Users: Individuals who interact with the telemetry system. Each user belongs to one or more roles.

- Roles: Named job functions within the organization that dictate which permissions users in a given role can exercise.

- Permissions: Authorized actions that can be performed on resources, such as reading telemetry data or configuring observability settings.

- Sessions: Instances linking users with activated roles within a specific context or timeframe.

Implementing RBAC in telemetry systems requires careful planning and consideration of organizational roles and corresponding access requirements. A well-thought-out RBAC design simplifies management while providing robust security against unauthorized data access.

To implement RBAC in telemetry systems, several technical steps need to be taken, from role definition to permission assignment and enforcement through access policies. Below is an overview of how to achieve an RBAC system for telemetry:

- Define Roles and Permissions: Establish a clear understanding of different roles needed within the organization, such as administrators, developers, and auditors, and assign appropriate permissions. For instance, auditors might require read-only access to telemetry data for compliance checks, while developers need access to configuration settings to fine-tune system operations.

- Access Control Systems: Implement access control systems to enforce RBAC policies, often achieved through modern Identity and Access Management (IAM) solutions integrated with observability platforms.

- Assign Roles to Users: Associate users with pre-defined roles, simplifying the process of onboarding new employees and modifying permissions as roles evolve.

- Enforce RBAC Policies: Apply RBAC policies across telemetry environments, ensuring that users can only access telemetry data and services aligned with their roles.

Here is an illustrative example in Python to demonstrate the implementation of a simple RBAC system using dictionaries to map users to roles and roles to permissions:

```
class RBAC:
    def __init__(self):
        # Define roles and their associated permissions
        self.roles_permissions = {
            "admin": {"read", "write", "configure"},
            "developer": {"read", "write"},
            "auditor": {"read"}
        }
        # Map users to roles
        self.users_roles = {
            "alice": "admin",
            "bob": "developer",
            "carol": "auditor"
```

```
    }
 def check_access(self, user, action):
     role = self.users_roles.get(user, None)
     if role and action in self.roles_permissions.get(role, set()):
         return f"Access granted for {action} to {user} ({role})"
     return f"Access denied for {action} to {user}"

# Example usage
rbac_system = RBAC()
print(rbac_system.check_access("alice", "configure"))
print(rbac_system.check_access("bob", "configure"))
```

This example highlights the assignment of permissions to roles and the subsequent mapping of users to roles, forming the basis of an RBAC system.

RBAC's adoption within telemetry systems presents manifold advantages:

- Scalability: Ideal for large organizations where user numbers may rapidly change. RBAC allows easy scalability with new users quickly assigned to pre-defined roles.

- Principle of Least Privilege: Users access only the telemetry data and resources necessary for their specific duties, minimizing potential security vulnerabilities through minimized permissions.

- Simplified Compliance and Auditability: Streamlined role assignment ensures that users comply with internal policies and regulatory mandates specific to telemetry. Audit logs can be straightforwardly generated to demonstrate user activity, crucial for compliance reporting and security investigations.

- Reduction in Administrative Complexity: Role definition reduces the complexity administrators typically encounter when setting individual permissions. Modifications in role permissions reflect across all users in that role without manual intervention, streamlining authorization management.

While RBAC provides pronounced benefits, its implementation is not without challenges. Key considerations include:

- Granular Role Definitions: Crafting overly broad roles may inadvertently provide more permissions than necessary, violating the principle of least privilege. Conversely, excessively granular roles can lead to a complex mesh of roles that overburdens administrators and users.

- Change Management: Organizational changes that affect roles, responsibilities, or permissions require vigilant and prompt updates in RBAC configurations. Automated tools and workflows aid in effective change management.

- Cultural and Training Aspects: Successful RBAC adoption depends on creating a culture that values security and understanding among users and IT staff. Continuous training programs teach employees the importance of their roles and their corresponding access privileges.

- Tooling Integration: Choose observability tools that seamlessly integrate with existing IAM solutions or implement custom RBAC solutions consistent with enterprise security architectures.

For practitioners, leveraging open-source tools and platforms that offer RBAC capabilities, such as Vault by HashiCorp, Kubernetes RoleBindings, or AWS IAM roles, ensures robust and efficient RBAC implementations in telemetry systems.

Below is an example of integrating RBAC using Kubernetes to manage access to telemetry metrics:

```
apiVersion: v1
kind: ServiceAccount
metadata:
  name: telemetry-viewer
---
apiVersion: rbac.authorization.k8s.io/v1
kind: Role
metadata:
  name: view-telemetry
rules:
- apiGroups: [""]
  resources: ["pods", "pods/log"]
  verbs: ["get", "watch", "list"]
---
apiVersion: rbac.authorization.k8s.io/v1
kind: RoleBinding
metadata:
  name: view-telemetry-binding
subjects:
- kind: ServiceAccount
  name: telemetry-viewer
```

```
roleRef:
  kind: Role
  name: view-telemetry
  apiGroup: ""
```

This Kubernetes setup illustrates RBAC in action, where a service account is granted permissions to view pods and logs, showcasing access control over telemetry data.

Implementing RBAC in telemetry systems ensures that access is tailored intricately to organizational structures and needs, allowing for optimized and secure management of sensitive data. With RBAC, organizations can confidently deploy observability solutions that reconcile the need for insight and data privacy, reflecting a secure and streamlined approach to access management, ultimately driving operational excellence and risk reduction.

9.6 Auditing and Monitoring Telemetry Systems

The proliferation of distributed architectures and the necessity for robust observability mandate sophisticated auditing and monitoring not only within system components but also across telemetry systems managing them. As telemetry systems gather vast amounts of data to provide insights into system performance and health, auditing and monitoring capabilities become critical. These capabilities ensure compliance, enhance security, and sustain operational integrity.

Understanding Auditing in Telemetry Systems

Auditing involves the systematic examination of telemetry systems to ensure compliance with policies and standards, detect anomalies, and track usage patterns. A telemetry system with auditing capabilities tracks actions, changes, data access, and system operations, thereby providing a reliable record of activities.

Key elements of auditing include:

- **Event Recording**: Captures detailed logs of events within the system, such as configuration changes, access attempts, and system errors. This feature aids in tracking usage patterns and detecting unauthorized activities.

- **Integrity Assurance**: Maintains the integrity of logs and audit trails, ensuring that records remain untampered. Techniques such as cryptographic signatures and hashing bolster this integrity.

- **Compliance Verification**: Demonstrates adherence to statutory, legal, and organizational requirements by logging all necessary activities and storing them securely for review.

Auditing serves as a cornerstone in establishing accountability and transparency in telemetry systems by providing stakeholders with the evidence required to support forensic analyses, compliance evaluations, and policy improvements.

Implementing Auditing Capabilities

Telemetry systems benefit immensely from integrated auditing subsystems that facilitate logging, monitoring, and reporting. Consider the following aspects when implementing auditing in telemetry environments:

- **Define Audit Requirements**: Establish the scope of auditing based on regulatory requirements, operational needs, and security objectives. Prioritize audit focus areas such as data access logs, configuration changes, and critical system events.

- **Log Management Systems**: Deploy robust logging frameworks and management systems to capture, aggregate, process, and store logs. Open-source platforms such as the ELK Stack (Elasticsearch, Logstash, Kibana) provide comprehensive log management, offering capabilities for real-time analysis and visualization.

Here is a Python snippet demonstrating the basic implementation of audit logging using the logging library:

```
import logging

# Configure audit logging
```

```
logger = logging.getLogger('telemetry_audit')
handler = logging.FileHandler('telemetry_audit.log')
formatter = logging.Formatter('%(asctime)s - %(levelname)s - %(message)s')
handler.setFormatter(formatter)
logger.addHandler(handler)
logger.setLevel(logging.INFO)

def audit_event(user, action, resource, status):
    message = f"User: {user}, Action: {action}, Resource: {resource}, Status: {status}"
    logger.info(message)

# Example usage
audit_event('admin', 'modify', 'config.yaml', 'success')
audit_event('guest', 'access', 'metrics', 'denied')
```

This example logs audit events to a file, capturing critical details such as user actions, the resources involved, and the outcomes.

- **Data Integrity Mechanisms**: Utilize cryptographic techniques to ensure that log data maintains its integrity. Hash the content of logs regularly to detect and prevent unauthorized changes.

- **Secure Storage and Access**: Store audit logs securely using encryption for confidentiality and access controls to limit manipulation and unauthorized viewing. Consider immutable storage solutions that provide built-in tamper-evidence capabilities.

- **Audit Reports**: Generate comprehensive reports from logs to support decision-making, compliance audits, and security analyses. Graphical visualization and summary tools in platforms such as Kibana enhance the interpretability of log data for stakeholders.

Monitoring Telemetry Systems in Real-Time

Monitoring, complementing auditing, offers continuous oversight of system activities and health, emphasizing real-time detection and alerting for anomalies, performance degradation, and security events. A robust telemetry monitoring framework encompasses data collection, alerting, visualization, and analysis capabilities.

Key Components of Telemetry Monitoring:

- **Data Collection Agents**: Deployed across infrastructure, capturing performance metrics, logs, and traces. Configured agents ensure comprehensive coverage of system components.

- **Aggregation and Processing**: Central systems consolidate data streams from various agents, perform initial processing, and store them for analysis. Logstash and Fluentd are popular tools for this purpose.

- **Alerting Engines**: Set thresholds and conditions for data, triggering alerts when metrics deviate from expected values, indicating potential issues. Tools like Prometheus with Alertmanager facilitate complex alerting workflows.

An example Prometheus configuration for monitoring CPU usage with alerts:

```
# Prometheus configuration to monitor CPU usage
- alert: HighCpuUsage
  expr: process_cpu_seconds_total > 1
  for: 5m
  labels:
    severity: warning
  annotations:
    summary: "High CPU usage detected"
    description: "CPU usage has exceeded normal operational parameters for over 5
        minutes."
```

This rule triggers an alert when CPU usage surpasses specific thresholds, indicating potential bottlenecks or misconfigurations.

- **Visualization and Analysis**: Deploy dashboards and visualization tools to interpret telemetry data visually on graphical interfaces. Grafana is frequently used to create informative dashboards that allow users to combine data from disparate sources and customize views according to organizational requirements.

Challenges and Best Practices

Telemetry system auditing and monitoring introduce challenges that require addressal through best practices:

- **Data Volume and Complexity**: Handling massive data streams presents storage, processing, and analysis challenges. Employ scalable architectures and cloud-based solutions capable of processing large datasets efficiently.

- **False Positives**: Monitoring systems with excessive threshold alerts may overwhelm teams with false positives, obscuring true anomalies. Careful calibration and machine learning models can reduce noise and improve signal clarity.

- **Security of Monitoring Systems**: Because monitoring systems are integral to security and observability, they themselves are attractive targets for attacks. Secure these systems using strong access controls, encryption, and regular security audits.

- **User Awareness and Training**: Educate engineers and administrators about the purpose and use of auditing and monitoring, covering how to interpret audit logs and respond to system alerts effectively.

- **Redundancy and Fail-Safes**: Implement fail-safe mechanisms and redundant configurations that ensure uninterrupted monitoring operations during failures or maintenance periods. High availability setups for monitoring components prevent loss of oversight.

The integration of robust auditing and monitoring processes within telemetry systems is an indispensable aspect of modern observability practices. These intertwined efforts bolster security, ensure compliance, and enable organizations to respond proactively to system anomalies, thereby sustaining operational excellence and stakeholder confidence. With a nuanced approach that leverages the latest in auditing and monitoring technology, organizations can address risks effectively while maximizing the value derived from telemetry data.

9.7 Incident Response for Observability Breaches

In increasingly complex digital environments, observability systems are pivotal in offering comprehensive insights into the state and performance of distributed applications and infrastructures. However, like any other component of an IT ecosystem, these systems are susceptible to breaches and cyber threats. An effective and robust incident response plan is essential in mitigating the impact of such breaches, facilitating swift recovery, and ensuring minimal disruption to business operations.

Incident response for observability breaches involves a structured approach that encompasses preparation, detection, containment, eradication, recovery, and lessons learned. This chapter delves into these critical phases, emphasizing the necessity of an agile, proactive, and well-coordinated incident response strategy.

- **Preparation: Building a Foundation for Response**

Effective incident response begins with meticulous preparation. Organizations must equip themselves with the necessary tools, resources, and processes to manage breaches efficiently.

- Policy Development: Establish a clear incident response policy, outlining roles, responsibilities, and procedures. It must define the scope of incidents, communication channels, and escalation paths.

- Incident Response Team (IRT): Formulate a dedicated team composed of individuals across various disciplines, such as security analysts, system administrators, legal advisors, and communications specialists. This team must be adequately trained, with periodic drills conducted to ensure readiness.

- Infrastructure Hardening: Implement security measures across observability systems, such as network segmentation, strong authentication mechanisms, and regular updates to reduce vulnerabilities that adversaries could exploit.

Tools like MISP (Malware Information Sharing Platform) can enhance preparation by facilitating threat intelligence sharing, providing insights on evolving threats and adversarial tactics.

- **Detection and Analysis: Identifying Breaches Quickly**

Detection of breaches within observability systems requires a sophisticated setup capable of continuously monitoring and analyzing telemetry data for anomalous activities.

283

- Monitoring and Alerting: Employ robust monitoring tools that can analyze logs, metrics, and traces from observability systems, configured to raise alerts upon detecting irregular patterns indicative of potential breaches. Tools like Splunk and Elasticsearch used with SIEM solutions can substantially bolster detection capabilities.

For example, a simplistic log monitoring script using Python could be:

```
import time
import logging

# Setup logging
logging.basicConfig(filename='incident_detection.log', level=logging.INFO)

def monitor_logs(log_file):
    with open(log_file, 'r') as logs:
        logs.seek(0, 2)  # Go to end of the file
        while True:
            line = logs.readline()
            if not line:
                time.sleep(0.2)
                continue
            if "suspicious_activity" in line:
                logging.info(f"Suspicious activity detected: {line.strip()}")

# Calling the log monitor function
monitor_logs('/var/log/application.log')
```

- Anomaly Detection: Implement machine learning algorithms to detect deviations from established baselines, recognizing patterns that may not be identifiable through traditional rules-based detection methods.

- Incident Classification: Upon detection of a breach, classify incidents based on their severity, scope, and potential impact. This classification aids in prioritizing response efforts and ensuring resources are directed appropriately.

- **Containment: Limiting the Impact of Breaches**

Once a breach is detected, rapid containment measures prevent further damage or data exfiltration. Containment strategies must be carefully crafted to maintain business continuity while securing critical assets.

284

- Immediate Response: Isolate affected systems or network segments to thwart further propagation of the breach. This may involve blocking anomalous traffic, disabling breached user accounts, or employing firewall rules to limit external access.

- Short-term and Long-term Containment: Focus short-term efforts on immediate remediation actions, while further planning long-term containment strategies such as deploying patches, reconfiguring network defenses, or adjusting security policies to thwart future attempts.

- **Eradication: Removing Threat Elements**

After containment, the next phase involves thoroughly eradicating malicious elements from affected systems. Organizations must ensure complete removal of malware, unauthorized access points, and any residual threats.

- Root Cause Analysis: Conduct a forensic investigation to ascertain how the breach occurred, identify vectors exploited by attackers, and eliminate vulnerabilities. This step is critical to preventing recurrences.

- Malware Removal and System Restoration: Utilize advanced anti-malware tools to cleanse affected systems, replacing or repairing corrupted or compromised files and configurations.

  For example, employing open-source tools such as ClamAV for malware removal might be scripted as follows:

```
#!/bin/bash

# Update ClamAV signatures
freshclam

# Scan system for malware
clamscan -r --bell -i /path/to/scan
```

- **Recovery: Returning to Normal Operations**

The recovery process aims to restore normalcy to observability systems while minimizing risk of re-compromise.

285

- System Restoration: Rebuild or restore affected systems using clean backups or system images that were verified for integrity.

- System Validation: Conduct thorough testing and validation to confirm that systems function correctly and without vulnerabilities. Consider using integrity monitoring tools to continuously verify system state post-recovery.

- **Lessons Learned: Reviewing and Improving**

An often overlooked yet crucial phase is the post-incident analysis, from which valuable lessons can be drawn to enhance future incident response efforts.

- Incident Review Meetings: Conduct retrospective meetings involving all stakeholders to review the incident timeline, assess the effectiveness of the response measures, and identify areas of improvement.

- Policy and Process Amendment: Update incident response plans, policies, and processes based on insights obtained from the incident review, ensuring preparedness for future breaches.

- Training and Awareness: Initiate training programs to propagate awareness generated from the incident across the organization, creating a more security-conscious culture.

Incident response for observability breaches is an integral aspect of managing and securing modern IT environments. With thorough preparation, effective detection mechanisms, strategic containment, diligent eradication, and comprehensive recovery procedures, organizations can significantly mitigate the impacts of breaches. Continuously refining incident response capabilities through lessons learned fosters a proactive and resilient organizational stance against evolving threats, safeguarding observability systems and the substantial insights they provide.

Chapter 10

Case Studies: Real-World Applications of OpenTelemetry

This chapter presents a series of case studies illustrating the practical application of OpenTelemetry across diverse industries. It examines how organizations in sectors such as e-commerce, finance, telecommunications, healthcare, and media streaming have implemented OpenTelemetry to enhance system performance, ensure compliance, and optimize operations. Each case provides insights into specific challenges addressed, solutions applied, and outcomes achieved, offering valuable lessons and best practices for employing OpenTelemetry in real-world scenarios.

10.1   E-commerce Platform Performance Monitoring

The exponential growth of e-commerce platforms necessitates the implementation of robust performance monitoring mechanisms to ensure an optimal user experience. One such method involves the integration of OpenTelemetry, a set of APIs, libraries, and agents used for the instrumentation of cloud-native software to gather data across complex distributed systems. This section delves into the practical application of OpenTelemetry in an e-commerce setting, focusing on optimizing website performance and enhancing customer experience.

E-commerce platforms, which inherently rely on a seamless user experience for revenue generation, encounter myriad performance issues such as slow loading times, inefficient resource allocation, and unpredictable system downtimes. The adoption of OpenTelemetry facilitates comprehensive monitoring and observability, allowing engineering teams to pre-emptively identify performance bottlenecks and mitigate potential system failures.

To effectively implement OpenTelemetry, the e-commerce platform followed a structured approach. Initial steps involved identifying critical user interactions and backend processes that directly impacted customer satisfaction. Key metrics such as page load time, transaction efficiency, server response times, and error rates were identified as primary indicators of performance. For each of these metrics, manual instrumentation was carried out using OpenTelemetry's robust API set.

Instrumenting the e-commerce platform began with tracing HTTP requests. The following code snippet demonstrates the basic setup for an HTTP server using OpenTelemetry:

```
from opentelemetry import trace
from opentelemetry.trace import Tracer
from opentelemetry.sdk.trace import TracerProvider
from opentelemetry.sdk.trace.export import SimpleExportSpanProcessor,
    ConsoleSpanExporter

# Set up tracing provider
trace.set_tracer_provider(TracerProvider())
tracer = trace.get_tracer(__name__)

# Add console exporter for visualization
span_processor = SimpleExportSpanProcessor(ConsoleSpanExporter())
```

```
trace.get_tracer_provider().add_span_processor(span_processor)

# Example function to trace HTTP requests
def http_request():
    with tracer.start_as_current_span("HTTP GET /products") as span:
        # Simulate a GET request
        span.add_event("Fetch product details")
        get_product_details()
```

The organization leveraged distributed tracing to visualize end-to-end transaction flows. Such visualization enabled the identification of latency hotspots within the system architecture. OpenTelemetry's ability to propagate context across different services and platforms was crucial. The propagation mechanism ensures that trace data collected from several microservices within the e-commerce ecosystem is correlated appropriately, providing a comprehensive view of the transaction path.

Moreover, the e-commerce platform capitalized on OpenTelemetry for redundancy reduction by integrating automatic metric collection and exporting. Here is a snippet demonstrating the integration of metrics in a way that supports automated capture and presentation:

```
from opentelemetry import metrics
from opentelemetry.sdk.metrics import MeterProvider
from opentelemetry.sdk.metrics.export import ConsoleMetricsExporter
from opentelemetry.sdk.metrics.export.controller import PushController

# Create MeterProvider and install it globally
meter_provider = MeterProvider()
metrics.set_meter_provider(meter_provider)
meter = metrics.get_meter(__name__)

# Export metrics to console
exporter = ConsoleMetricsExporter()
controller = PushController(meter, exporter, 5)

# Record metrics automatically
response_time = meter.create_value_recorder("response_time", unit="ms")
labels = {"service.name": "ecommerce-platform"}

def simulate_transaction(duration):
    response_time.record(duration, labels)
```

The continuous collection and exporting of these performance metrics allowed stakeholders to perform long-term analyses, extract insights, and make data-driven decisions regarding infrastructure optimization and resource allocation. By focusing analytical efforts on these metrics, the platform's engineering team could prioritize code refactoring exer-

289

cises, optimize SQL queries, improve caching strategies, and enhance the throughput of critical endpoints.

While implementing OpenTelemetry, there were notable challenges, particularly concerning data volume. Consequently, the organization was compelled to implement a data sampling strategy that ensured the transmitted data did not overwhelm storage capacities while still retaining statistical fidelity. Sampling techniques, such as Probabilistic and Rate Limiting sampling, were employed. These methods aid in reducing the volume of telemetry data processed and stored:

```
from opentelemetry.sdk.trace.sampling import TraceIdRatioBased

# Define a sampling policy
sampling_policy = TraceIdRatioBased(0.25) # Sample 25% of the traces
trace.get_tracer_provider().sampler = sampling_policy
```

The system architecture was designed to utilize lateral (horizontal) scaling techniques, as opposed to purely vertical scaling, to address increased loads. The e-commerce company leveraged cloud-native solutions to dynamically adjust resource availability in response to the patterns identified by OpenTelemetry. By observing system behavior under varying loads, the platform could consider dynamically responsive elasticity within the cloud environment.

In furtherance of these efforts, dashboards were configured using observability tools to display data collected through OpenTelemetry. These dashboards facilitated real-time monitoring, enabling engineers to detect anomalies swiftly and act accordingly. Technologies such as Prometheus, Grafana, and Jaeger proved invaluable, contributing to the analytics framework by visualizing trace data and rendering it intelligible.

The integration of alerting mechanisms marked another essential aspect. With the aid of OpenTelemetry, alerts were generated when certain defined thresholds were breached. The organization defined error rate thresholds and set latency alarms, thus allowing the operations team to undertake remedial measures proactively.

Finally, it should be highlighted that the implementation of OpenTelemetry goes beyond mere technical execution. It necessitated a culture shift within the organization. Development, operations, and business teams cooperatively defined the critical performance indicators, and sustained alignment was achieved through an ongoing feedback loop ensuring continuous improvement.

E-commerce platform performance monitoring via OpenTelemetry constitutes a milestone in enhancing operational efficiency and customer satisfaction. Through structured and persistent monitoring, businesses can navigate dynamic market demands and technological complexities with greater agility and assurance. This endeavor underscores the growing importance of observability within modern software development, profoundly impacting an organization's capability to deliver quality services in a competitive landscape.

10.2 Financial Services Use Case

In the financial services sector, operational reliability and security are paramount. Firms must ensure compliance with stringent regulatory standards while concurrently optimizing transaction processes to maintain competitive advantage. This section explores a financial services firm's implementation of OpenTelemetry to achieve these objectives. Through advanced monitoring and observability, the firm enhanced transaction security and compliance, leveraging OpenTelemetry's capabilities to address complexities inherent in financial operations.

The financial firm initiated the implementation of OpenTelemetry by performing a thorough assessment of its existing infrastructure to identify areas in need of observability improvements. Emphasis was placed on safeguarding sensitive data and ensuring robust transaction integrity. An architecture overhaul was deemed necessary, with a shift towards incorporating distributed tracing and metric collection using OpenTelemetry as a cornerstone of the monitoring strategy.

The firm focused on key operations within financial transactions, such as payment processing, fund transfers, and market transactions. Each transaction's lifecycle was instrumented to gather telemetry data that provided insights into latency, transaction verification failures, error occurrences, and any anomalous activities. The code excerpt below illustrates how tracing was employed to monitor transaction processing:

```
from opentelemetry import trace
```

```
from opentelemetry.trace import Tracer
from opentelemetry.sdk.trace import TracerProvider
from opentelemetry.sdk.trace.export import BatchSpanProcessor, ConsoleSpanExporter


trace.set_tracer_provider(TracerProvider())
tracer = trace.get_tracer(__name__)

# Setting up exporters
exporter = ConsoleSpanExporter()
span_processor = BatchSpanProcessor(exporter)
trace.get_tracer_provider().add_span_processor(span_processor)

# Transaction processing tracing
def process_transaction(transaction_id):
    with tracer.start_as_current_span("process_transaction") as span:
        span.set_attribute("transaction.id", transaction_id)
        validate_transaction(transaction_id)
        execute_transaction(transaction_id)
```

Such instrumentation provided end-to-end visibility into how transactions traversed through multiple services and identified bottlenecks
that were promptly addressed to reduce latency.

Complementary to tracing, the firm incorporated metrics collection
to detail each service's performance involved in the transaction chain.
The telemetry data collected were pivotal for auditing processes, ensuring compliance with financial regulations like the Payment Card Industry Data Security Standard (PCI DSS) and the Sarbanes-Oxley Act.
Furthermore, these data facilitated predictive analytics by feeding into
machine learning models that forecast transaction anomalies, thereby
preempting fraud or unauthorized access.

```
from opentelemetry import metrics
from opentelemetry.sdk.metrics import MeterProvider
from opentelemetry.sdk.metrics.export import ConsoleMetricsExporter
from opentelemetry.sdk.metrics.export.controller import PushController

meter_provider = MeterProvider()
metrics.set_meter_provider(meter_provider)
meter = metrics.get_meter(__name__)

exporter = ConsoleMetricsExporter()
controller = PushController(meter, exporter, 10)

# Defining metrics
transaction_latency = meter.create_value_recorder("transaction_latency", unit="ms
    ", description="Time taken to process a transaction")
fraud_attempt_counter = meter.create_counter("fraud_attempt_counter")

def record_transaction_metrics(latency, is_fraud):
    transaction_latency.record(latency, {"region": "NA"})
```

```
if is_fraud:
    fraud_attempt_counter.add(1, {"alert": "suspected"})
```

The financial firm diligently designed alerting mechanisms based on these telemetry inputs. A hybrid detection approach was implemented, which combined predefined metric thresholds with anomaly detection algorithms. Such a strategy catered to catching both known vulnerabilities and novel threats. This made the alerting system dynamic, responsive, and significantly reduced false positive rates.

An integral part of the OpenTelemetry deployment was the formulation of precise sampling strategies, given the financial sector's vast transaction volumes. Adaptive sampling methods were intelligently used to ensure that only critical transaction traces were fully captured for further analysis, thereby easing the burden on data storage resources while maintaining comprehensive observability.

```
from opentelemetry.sdk.trace.sampling import AlwaysOnSampler, AlwaysOffSampler

# Using Conditional Sampling
if is_high_value_transaction():
    sampling_policy = AlwaysOnSampler() # Capture all traces for high-value
        transactions
else:
    sampling_policy = AlwaysOffSampler() # Sample less for regular transactions

trace.get_tracer_provider().sampler = sampling_policy
```

Another salient focus was data privacy; the financial firm employed sanitization protocols to anonymize telemetry data, ensuring compliance with data protection regulations such as the General Data Protection Regulation (GDPR). This step was crucial to balance between gleaning actionable insights from sensitive data while ensuring customer privacy is respected.

Beyond technical advancements, the OpenTelemetry implementation catalyzed collaborative transformation within the organization. Cross-departmental alignment was fostered among IT, compliance, risk assessment, and customer service teams. The interconnectedness facilitated by OpenTelemetry's insights spawned a unified approach to problem-solving and decision-making.

Dashboards and visualizations proved invaluable for non-technical stakeholders, enabling streamlined monitoring of financial operations. Visual tools like Grafana displayed real-time metrics and transaction paths, offering intuitive insights into system status for executive management, who could then swiftly align business decisions with operational realities.

The successes experienced in utilizing OpenTelemetry extended beyond immediate gains such as improved compliance and security. The resultant data architecture served as a foundation for upcoming initiatives like real-time customer experience analytics and AI-based trading systems, elevating innovation prospects within the institution.

The strategic use of OpenTelemetry within a financial services context underscores its critical role in fortifying transaction security and ensuring regulatory compliance. As financial services ecosystems grow in complexity, the need for robust, holistic, and transparent observability mechanisms becomes indispensable. OpenTelemetry offers such an integrative solution, positioning firms to navigate regulatory landscapes effectively while keeping pace with technological advancements.

10.3 Telecommunications Network Monitoring

Telecommunications networks form the foundation of global connectivity, with service providers facing the continuous challenge of maintaining optimal performance across complex, distributed systems. Effective network monitoring is critical for ensuring seamless communication and preventing service degradation. This section discusses the integration and utilization of OpenTelemetry for monitoring telecommunications networks, focusing on optimized traffic monitoring and diagnostics capabilities.

The telecommunications provider under consideration embarked on integrating OpenTelemetry after identifying the need for enhanced visibility into network performance, congestion points, and anomaly detection. This decision arose from the complexities of their expansive network infrastructure, which spanned multiple geographies and technologies, including wireless, fiber optics, and satellite communications.

Central to the provider's strategy was the deployment of OpenTelemetry to gauge network health indicators such as latency, bandwidth utilization, jitter, and packet loss. These metrics collectively influence the quality of service (QoS) provided to end users, making their continuous monitoring imperative. The organization started by implementing tracing and metrics collection to capture detailed network performance data.

Network packets were instrumented using OpenTelemetry's tracing capabilities, enabling detailed insights into data flow across numerous network nodes. The code block below illustrates a Python snippet for instrumenting packet flow tracing:

```
from opentelemetry import trace
from opentelemetry.trace import Tracer
from opentelemetry.sdk.trace import TracerProvider
from opentelemetry.sdk.trace.export import BatchSpanProcessor, ConsoleSpanExporter


# Set up tracing provider
trace.set_tracer_provider(TracerProvider())
tracer = trace.get_tracer(__name__)

# Configure span processor
span_processor = BatchSpanProcessor(ConsoleSpanExporter())
trace.get_tracer_provider().add_span_processor(span_processor)

# Network packet processing trace
def process_packet(packet_id, source, destination):
    with tracer.start_as_current_span("process_packet") as span:
        span.set_attribute("packet.id", packet_id)
        span.set_attribute("packet.source", source)
        span.set_attribute("packet.destination", destination)
        # Perform packet processing
        analyze_packet_flow()
```

Traces collected this way illuminated the end-to-end path of data packets, uncovering latency and bottleneck instances at specific nodes such as routers, switches, and base stations. This visualization enabled network engineers to pinpoint failure points or areas necessitating resource upgrades precisely.

In addition to traces, metrics were continuously gathered, offering a broader perspective of network operations. Metrics, such as throughput and error rate, were categorized by geographic region, aiding in localized assessments of service quality and operational efficiency. The metrics instrumentation example below showcases capturing standard network metrics:

```
from opentelemetry import metrics
from opentelemetry.sdk.metrics import MeterProvider
from opentelemetry.sdk.metrics.export import ConsoleMetricsExporter
from opentelemetry.sdk.metrics.export.controller import PushController

# Create MeterProvider and install it globally
meter_provider = MeterProvider()
metrics.set_meter_provider(meter_provider)
meter = metrics.get_meter(__name__)

# Export metrics to console
exporter = ConsoleMetricsExporter()
controller = PushController(meter, exporter, 5)

# Define network-related metrics
bandwidth_usage = meter.create_value_recorder("bandwidth_usage", unit="Mbps")
packet_loss = meter.create_counter("packet_loss")

def update_network_metrics(bandwidth, loss_count):
    bandwidth_usage.record(bandwidth, {"area": "Urban"})
    packet_loss.add(loss_count, {"cause": "Congestion"})
```

The telecommunications firm adopted a sophisticated setup for data aggregation from numerous network devices and endpoints, recognizing the sheer volume and velocity of data in telecommunications networks. In response, they employed high throughput data pipelines capable of handling petabytes of telemetry data, ensuring scalable and fault-tolerant ingestion into distributed storage.

Given the high data rates, adaptive sampling was employed to selectively capture vital traces that sufficiently represented network conditions without exhaustive recording, thus achieving storage efficiency and focused analysis:

```
from opentelemetry.sdk.trace.sampling import TraceIdRatioBased

# Determine dynamic sampling rate based on network load
def determine_sampling_rate():
    current_network_load = measure_network_load()
    if current_network_load > THRESHOLD_HIGH:
        return TraceIdRatioBased(0.05)
    elif current_network_load > THRESHOLD_MEDIUM:
        return TraceIdRatioBased(0.10)
    else:
        return TraceIdRatioBased(0.20)

trace.get_tracer_provider().sampler = determine_sampling_rate()
```

Dashboards and visualizations were essential components of the diagnostic processes. Stateful visualizations with data series illustrations of network throughput over time periods helped operations teams identify traffic patterns and anomalies. Grafana dashboards were used prolifically to visualize metrics and render complex telemetry data as actionable insights.

The firm's network operations center (NOC) leveraged these insights for decision-making and corrective actions. Alerts generated from defined thresholds provided proactive notifications of worsening conditions. Automated response systems were deployed to reroute traffic upon detection of high packet loss or extended latency beyond acceptable service levels, maintaining an uninterrupted communication flow.

Furthermore, the organization executed a comprehensive culture shift to support this technological transformation, encouraging cross-functional collaborations among network engineers, IT teams, compliance officers, and business units. This interdisciplinary approach was crucial to aligning technical objectives with customer service deliverables and regulatory requirements.

OpenTelemetry is not just a technical solution but a transformational tool that serves the evolving needs of modern telecommunications networks. The insights gained through its implementation position service providers to minimize disruptions, ensure compliance, and offer superior quality communication services consistently. As telecommunications technology advances, incorporating OpenTelemetry will continually support optimized network management strategies and foster an adaptive, responsive telecommunications landscape.

10.4 Healthcare Application Observability

Healthcare applications are central to modern medical practices, facilitating patient management, diagnostics, and record-keeping. The integration of technology into healthcare systems necessitates advanced observability to ensure critical applications function seamlessly and securely. This section examines how a healthcare institution employed OpenTelemetry to enhance application observability, ultimately improving patient care and data management.

The healthcare organization's primary objectives in adopting Open-

Telemetry included achieving comprehensive visibility into application performance, ensuring data integrity, and maintaining compliance with healthcare regulations such as Health Insurance Portability and Accountability Act (HIPAA).

The deployment of OpenTelemetry commenced with an extensive evaluation of existing infrastructure to determine areas where observability was most needed. The organization prioritized systems involving electronic health records (EHR), appointment scheduling, telemedicine interfaces, and lab results processing due to their critical role in clinical workflows.

Central to the OpenTelemetry strategy was implementing distributed tracing to gain insights into complex transactions across these systems. Tracing allowed the institution to monitor request propagation through microservices powering healthcare services, revealing latencies, errors, and points of failure. The following code illustrates how to instrument an EHR system for tracing:

```
from opentelemetry import trace
from opentelemetry.sdk.trace import TracerProvider
from opentelemetry.sdk.trace.export import BatchSpanProcessor, ConsoleSpanExporter


# Set tracer provider
trace.set_tracer_provider(TracerProvider())
tracer = trace.get_tracer(__name__)

# Export spans to console for debugging
exporter = ConsoleSpanExporter()
span_processor = BatchSpanProcessor(exporter)
trace.get_tracer_provider().add_span_processor(span_processor)

def retrieve_patient_record(patient_id):
    with tracer.start_as_current_span("retrieve_patient_record") as span:
        span.set_attribute("patient.id", patient_id)
        access_medical_records(patient_id)
```

Tracing revealed critical paths within patient data retrieval processes, highlighting areas affected by network latency or inefficiencies in service communication. This information guided optimization efforts, significantly enhancing response times for healthcare practitioners accessing patient data.

In addition to tracing, comprehensive metrics collection was integrated to provide quantitative insights into application performance. Metrics such as response times, error rates, and system load were crucial for evaluating the efficiency and reliability of healthcare applications. The following code snippet demonstrates capturing performance metrics:

```
from opentelemetry import metrics
from opentelemetry.sdk.metrics import MeterProvider
from opentelemetry.sdk.metrics.export import ConsoleMetricsExporter
from opentelemetry.sdk.metrics.export.controller import PushController

# Create MeterProvider and install it globally
meter_provider = MeterProvider()
metrics.set_meter_provider(meter_provider)
meter = metrics.get_meter(__name__)

# Export metrics to console to observe values
exporter = ConsoleMetricsExporter()
controller = PushController(meter, exporter, 5)

# Define metrics for application performance
response_time_recorder = meter.create_value_recorder("response_time", unit="ms")
operation_failure_counter = meter.create_counter("operation_failures")

def capture_metrics(response_time, failures):
    response_time_recorder.record(response_time, {"service": "EHR"})
    operation_failure_counter.add(failures, {"service": "EHR"})
```

Utilizing comprehensive performance data, healthcare IT teams were enabled to perform trend analyses that informed infrastructure scaling and load balancing adjustments during peak usage periods such as during pandemics or health crises.

A salient feature of the OpenTelemetry deployment was rigorous data control measures ensuring compliance with HIPAA mandates on patient data protection. Data anonymization and encryption practices were established to safeguard telemetry data, limiting exposure risk while preserving the analytic value of collected metrics and traces.

```
from cryptography.fernet import Fernet

# Generate a key for encryption
key = Fernet.generate_key()
cipher_suite = Fernet(key)

def encrypt_data(data):
    encrypted_data = cipher_suite.encrypt(data.encode())
    return encrypted_data

def decrypt_data(encrypted_data):
    decrypted_data = cipher_suite.decrypt(encrypted_data).decode()
    return decrypted_data

# Example of encrypting a patient ID
patient_id = "12345"
```

```
encrypted_patient_id = encrypt_data(patient_id)
```

Through these measures, the healthcare institution maintained a balance between operational transparency for internal analytics and the privacy expectations mandated by legal regulations.

Dashboards and analytics platforms were pivotal for operational stakeholders, offering real-time and historical perspectives on application performance. Visualization tools such as Kibana and Grafana transformed masses of telemetry data into intuitive charts and alerts, driving informed decision-making processes.

By visualizing metrics, staff could quickly detect deviations from normal operation patterns, enabling timely interventions to address emerging issues before they could impact patient care. This proactive approach marked a significant shift from reactive break-fix methodologies that were traditionally employed.

Moreover, developing a culture open to data-driven improvements was essential. Multidisciplinary workshops and futures-thinking sessions facilitated communication across clinical, operational, and technical teams. The collective effort significantly enhanced the institution's observability, ultimately fostering a patient-centered operational framework motivated by a shared commitment to quality improvement.

Implementing OpenTelemetry led to notable advances in system resilience, equipping the healthcare organization to adapt quickly to evolving operational demands and technological advancements. The institution's leadership highlighted how data transparency enabled through observability cultivated trust among stakeholders, further reinforcing the institution's reputation for excellence in care delivery.

Overall, the integration of OpenTelemetry in healthcare applications underlines its capacity to drive meaningful enhancements not only in system reliability and efficiency but also in elevating the quality of patient outcomes. As the sector continues to embrace digital transformation, comprehensive observability will remain a cornerstone of successful healthcare IT strategies.

10.5 Media Streaming Service Optimization

In today's digital age, media streaming services are an integral part of entertainment, delivering a vast array of content on-demand to viewers worldwide. The performance and quality of these services are critical as buffering issues, playback failures, or latencies can significantly impact user satisfaction and service retention. This section explores how a media streaming company employed OpenTelemetry to troubleshoot streaming issues and optimize delivery networks, ultimately enhancing the user experience while optimizing resource utilization.

For a media streaming service, key objectives include minimizing latency, ensuring smooth playback, and efficiently utilizing bandwidth. To address these challenges, the company undertook a comprehensive observability strategy using OpenTelemetry. The deployment aimed to collect telemetry data that provided a granular view of service performance, supported by advanced analytics to identify and resolve performance bottlenecks.

The media streaming environment presented unique challenges due to its scale and complexity. With a distributed content delivery network (CDN) handling varying traffic loads, it required end-to-end visibility from content servers to client applications. OpenTelemetry tracing was chosen to provide insights into data flow across these distributed systems. The following example demonstrates how tracing was implemented in a media streaming context:

```
import { trace } from '@opentelemetry/api';
import { NodeTracerProvider } from '@opentelemetry/sdk-trace-node';
import { ConsoleSpanExporter, SimpleSpanProcessor } from '@opentelemetry/sdk-
    trace-base';

// Initialize tracer provider
const tracerProvider = new NodeTracerProvider();
tracerProvider.addSpanProcessor(new SimpleSpanProcessor(new ConsoleSpanExporter
    ()));
tracerProvider.register();

// Create a tracer
const tracer = trace.getTracer('media-streaming-service');

// Function to trace video streaming session
function streamVideo(sessionId, contentId) {
  const span = tracer.startSpan('stream_video', {
```

```
    attributes: { 'session.id': sessionId, 'content.id': contentId }
  });

  // Simulate streaming logic
  fetchContent(contentId).then(content => {
    serveContent(content);
    span.end();
  }).catch(err => {
    span.recordException(err);
    span.setStatus({ code: 2, message: 'Streaming error' });
    span.end();
  });
}
```

This tracing setup allowed the streaming service to monitor streaming sessions, capturing signals related to request-response cycles, jitter, buffering frequencies, and any errors encountered during stream
delivery. Such detailed tracing enabled rapid identification of performance issues, particularly those that only manifested under specific
traffic conditions or client configurations.

In complement to tracing, effective metrics collection was established
across various nodes within the CDN. Metrics such as playback start
time, buffering ratio, and bitrate switches offered crucial visibility into
user-perceived performance aspects. The following code snippet illustrates the metrics collection approach:

```
import { metrics } from '@opentelemetry/api';
import { MeterProvider, ConsoleMetricExporter, PeriodicExportingMetricReader }
    from '@opentelemetry/sdk-metrics-base';

// Set up MeterProvider
const meterProvider = new MeterProvider();
const meter = meterProvider.getMeter('media-streaming-metrics');

// Export metrics to console
meter.addPeriodicMetricReader(new PeriodicExportingMetricReader({
  exporter: new ConsoleMetricExporter(),
  exportIntervalMillis: 30000
}));

// Define streaming-related metrics
const startupTime = meter.createHistogram('playback_start_time', {
  description: 'Time taken to start video playback', unit: 'ms'
});

const bufferingRatio = meter.createUpDownCounter('buffering_ratio', {
  description: 'Ratio of buffering time to playback time'
});

function recordMetrics(startup, buffering, totalPlayback) {
  startupTime.record(startup);
```

```
  bufferingRatio.add(buffering / totalPlayback);
}
```

With such metrics in place, the streaming service was able to perform real-time analytics to optimize adaptive bitrate algorithms, balancing between the best possible quality and playback stability based on current network conditions.

Given the global reach of media content, adaptive sampling strategies were implemented in OpenTelemetry to manage data volumes without overwhelming storage capabilities or analysis platforms. By sampling traces and metrics intelligently, only the most impactful data points were processed for thorough investigation:

```
import { TraceIdRatioBasedSampler } from '@opentelemetry/core';

// Adaptive sampling setup
const networkCondition = determineNetworkConditions();
const samplingRate = networkCondition === 'high' ? 0.1 : (networkCondition === '
    medium' ? 0.2 : 0.5);

const sampler = new TraceIdRatioBasedSampler(samplingRate);
tracerProvider.register({
  sampler: sampler
});
```

The streaming company leveraged visualization tools such as Grafana to set up comprehensive dashboards that displayed telemetry data across user devices, geographic regions, and time zones. This visualization empowered operations teams to pinpoint geographic-specific issues quickly, like regional CDN node failures or ISP-related throttling that affected service quality.

Automation and alerting became crucial components of the observability framework, where predefined thresholds in telemetry data triggered automated workflows to address disruptions proactively. For instance, if the buffering ratio exceeded a certain threshold, automated load balancing routines redistributed traffic to less loaded servers within the CDN.

An additional facet of the observability strategy involved machine learning integration. The streaming company fed telemetry data into machine learning models that predicted user churn risk based on streaming quality metrics. This predictive analytics enabled targeted interventions, such as notifying users of network tips during poor connectivity or suggesting lower bitrate streams to avoid interruptions.

```
from sklearn.ensemble import RandomForestClassifier
import numpy as np

# Assume historical data for model training
features = np.array([[20, 0.1, 6], [50, 0.4, 3], [15, 0.05, 9]]) # Example: [startup,
    buffering_ratio, bitrate_switch]
labels = np.array([1, 0, 1]) # 1 indicates potential churn, 0 indicates satisfied user

# Train a classifier
classifier = RandomForestClassifier(n_estimators=100)
classifier.fit(features, labels)

# Predict churn risk for a new session
new_user_session = np.array([[30, 0.2, 5]])
churn_risk = classifier.predict(new_user_session)
```

This forward-thinking approach demonstrated the potential of combining telemetry data with advanced analytics to not only resolve past performance issues but also anticipate and mitigate future risks.

Culturally, the adoption of OpenTelemetry fostered collaborative dialogues across development, operations, and business teams. By establishing observability as a shared responsibility, all stakeholders were vested in continuously refining the service delivery model, ultimately enriching product offerings and enhancing customer engagement.

The integration of OpenTelemetry for media streaming service optimization exemplifies the dynamic, multi-dimensional capabilities of observability practices. Such endeavors ensure that content delivery remains robust and consistent, providing users with exceptional viewing experiences while equipping service providers with the tools needed to adapt to ever-evolving technological landscapes.

10.6 Retail Supply Chain Management

The retail sector is characterized by intricate supply chains that synchronize the flow of goods from manufacturers to consumers. Effective supply chain management is pivotal for sustaining competitive advantage, ensuring timely deliveries, and minimizing operational costs. This section discusses how a retail company employed OpenTelemetry to enhance observability across its supply chain network, driving efficiencies and achieving precise, data-driven decision-making.

Retail supply chains encompass multiple facets such as procurement, transportation, distribution, inventory management, and demand forecasting. The interplay amongst these activities makes end-to-end visibility critical for preempting disruptions and optimizing performance. The company in focus adopted OpenTelemetry to capture telemetry data that illuminated these intricate processes, thereby enhancing visibility and control.

The initial phase of implementation focused on instrumenting critical supply chain processes using OpenTelemetry's tracing capabilities to gather real-time insights into item flows from suppliers to warehouses, and ultimately to retail outlets. Tracing was employed across all touchpoints, from order processing and shipment tracking to warehouse logistics. The following Python-based example demonstrates this tracing:

```
from opentelemetry import trace
from opentelemetry.sdk.trace import TracerProvider
from opentelemetry.sdk.trace.export import BatchSpanProcessor, ConsoleSpanExporter


# Initialize tracer provider
trace.set_tracer_provider(TracerProvider())
tracer = trace.get_tracer('retail-supply-chain')

# Add exporter to the processor
exporter = ConsoleSpanExporter()
span_processor = BatchSpanProcessor(exporter)
trace.get_tracer_provider().add_span_processor(span_processor)

# Function to trace order fulfillment
def fulfill_order(order_id, warehouse_id):
    with tracer.start_as_current_span("fulfill_order") as span:
        span.set_attribute("order.id", order_id)
        span.set_attribute("warehouse.id", warehouse_id)
        span.add_event("Start Picking Goods")
        pick_goods(order_id, warehouse_id)
        span.add_event("Goods Picked")
        initiate_shipment(order_id)
```

Such observability into supply chain operations allowed the company to ascertain potential delays, assess the efficiency of logistics providers, and streamline warehouse operations through a detailed evaluation of time taken across different stages.

In complement to tracing, the implementation of comprehensive metrics was pivotal for evaluating supply chain performance. Key performance indicators (KPIs) such as order fulfillment cycle time, inventory turnover rates, and transportation reliability indexes were automatically computed through continuous metrics capture. The code snippet below demonstrates the process of collecting supply chain metrics:

```
from opentelemetry import metrics
from opentelemetry.sdk.metrics import MeterProvider
from opentelemetry.sdk.metrics.export import ConsoleMetricsExporter
from opentelemetry.sdk.metrics.export.controller import PushController

# Initialize meter provider
meter_provider = MeterProvider()
metrics.set_meter_provider(meter_provider)
meter = meter_provider.get_meter('retail-supply-chain-metrics')

# Export metrics to console
exporter = ConsoleMetricsExporter()
controller = PushController(meter, exporter, 5)

# Define metrics for the supply chain
fulfillment_time = meter.create_histogram('order_fulfillment_time', unit='hours')
inventory_levels = meter.create_up_down_counter('inventory_levels')

def update_metrics(fulfillment_duration, inventory_count):
    fulfillment_time.record(fulfillment_duration, labels={"region": "East"})
    inventory_levels.add(inventory_count, labels={"product_category": "Electronics
        "})
```

The deployment of these metrics enabled comprehensive analysis of supply chain workflows, facilitating real-time decision making that accounted for factors like demand fluctuations and stockouts, vastly improving overall efficiency.

An intelligent sampling strategy was critical given the scale and data volume inherent in retail supply chains. The firm adopted sophisticated probabilistic sampling methods to ensure that the most consequential telemetry data were analyzed, while less significant datasets were filtered out to achieve processing efficiency:

```
from opentelemetry.sdk.trace.sampling import TraceIdRatioBased

# Define sampling rate based on strategic priorities
def define_sampling_strategy(order_priority):
    if order_priority == 'High':
        return TraceIdRatioBased(0.5) # 50% of high-priority orders traced
    elif order_priority == 'Medium':
        return TraceIdRatioBased(0.2)
    else:
        return TraceIdRatioBased(0.1)

tracer.get_tracer_provider().sampler = define_sampling_strategy('High')
```

Data visualization and dashboarding were integral to gaining actionable insights from the observed data. Tools such as Grafana and Kibana enabled the transformation of raw telemetry data into meaningful dashboards, providing clarity on supply chain performance across various nodes and facilitating performance comparisons by geographical regions.

Furthermore, the integration of artificial intelligence (AI) and machine learning (ML) enhanced the predictive analytics space within supply chain management. By feeding telemetry into ML models, the company could predict disruptions, optimize inventory levels, and forecast demand with greater precision. The subsequent example illustrates employing machine learning for demand prediction:

```
from sklearn.linear_model import LinearRegression
import numpy as np

# Assume historical demand data
historical_demand = np.array([[100, 50], [120, 55], [150, 60]])
sales_next_week = np.array([105, 130, 160])

# Train a model for demand forecasting
model = LinearRegression()
model.fit(historical_demand, sales_next_week)

# Forecast demand for upcoming week
current_factors = np.array([[110, 52]])
predicted_demand = model.predict(current_factors)
```

The outcomes of employing AI to bolster supply chain observability were profound, allowing the company to anticipate seasonal spikes and variably allocate resources, reducing wastage while maximizing availability.

To drive these initiatives, fostering a collaborative ecosystem across supply chain stakeholders was essential. This ecosystem enabled seamless communication between suppliers, logistics partners, warehouse operatives, and retail outlets. OpenTelemetry data catalyzed this cooperation, transforming disparate operations into a cohesive supply network characterized by adaptive and agile responses to market demands.

Finally, compliance and data privacy considerations were meticulously addressed. Transparent processes were documented to ensure adherence to international trade regulations and data protection laws such as the General Data Protection Regulation (GDPR). Anonymizing sensitive transactional data before analysis ensured compliance while preserving analytical integrity.

In culmination, the integration of OpenTelemetry into retail supply chain management underscored its role as a transformative lever, offering unprecedented levels of transparency and control. Real data-driven insights facilitated by OpenTelemetry empowered the company to not only fine-tune operations but also proactively adapt to dynamic retail landscapes. As retail trends continue to evolve, the strategic implementation of observability solutions will invariably remain at the forefront, driving efficiencies and elevating service delivery.

10.7 Lessons Learned from OpenTelemetry Deployments

The implementation of OpenTelemetry across diverse industry sectors has provided insightful lessons about observability's vital role in optimizing complex systems. This section distills key takeaways from deploying OpenTelemetry, offering valuable insights into challenges encountered, strategies employed, and best practices developed. Organizations, ranging from finance, healthcare, telecommunications to media and retail, reveal diverse learnings applicable universally, underscoring the significance of establishing robust observability into operational workflows.

One pivotal lesson early in OpenTelemetry deployments was the importance of defining clear objectives and metrics for observability. Organizations experienced varying degrees of success often correlated with initial clarity around what to observe. Precise scoping prevents unnecessary complexity and circumvents excessive data collection, focusing resources on key performance indicators. Organizations found it beneficial to align measurement objectives closely with organizational goals and customer needs to foster accountability and strategic alignment.

Environments highly benefited from OpenTelemetry's ability to instrument distributed systems seamlessly, unifying telemetry data across diverse services and platforms. However, one operational realization was the criticality of standardized instrumentation practices. Differences in trace and metric definitions led to inconsistent data, impeding comparability and insights. Establishing common practices and taxonomy across development teams became fundamental, paving the way for coherent telemetry analysis.

A technical consideration frequently encountered concerned data handling rules to prevent storage and processing overloads. OpenTelemetry deployers identified the necessity of adept data governance measures, balancing data fidelity with resource constraints. Implementing intelligent sampling strategies reduced data volumes significantly while retaining comprehensive visibility. Below is a coding illustration for dynamic sampling configuration, embracing such efficiency:

```
from opentelemetry.sdk.trace import Sampler
from opentelemetry.sdk.trace.sampling import TraceIdRatioBased

class ContextualSampler(Sampler):
    def __init__(self, thresholds):
        self.thresholds = thresholds

    def should_sample(self, trace_id, span_name, attributes, links):
        # Dynamically adjust based on context
        importance = attributes.get('importance', 'normal')
        ratio = self.thresholds.get(importance, 0.1)
        return TraceIdRatioBased(ratio).should_sample(trace_id, span_name,
            attributes, links)

# Example usage of ContextualSampler
contextual_sampler = ContextualSampler({'high': 0.5, 'normal': 0.1, 'low': 0.01})
```

The strategic implementation of dashboards and alerting systems also emerged as a critical influence on observability outcomes. Deployers frequently encountered a paradox where robust telemetry collection was undermined by inadequate data visualization and alerting capabilities. Effective dashboards transform raw data into actionable insights, necessitating intuitive designs and integrations with team workflows. Many organizations have utilized platforms like Grafana and Prometheus to bridge this gap, allowing for real-time monitoring and fostering proactive responses to anomalies.

Integrating and maintaining secure, compliant data practices within OpenTelemetry implementations became an unmistakable necessity, emphasized especially in heavily regulated industries like finance and healthcare. Solutions often involved encrypting sensitive data while maintaining operational accessibility, a challenging yet essential balance. Qualitative practices, such as pseudonymization and access controls, complemented technical solutions to address data security com-

309

prehensively.

```
from cryptography.fernet import Fernet

key = Fernet.generate_key()
cipher = Fernet(key)

def encrypt_telemetry_data(data):
    encrypted_data = cipher.encrypt(data.encode())
    return encrypted_data

def decrypt_telemetry_data(encrypted_data):
    decrypted_data = cipher.decrypt(encrypted_data).decode()
    return decrypted_data

# Example usage
data = "sensitive_telemetry_info"
encrypted_data = encrypt_telemetry_data(data)
```

Another resounding lesson focused on the cultural transformation inherent in successful OpenTelemetry deployments. Observability, although technical by nature, necessitates collaborative mindsets across cross-functional teams, bridging IT, operations, and business units. Comprehensively involving diverse perspectives from stakeholders facilitated a shared ownership of observability processes, enriching organizational learning and iterative refinement.

Institutional patience was often cited as a virtue in these deployments. Implementing OpenTelemetry is a significant undertaking, requiring iterative trial, refinement, and scaling to achieve its full potential. Organizations stressed the importance of committing to continuous learning cycles to optimize telemetry strategies while adapting to evolving organizational needs and technological advancements.

Finally, exploitability represents a crucial dimension of observability, often unanticipated until initial implementation phases stabilize. The prospect of expanding OpenTelemetry's utilizations—from improving system stability to advancing strategic initiatives like predictive analytics and service innovation—illustrated the expansive value proposition of embracing comprehensive observability frameworks. This led many organizations to explore integrations with machine learning platforms, as demonstrated in the example below:

```
import pandas as pd
from sklearn.ensemble import RandomForestClassifier

# Example: Load telemetry data for training
data = pd.read_csv('telemetry_data.csv')
```

```
# Train a classifier for anomaly detection
model = RandomForestClassifier()
X = data.drop('anomaly', axis=1)
y = data['anomaly']
model.fit(X, y)

# Predict anomalies for new data
new_data = pd.read_csv('new_telemetry_data.csv')
predictions = model.predict(new_data)
```

Efficient deployment of OpenTelemetry reveals an array of poignant lessons for organizations striving to enhance observability. Establishing structured, goal-driven observability practices, fostering alignment and collaboration, and harnessing flexible technical solutions lay at the heart of these lessons. As industries increasingly gravitate towards more complex systems, the insights harvested from OpenTelemetry implementations will continue to offer pathways for achieving superior operational resilience and innovation.

Printed in Dunstable, United Kingdom